Discourse
Analysis
as Theory and Method

Discourse
Analysis
as Theory and Method

Marianne Jørgensen and Louise Phillips

SAGE Publications
London • Thousand Oaks • New Delhi

First published 2002

 SAGE Publications Ltd
6 Bonhill Street
London EC2A 4PU

SAGE Publications Inc
2455 Teller Road
Thousand Oaks, California 91320

SAGE Publications India Pvt Ltd
32, M-Block Market
Greater Kailash - I
New Delhi 110 048

British Library Cataloguing in Publication data

A catalogue record for this book is available from
the British Library.

ISBN 0 7619 7111 4
ISBN 0 7619 7112 2 (pbk)

Library of Congress Control Number available

Typeset by C&M Digitals (P) Ltd., Chennai, India
Printed in Great Britain by TJ International Ltd, Padstow,
Cornwall

Contents

Preface

A preface is used to place the text in a wider context. It informs the reader about how the text has come into existence, and how it is to be read. Or, using concepts we will apply later in the book, it suggests how the text has been produced and how it is to be consumed. The preface navigates the text between the individual and the collective. As authors, we know that we are not the exclusive originators; rather, the text is indebted to other texts and to discussions with other people. And as authors let go of their texts in publishing them, they also let go of their control of the text. Readers may find quite different messages in the text from those expected by the author.

Attempting to domesticate the unruly readers, the preface often provides guidelines for the reading of the text. By stating the intentions of the book, authors hope to reduce the readers' possibilities for alternative interpretations. The intention of this book is to provide an introduction to the large, interdisciplinary field of social constructionist discourse analysis. In the book, we demonstrate the scope of the field by presenting and discussing three different approaches to discourse analysis – Laclau and Mouffe's discourse theory, critical discourse analysis and discursive psychology. We aim to delineate the distinctive theoretical and methodological features of each of the approaches, and, by presenting a range of empirical examples, we hope to provide inspiration for new discourse analytical studies. In addition, by outlining and discussing the philosophical premises common to all forms of social constructionist discourse analysis, we aim to facilitate the design of research frameworks which draw on more than one of the approaches.

Of course, all of these issues cannot be covered fully by one single book. Some discussions we only touch on briefly, we condense the theories, and the methodological tools we present are only a small selection of the possibilities each approach provides. In that sense, the book should be read as an appetiser, encouraging the reader to engage in further exploration of the field of discourse analysis.

After having negotiated the meaning potentials of the text on its way to the reader, the preface is also used to acknowledge debts. This book has its origins in the Department of Communication at the University of Roskilde in Denmark, and we would like to thank the department for support in all phases of our project. Since the very first version of the text appeared, many people have taken the time to read it, to discuss it with us and to make comments and suggestions concerning both form and content. We remain indebted to all of these people. Students in the different departments in which we have taught discourse analysis have contributed immensely through specific comments to the text and through more general discussions of discourse analytical issues. Likewise, colleagues, families and friends have both challenged and supported us, thus making highly appreciated imprints on the text.

While vivid in our minds and hearts, all these people remain anonymous in this preface, as we restrict ourselves to mentioning only a few of the helping hands that have seen us through the final phase of the process. The Danish Social Science Research Council gave financial support for the preparation of the English-language manuscript. Ebbe Klitgård and Laura Trojaborg produced the first draft translation of the Danish-language edition on which the book builds. Alfred Phillips spent weeks working with the translation of the text. Erik Berggren, Lilie Chouliaraki, Torben Dyrberg, Norman Fairclough, Henrik Larsen and Chantal Mouffe all offered valuable comments to almost-final drafts of individual chapters.

We have not been able to implement all of the good ideas given to us along the road about how to change and expand the text. But we have incorporated many suggestions, and the discussions we have had with people have stimulated us to rewrite and elaborate on the text. Without all our discussion partners, the book would never have become what it is.

In this preface the writing of the text has been attributed to collective processes in which many people have made an imprint. It may sound as if the authors have done nothing themselves. But with the traditional concluding remark, that the author takes full responsibility for any errors and mistakes in the text, some measure of authority as authors is modestly reclaimed.

Through this preface, then, we have made an attempt to exert control over the text. Now, the rest is in your hands.

Marianne W. Jørgensen and Louise J. Phillips

Acknowledgements

We are grateful to Sheffield Hallam University and the University of Newcastle upon Tyne for permission to reproduce advertisements which appeared in the Times Higher Education Supplement on 22 May 1992.

1 The Field of Discourse Analysis

For at least ten years now, 'discourse' has been a fashionable term. In scientific texts and debates, it is used indiscriminately, often without being defined. The concept has become vague, either meaning almost nothing, or being used with more precise, but rather different, meanings in different contexts. But, in many cases, underlying the word 'discourse' is the general idea that language is structured according to different patterns that people's utterances follow when they take part in different domains of social life, familiar examples being 'medical discourse' and 'political discourse'. 'Discourse analysis' is the analysis of these patterns.

But this common sense definition is not of much help in clarifying what discourses are, how they function, or how to analyse them. Here, more developed theories and methods of discourse analysis have to be sought out. And, in the search, one quickly finds out that discourse analysis is not just one approach, but a series of interdisciplinary approaches that can be used to explore many different social domains in many different types of studies. And there is no clear consensus as to what discourses are or how to analyse them. Different perspectives offer their own suggestions and, to some extent, compete to appropriate the terms 'discourse' and 'discourse analysis' for their own definitions. Let us begin, however, by proposing the preliminary definition of a discourse as *a particular way of talking about and understanding the world (or an aspect of the world)*.

In this chapter, three different approaches to social constructionist discourse analysis will be introduced – Ernesto Laclau and Chantal Mouffe's discourse theory, critical discourse analysis, and discursive psychology. In the three following chapters, we will present the approaches individually. All three approaches share the starting point that our ways of talking do not neutrally reflect our world, identities and social relations but, rather, play an active role in creating and changing them. We have selected these approaches from the range of different perspectives within discourse analysis on the grounds that we think that they represent particularly fruitful theories and methods for research in communication, culture and society. They can be applied in analysis of many different social domains, including organisations and institutions, and in exploration of the role of language use in broad societal and cultural developments such as globalisation and the spread of mass mediated communication.

Let us give a few examples of possible applications of discourse analysis. For instance, it can be used as a framework for analysis of national identity. How can we understand national identities and what consequences does the division of the world into nation states have? Many different forms of text and talk could be selected for analysis. The focus could be, for instance, the discursive construction of national identity in textbooks about British history. Alternatively, one could choose to explore the significance of national identity for interaction between people in an organisational context such as a workplace. Another research topic could be the ways in which expert knowledge is conveyed in the mass media and the implications for questions of power and democracy. How are claims to expert knowledge constructed and contested in the mass media and how are competing knowledge claims 'consumed' by media audiences? The struggle between different knowledge claims could be understood and empirically explored as a struggle between different discourses which represent different ways of understanding aspects of the world and construct different identities for speakers (such as 'expert' or 'layperson').

The three approaches on which we have chosen to focus as frameworks for discourse analysis share certain key premises about how entities such as 'language' and 'the subject' are to be understood. They also have in common the aim of carrying out *critical* research, that is, to investigate and analyse power relations in society and to formulate normative perspectives from which a critique of such relations can be made with an eye on the possibilities for social change. At the same time, though, each perspective has a range of distinctive philosophical and theoretical premises, including particular understandings of discourse, social practice and critique, which lead to particular aims, methods and empirical focal points. The purpose of this introductory chapter is to outline the field to which social constructionist approaches to discourse analysis belong.[1] We are interested both in those aspects which are common to all approaches – and, in particular, to our three approaches – and in those aspects in relation to which the approaches diverge.

The approaches are similar to one another in their social constructionist starting point, in their view of language, stemming from structuralist and poststructuralist linguistics, and in their understanding of the individual based on a version of structuralist Marxism. In this chapter, we will present these common roots and sources of theoretical inspiration, and during our account will touch on a series of concepts – for example, 'power' and 'ideology' – that often accompany the concept of discourse.

Notwithstanding the shared premises, important differences exist between the approaches. First, there is disagreement as to the 'scope' of discourses: do they constitute the social completely, or are they themselves partly constituted by other aspects of the social? Secondly, the approaches also vary with respect to their focus of analysis. Some analyse people's discourse in everyday social interaction, others prefer a more abstract mapping of the discourses that circulate in society. We will elaborate on these points of divergence towards the end of the chapter.

The division of the field into three approaches among which there are both similarities and differences should, to some extent, be understood as a construction of our own. We have picked out the three approaches and have chosen to allot one chapter to each and to compare and contrast them to one another in Chapter 5, in order to provide a clear introduction to the field of discourse analysis. This representation should not be taken to be a neutral description or transparent reflection of the field. With respect to our choice of approaches, we cover only three approaches within the field of social constructionist discourse analysis, excluding, for example, the Foucauldian approach.[2] And in relation to our identification of points of convergence and divergence among the three approaches, we acknowledge that comparison between the approaches is not a straightforward exercise. The three approaches emanate from different disciplines and have their own distinctive characteristics. At the same time, many discourse analysts work across disciplinary borders, and there are many theoretical points and methodological tools that cannot be assigned exclusively to one particular approach.

A COMPLETE PACKAGE

Although discourse analysis can be applied to all areas of research, it cannot be used with all kinds of theoretical framework. Crucially, it is not to be used as a method of analysis detached from its theoretical and methodological foundations. Each approach to discourse analysis that we present is not just a method for data analysis, but a theoretical and methodological whole – a complete package. The package contains, first, philosophical (ontological and epistemological) premises regarding the role of language in the social construction of the world, second, theoretical models, third, methodological guidelines for how to approach a research domain, and fourth, specific techniques for analysis. In discourse analysis, *theory* and *method* are intertwined and researchers must accept the basic philosophical premises in order to use discourse analysis as their method of empirical study.

It is important to stress that, while the content of the package should form an integrated whole, it is possible to create one's own package by combining elements from different discourse analytical perspectives and, if appropriate, non-discourse analytical perspectives. Such *multiperspectival* work is not only permissible but positively valued in most forms of discourse analysis. The view is that different perspectives provide different forms of knowledge about a phenomenon so that, together, they produce a broader understanding. Multiperspectival work is distinguished from an eclecticism based on a mishmash of disparate approaches without serious assessment of their relations with each other. Multiperspectivalism requires that one weighs the approaches up against each other, identifying what kind of (local) knowledge each approach can supply and modifying the approaches in the light of these considerations.[3]

In order to construct a coherent framework, it is crucial to be aware of the philosophical, theoretical and methodological differences and similarities among the approaches. Obviously, this requires an overview of the field. The aim of our presentation of the three perspectives in the following three chapters is to contribute to the acquisition of this overview by introducing the key features of three important discourse analytical approaches as well as the central themes in academic debates concerning these features. In addition, we will provide extensive references and suggestions for further reading.

Key Premises

The three approaches on which we have chosen to concentrate are all based on social constructionism.[4] Social constructionism is an umbrella term for a range of new theories about culture and society.[5] Discourse analysis is just one among several social constructionist approaches but it is one of the most widely used approaches within social constructionism.[6] Furthermore, many use approaches that have the same characteristics as those of discourse analysis without defining them as such. We will first provide a brief outline of the general philosophical assumptions that underpin most discourse analytical approaches, drawing on the accounts of social constructionism given by Vivien Burr (1995) and Kenneth Gergen (1985). Then we will focus specifically on the assumptions about language and identity that all discourse analytical approaches embrace.

Burr (1995: 2) warns about the difficulty of giving one description that seeks to cover all social constructionist approaches, since they are so manifold and diverse. This notwithstanding, in Burr (1995: 2–5) she lists four premises shared by all social constructionist approaches, building on Gergen (1985). These premises are also embraced by our three approaches. They are as follows:[7]

- *A critical approach to taken-for-granted knowledge*
  Our knowledge of the world should not be treated as objective truth. Reality is only accessible to us through categories, so our knowledge and representations of the world are not reflections of the reality 'out there', but rather are products of our ways of categorising the world, or, in discursive analytical terms, products of discourse (Burr 1995: 3; Gergen 1985: 266–7). This premise will be explained further on (p. 9–12.)
- *Historical and cultural specificity* (Burr 1995: 3)
  We are fundamentally historical and cultural beings and our views of, and knowledge about, the world are the 'products of historically situated interchanges among people' (Gergen 1985: 267). Consequently, the ways in which we understand and represent the world are historically and culturally specific and *contingent*: our worldviews and our identities could have been different, and they can change over time. This view that all knowledge is contingent is an *anti-foundationalist* position that stands in opposition to the foundationalist-view that knowledge can be grounded on a solid, metatheoretical base that transcends contingent human actions. Discourse is a form of social action that plays a part in producing the social world – including knowledge, identities and social relations – and thereby in maintaining specific social patterns. This view is *anti-essentialist*: that the social world is constructed socially and discursively implies that its character is not pre-given or determined by external conditions, and that people do not possess a set of fixed and authentic characteristics or essences.
- *Link between knowledge and social processes*
  Our ways of understanding the world are created and maintained by social processes (Burr 1995: 4; Gergen 1985: 268). Knowledge is created through social interaction in which we construct common truths and compete about what is true and false.

- *Link between knowledge and social action*
  Within a particular worldview, some forms of action become
  natural, others unthinkable. Different social understandings of the
  world lead to different social actions, and therefore the social construction of knowledge and truth has social consequences (Burr 1995: 5,
  Gergen 1985: 268–269).

Some critics of social constructionism have argued that if all knowledge
and all social identities are taken to be contingent, then it follows that
everything is in flux and there are no constraints and regularities in social
life. There are certainly social constructionist theorists, such as Kenneth
Gergen and Jean Baudrillard, who might be interpreted in this way. But,
by and large, we believe that this is a caricature of social constructionism. Most social constructionists, including adherents of our three
approaches, view the social field as much more rule-bound and regulative. Even though knowledge and identities are always contingent *in
principle*, they are always relatively inflexible in specific situations.
Specific situations place restrictions on the identities which an individual
can assume and on the statements which can be accepted as meaningful.
We will resume this discussion in the next chapter in relation to Laclau
and Mouffe's discourse theory.

The Three Approaches

The key premises of social constructionism have roots in French poststructuralist theory and its rejection of totalising and universalising
theories such as Marxism and psychoanalysis. But both social constructionism and poststructuralism are disputed labels and there is no consensus about the relationship between the two. We understand social
constructionism as a broader category of which poststructuralism is a
subcategory. All our discourse analytical approaches draw on structuralist and poststructuralist language theory, but the approaches vary as
to the extent to which the poststructuralist label applies.
Ernesto Laclau and Chantal Mouffe's discourse theory, which we
present in Chapter 2, is the 'purest' poststructuralist theory in our selection. The theory has its starting point in the poststructuralist idea that
discourse constructs the social world in meaning, and that, owing to the
fundamental instability of language, meaning can never be permanently
fixed. No discourse is a closed entity: it is, rather, constantly being transformed through contact with other discourses. So a keyword of the theory
is *discursive struggle*. Different discourses – each of them representing

particular ways of talking about and understanding the soc\
engaged in a constant struggle with one other to achieve he\
is, to fix the meanings of language in their own way. Hege\
can provisionally be understood as the dominance of one par\
spective. We will elaborate on this in Chapter 2.

Critical discourse analysis, which we discuss in Chapter 3 wit\
focus on Norman Fairclough's approach, also places weight on th ...tive
role of discourse in constructing the social world. But, in contrast to
Laclau and Mouffe, Fairclough insists that discourse is just one among
many aspects of any social practice. This distinction between discourse
and non-discourse represents a remnant of more traditional Marxism in
Fairclough's theory, rendering critical discourse analysis less poststructuralist than Laclau and Mouffe's discourse theory.

A central area of interest in Fairclough's critical discourse analysis is the
investigation of *change*. Concrete language use always draws on earlier discursive structures as language users build on already established meanings.
Fairclough focuses on this through the concept of *intertextuality* – that is,
how an individual text draws on elements and discourses of other texts. It
is by combining elements from different discourses that concrete language
use can change the individual discourses and thereby, also, the social and
cultural world. Through analysis of intertextuality, one can investigate both
the reproduction of discourses whereby no new elements are introduced
and discursive change through new combinations of discourse.

Discursive psychology, the subject of Chapter 4, shares critical discourse
analysis' empirical focus on specific instances of language use in social
interaction. But the aim of discursive psychologists is not so much to
analyse the changes in society's 'large-scale discourses', which concrete
language use can bring about, as to investigate how people use the available discourses flexibly in creating and negotiating representations of the
world and identities in talk-in-interaction and to analyse the social consequences of this. Despite the choice of label for this approach – 'discursive
psychology' – its main focus is not internal psychological conditions.
Discursive psychology is an approach to social psychology that has developed a type of discourse analysis in order to explore the ways in which
people's selves, thoughts and emotions are formed and transformed
through social interaction and to cast light on the role of these processes
in social and cultural reproduction and change. Many discursive psychologists draw explicitly on poststructuralist theory, but with different results
than, for example, Laclau and Mouffe. In discursive psychology, the stress
is on individuals both as products of discourse *and* as producers of discourse in specific contexts of interaction whereas Laclau and Mouffe's discourse theory tends to view individuals solely as subjects of discourse.

In Chapters 3 and 4 on respectively critical discourse analysis and discursive psychology, we set out the theoretical foundations and methodological guidelines for discourse analysis and present some concrete examples of discourse analysis within each tradition. Laclau and Mouffe's discourse theory, however, is short on specific methodological guidelines and illustrative examples. To compensate for this, we have extrapolated from their theory a range of analytical tools which we present in Chapter 2 together with an example of analysis based on some of these tools. The purpose of the guidelines and examples in the three chapters is to provide insight into how to apply the different approaches to discourse analysis in empirical work. In each of the chapters, we delineate the distinctive features of each perspective, whilst indicating the aspects which they share with one or both of the other perspectives. Throughout, we stress the links between theory and method. In Chapter 5, we home in on the theoretical and methodological differences and similarities among the approaches. We compare the approaches, weigh up their strengths and weaknesses, and point at ways in which they can supplement one other. Finally, we address some questions that are relevant to all the approaches. How do we delimit a discourse? How can we get started doing discourse analysis? How can we do multiperspectival research combining different discourse analytical approaches and different non-discourse analytical approaches? As in the other chapters, we present illustrative examples of ways of tackling these questions in empirical research. The final chapter of the book presents a discussion of the nature of critical research within the paradigm of social constructionism. Here, we discuss and evaluate a range of attempts to deal with the problems of doing critical research along social constructionist lines, focusing on their different stances in relation to the question of relativism and the status of truth and knowledge.[8]

FROM LANGUAGE SYSTEM TO DISCOURSE

In addition to general social constructionist premises, all discourse analytical approaches converge with respect to their views of language and the subject. In order to provide a common base for the discussions in the coming chapters, we will now introduce the views that the approaches share followed by the main points of divergence.

Discourse analytical approaches take as their starting point the claim of structuralist and poststructuralist linguistic philosophy, that our access to reality is always through language. With language, we create representations of reality that are never mere reflections of a pre-existing reality but contribute to constructing reality. That does not mean that reality itself does not exist. Meanings and representations are real. Physical objects also exist, but they only gain meaning through discourse.

Let us take as an example a flood associated with a river overflowing its banks. The rise in the water level that leads to the flood is an event that takes place independently of people's thoughts and talk. Everybody drowns if they are in the wrong place, irrespective of what they think or say. The rise in the water level is a material fact. But as soon as people try to ascribe meaning to it, it is no longer outside discourse. Most would place it in the category of 'natural phenomena', but they would not necessarily describe it in the same way. Some would draw on a meteorological discourse, attributing the rise in the water level to an unusually heavy downpour. Others might account for it in terms of the El Niño phenomenon, or see it as one of the many global consequences of the 'greenhouse effect'. Still others would see it as the result of 'political mismanagement', such as the national government's failure to commission and fund the building of dykes. Finally, some might see it as a manifestation of God's will, attributing it to God's anger over a people's sinful way of life or seeing it as a sign of the arrival of Armageddon. The rise in the water level, as an event taking place at a particular point in time, can, then, be ascribed meaning in terms of many different perspectives or discourses (which can also be combined in different ways). Importantly, the different discourses each point to different courses of action as possible and appropriate such as the construction of dykes, the organisation of political opposition to global environmental policies or the national government, or preparation for the imminent Armageddon. Thus the ascription of meaning in discourses works to constitute and change the world.

Language, then, is not merely a channel through which information about underlying mental states and behaviour or facts about the world are communicated. On the contrary, language is a 'machine' that generates, and as a result constitutes, the social world. This also extends to the constitution of social identities and social relations. It means that *changes* in discourse are a means by which the social world is changed. Struggles at the discursive level take part in changing, as well as in reproducing, the social reality.

The understanding of language as a system, which is not determined by the reality to which it refers, stems from the structuralist linguistics that followed in the wake of Ferdinand de Saussure's pioneering ideas around the beginning of this century. Saussure argued that signs consist of two sides, form (signifiant) and content (signifié), and that the relation between the two is *arbitrary* (Saussure 1960). The meaning we attach to words is not inherent in them but a result of social conventions whereby we connect certain meanings with certain sounds. The sound or the written image of the word 'dog', for example, has no natural connection to the image of a dog that appears in our head when we hear the word. That we understand what others mean when they say 'dog' is due to the social convention that has taught us that the word 'dog' refers to the four-legged animal that barks. Saussure's point is that the meaning of individual signs is determined by their relation to other signs: a sign gains its specific value from being different from other signs. The word 'dog' is different from the words 'cat' and 'mouse' and 'dig' and 'dot'. The word 'dog' is thus part of a network or *structure* of other words from which it differs; and it is precisely from everything that it is not that the word 'dog' gets its meaning.

Saussure saw this structure as a social institution and therefore as changeable over time. This implies that the relationship between language and reality is also arbitrary, a point developed in later structuralist and poststructuralist theory. The world does not itself dictate the words with which it should be described, and, for example, the sign 'dog' is not a natural consequence of a physical phenomenon. The form of the sign is different in different languages (for example, 'chien' and 'Hund'), and the content of the sign also changes on being applied in new situations (when, for example, saying to a person, 'you're such a dog').

Saussure advocated that the structure of signs be made the subject matter of linguistics. Saussure distinguished between two levels of language, *langue* and *parole*. *Langue* is the structure of language, the network of signs that give meaning to one another, and it is fixed and unchangeable. *Parole*, on the other hand, is situated language use, the signs actually used by people in specific situations. *Parole* must always draw on *langue*, for it is the structure of language that makes specific statements possible. But in the Saussurian tradition *parole* is often seen as random and so vitiated by people's mistakes and idiosyncrasies as to disqualify it as an object of scientific research. Therefore, it is the fixed, underlying structure, *langue*, which has become the main object of linguistics.

Poststructuralism takes its starting point in structuralist theory but modifies it in important respects. Poststructuralism takes from structuralism the idea that signs derive their meanings not through their relations to reality but through internal relations within the network of signs; it rejects structuralism's view of language as a stable, unchangeable and totalising structure and it dissolves the sharp distinction between *langue* and *parole*.

First we turn to the poststructuralist critique of the stable, unchangeable structure of language. As we have mentioned, in Saussure's theory, signs acquire their meaning by their difference from other signs. In the Saussurian tradition, the structure of language can be thought of as a fishing-net in which each sign has its place as one of the knots in the net. When the net is stretched out, the knot is fixed in position by its distance from the other knots in the net, just as the sign is defined by its distance from the other signs. Much of structuralist theory rests on the assumption that signs are locked in particular relationships with one another: every sign has a particular location in the net and its meaning is fixed. Later structuralists and poststructuralists have criticised this conception of language; they do not believe that signs have such fixed positions as the metaphor of the fishing-net suggests. In poststructuralist theory, signs still acquire their meaning by being different from other signs, but those signs from which they differ can change according to the context in which they are used (see Laclau 1993a: 433). For instance, the word 'work' can, in certain situations, be the opposite of 'leisure' whereas, in other contexts, its opposite is 'passivity' (as in 'work in the garden'). It does not follow that words are open to all meanings – that would make language and communication impossible – but it does have the consequence that words cannot be fixed with one or more definitive meaning(s). The metaphor of the fishing-net is no longer apt since it cannot be ultimately determined where in the net the signs should be placed in relation to one another. Remaining with the metaphor of 'net', we prefer to use the *internet* as a model, whereby all links are connected with one another, but links can be removed and new ones constantly emerge and alter the structure.

Structures do exist but always in a temporary and not necessarily consistent state. This understanding provides poststructuralism with a means of solving one of structuralism's traditional problems, that of *change*. With structuralism's focus on an underlying and fixed structure, it is impossible to understand change, for where would change come from? In poststructuralism, the structure becomes changeable and the meanings of signs can shift in relation to one another.

But what makes the meanings of signs change? This brings us to poststructuralism's second main critique of traditional structuralism, bearing on the latter's sharp distinction between *langue* and *parole*. As mentioned, *parole* cannot be an object of structuralist study because situated language use is considered too arbitrary to be able to say anything about the structure, *langue*. In contrast to this, poststructuralists believe that it is in concrete language use that the structure is created, reproduced and changed. In specific speech acts (and writing), people draw on the structure – otherwise speech would not be meaningful – but they may also challenge the structure by introducing alternative ideas for how to fix the meaning of the signs.

Not all discourse analytical approaches subscribe explicitly to post-structuralism, but all can agree to the following main points:

- Language is not a reflection of a pre-existing reality.
- Language is structured in patterns or discourses – there is not just one general system of meaning as in Saussurian structuralism but a series of systems or discourses, whereby meanings change from discourse to discourse.
- These discursive patterns are maintained and transformed in discursive practices.
- The maintenance and transformation of the patterns should therefore be explored through analysis of the specific contexts in which language is in action.

Foucault's Archaeology and Genealogy

Michel Foucault has played a central role in the development of discourse analysis through both theoretical work and empirical research. In almost all discourse analytical approaches, Foucault has become a figure to quote, relate to, comment on, modify and criticise. We will also touch on Foucault, sketching out his areas of contribution to discourse analysis – not only in order to live up to the implicit rules of the game, but also because all our approaches have roots in Foucault's ideas, while rejecting some parts of his theory.

Traditionally, Foucault's work is divided between an early 'archaeological' phase and a later 'genealogical' phase, although the two overlap, with Foucault continuing to use tools from his archaeology in his later works. His discourse theory forms part of his archaeology. What he is interested in studying 'archaeologically' are the rules that determine which statements are accepted as meaningful and true in a particular historical epoch. Foucault defines a discourse as follows:

> We shall call discourse a group of statements in so far as they belong to the same discursive formation [...Discourse] is made up of a limited number of statements for which a group of conditions of existence can be defined. Discourse in this sense is not an ideal, timeless form [...] it is, from beginning to end, historical – a fragment of history [...] posing its own limits, its divisions, its transformations, the specific modes of its temporality. (Foucault 1972: 117)

Foucault adheres to the general social constructionist premise that knowledge is not just a reflection of reality. Truth is a discursive construction and different regimes of knowledge determine what is true and false. Foucault's aim is to investigate the structure of different regimes of knowledge – that is, the rules for what can and cannot be said and the rules for what is considered to be true and false. The starting point is that although we have, in principle, an infinite number of ways to formulate statements, the statements that are produced within a specific domain are rather similar and repetitive. There are innumerable statements that are never uttered, and would never be accepted as meaningful. The historical rules of the particular discourse delimit what it is possible to say.[9]

The majority of contemporary discourse analytical approaches follow Foucault's conception of discourses as relatively rule-bound sets of statements which impose limits on what gives meaning. And they build on his ideas about truth being something which is, at least to a large extent, created discursively. However, they all diverge from Foucault's tendency to identify only one knowledge regime in each historical period; instead, they operate with a more conflictual picture in which different discourses exist side by side or struggle for the right to define truth.

In his genealogical work, Foucault developed a theory of *power/ knowledge*. Instead of treating agents and structures as primary categories, Foucault focuses on power. In common with discourse, power does not belong to particular agents such as individuals or the state or groups with particular interests; rather, power is spread across different social practices. Power should not be understood as exclusively oppressive but as *productive*; power constitutes discourse, knowledge, bodies and subjectivities:

> What makes power hold good, what makes it accepted, is simply the fact that it does not only weigh on us as a force that says no, but that it traverses and produces things, it induces pleasure, forms knowledge, produces discourse. It needs to be considered as a productive network which runs through the whole social body, much more than as a negative instance whose function is repression. (Foucault 1980: 119)

Thus power provides the conditions of possibility for the social. It is in power that our social world is produced and objects are separated from one another and thus attain their individual characteristics and relationships to one another. For instance, 'crime' has gradually been created as an area with its own institutions (e.g. prisons), particular subjects (e.g. 'criminals') and particular practices (e.g. 'resocialisation'). And power is always bound up with knowledge – power and knowledge presuppose one another. For example, it is hard to imagine the modern prison system without criminology (Foucault 1977).

Power is responsible *both* for creating our social world *and* for the particular ways in which the world is formed and can be talked about, ruling out alternative ways of being and talking. Power is thus both a productive and a constraining force. Foucault's conception of power is adhered to by Laclau and Mouffe's discourse theory and discursive psychology, while critical discourse analysis is more ambivalent towards it. We discuss the position of critical discourse analysis in Chapter 3.

With respect to *knowledge*, Foucault's coupling of power and knowledge has the consequence that power is closely connected to discourse. Discourses contribute centrally to producing the subjects we are, and the objects we can know something about (including ourselves as subjects). For all the approaches, adherence to this view leads to the following research question: *how is the social world, including its subjects and objects, constituted in discourses?*

Foucault's concept of power/knowledge also has consequences for his conception of *truth*. Foucault claims that it is not possible to gain access to universal truth since it is impossible to talk from a position outside discourse; there is no escape from representation. *'Truth effects'* are created within discourses. In Foucault's archaeological phase, 'truth' is understood as a system of procedures for the production, regulation and diffusion of statements. In his genealogical phase, he makes a link between truth and power, arguing that 'truth' is embedded in, and produced by, systems of power. Because truth is unattainable, it is fruitless to ask whether something is true or false. Instead, the focus should be on *how* effects of truth are created in discourses. What is to be analysed are the discursive processes through which discourses are constructed in ways that give the impression that they represent true or false pictures of reality.

THE SUBJECT

It is also Foucault who provided the starting point for discourse analysis' understanding of the subject. His view is, as already noted, that subjects are created in discourses. He argues that 'discourse is not the majestically unfolding manifestation of a thinking, knowing, speaking subject' (Foucault 1972: 55). Or as Steinar Kvale expresses the position, 'The self no longer uses language to express itself; rather language speaks through the person. The individual self becomes a medium for the culture and its language' (Kvale 1992: 36).

This is very different from the standard Western understanding of the subject as an autonomous and sovereign entity. According to Foucault, the subject is *decentred*. Here, Foucault was influenced by his teacher, Louis Althusser.

Althusser's structural Marxist approach links the subject closely to ideology: the individual becomes an ideological subject through a process of interpellation whereby discourses appeal to the individual as a subject. First, we will outline Althusser's understanding of ideology and, following that, his understanding of interpellation. Althusser defines *ideology* as a system of representations that masks our true relations to one another in society by constructing imaginary relations between people and between them and the social formation (Althusser 1971). Thus ideology is a distorted recognition of the real social relations. According to Althusser, all aspects of the social are controlled by ideology, which functions through 'the repressive state apparatus' (e.g. the police) and 'the ideological state apparatus' (e.g. the mass media).

Interpellation denotes the process through which language constructs a social position for the individual and thereby makes him or her an ideological subject:

> [I]deology 'acts' or 'functions' in such a way that it 'recruits' subjects among the individuals (it recruits them all), or 'transforms' the individuals into subjects (it transforms them all) by that very precise operation which I have called *inter-pellation* or hailing, and which can be imagined along the lines of the most commonplace everyday police (or other) hailing: 'Hey, you there!' Assuming that the theoretical scene I have imagined takes place in the street, the hailed individual will turn round – [...] he becomes a *subject*. (Althusser 1971: 174; italics in original, note omitted)

Let us take as an example public information material about health in late modernity, which interpellates readers as consumers with personal responsibility for the care of their bodies through a proper choice of lifestyle. By accepting the role as addressees of the text, we affiliate ourselves to the subject position that the interpellation has created. In so doing, we reproduce the ideology of consumerism and our position as subjects in a consumer culture. By taking on the role of subject in a consumer culture, we accept that certain problems are constructed as personal problems that the individual carries the responsibility for solving, instead of as public problems that demand collective solutions.

Althusser assumes that we always accept the subject positions allocated to us and thereby become subjects of ideology; there is no chance of resistance:

Experience shows that the practical telecommunications of hailings is such that they hardly ever miss their man: verbal call or whistle, the one hailed always recognizes that it is really him who is being hailed. (Althusser 1971: 174)

As we are going to see in the section below, this is just one of the aspects of Althusser's theory which has been subjected to heavy criticism by many including by the majority of discourse analytical approaches.

Rejection of Determinism

Althusser's theory had a great influence on cultural studies approaches to communication studies in the 1970s. The research focus was on texts (mainly mass media texts), not on text production or reception since researchers took the ideological workings and effects of texts for granted. Meanings were treated as if they were unambiguously embedded in texts and passively decoded by receivers. To a large extent, cultural studies – strongly influenced by Althusser – was based on the idea that a single ideology (capitalism) was dominant in society, leaving no real scope for effective resistance (the 'dominant ideology thesis').

But since the end of the 1970s, Althusser's perspective has been criticised in several ways. First, the question was raised as to the possibilities for resistance against the ideological messages that are presented to the subject – the question of the subject's *agency* or freedom of action. The media group at the Centre for Contemporary Cultural Studies in Birmingham, led by Stuart Hall, pointed, in this respect, to the complexity of media reception (Hall et al. 1980). According to Hall's 'encoding/decoding' theory, recipients were able to interpret or 'decode' messages by codes other than the code which was 'encoded' in the text (Hall 1980). The theory was based *inter alia* on Gramsci's theory of hegemony, which ascribes a degree of agency to all social groups in the production and negotiation of meaning (Gramsci 1991). Today there is a consensus in cultural studies, communication research and discourse analysis that the dominant ideology thesis underestimated people's capacity to offer resistance to ideologies. Some contributions to communications and cultural studies may even tend to overestimate people's ability to resist media messages (see, for example, Morley 1992 for a critique of this tendency), but usually discourse analysts take into account the role of textual features in setting limits on how the text can be interpreted by its recipients.

Second, all three of the discourse analytical approaches presented in our book reject the understanding of the social as governed by one totalising ideology. Just as they replace Foucault's monolithic view of knowledge regimes with a more pluralistic model in which many discourses compete, they dismiss Althusser's theory that one ideology controls all discourse. It follows from this that subjects do not become interpellated in just one subject position: different discourses give the subject different, and possibly contradictory, positions from which to speak.

The different approaches have developed different concepts of the subject which we will discuss in the following chapters. But generally speaking, it can be said that all the approaches see the subject as created in discourses – and therefore as decentred – the constitution of subjects being a key focus of empirical analysis. However, the approaches differ as to the degree of emphasis given to the subject's 'freedom of action' within the discourse – that is, they differ as to their position in the debate about the relationship between structure and agent. Laclau and Mouffe's discourse theory largely follows Foucault, viewing the individual as determined by structures, whereas critical discourse analysis and discursive psychology to a greater extent are in line with Roland Barthes' slogan that people are both 'masters and slaves of language' (Barthes 1982). Thus the latter two approaches stress that people use discourses as resources with which they create new constellations of words – sentences that have never before been uttered. In talk, language users select elements from different discourses which they draw on from mass mediated and interpersonal communication. This may result in new hybrid discourses. Through producing new discourses in this way, people function as agents of discursive and cultural change. As the critical discourse analyst, Fairclough, expresses it, 'Individual creative acts cumulatively establish restructured orders of discourse' (1989: 172). However, even in those approaches in which the subject's agency and role in social change are brought to the foreground, discourses are seen as frameworks that limit the subject's scope for action and possibilities for innovation. Critical discourse analysis and discursive psychology each present a theoretical foundation and specific methods for analysis of the dynamic discursive practices through which language users act as both discursive products and producers in the reproduction and transformation of discourses and thereby in social and cultural change.

The third and final controversial point in Althusser's theory is the concept of ideology itself. Most concepts of ideology, including Althusser's, imply that access to absolute truth is attainable. Ideology distorts real social relations, and, if we liberated ourselves from ideology, we would gain access to them and to truth. As we saw, this is an understanding that Foucault rejects completely. According to Foucault, truth, subjects and relations between subjects are created in discourse, and there is no possibility of getting behind the discourse to a 'truer' truth. Hence Foucault has no need of a concept of ideology. Laclau and Mouffe's discourse theory has adopted this position, and its concept of ideology is practically empty. In contrast, critical discourse analysis and discursive psychology do not reject the Marxist tradition completely on this point: both approaches are interested in the ideological effects of discursive practices. While they adhere to Foucault's view of power, treating power as productive rather than as pure compulsion, they also attach importance to the patterns of dominance, whereby one social group is subordinated to another. The idea is also retained – at least, in Fairclough's critical discourse analysis – that one can distinguish between discourses that are ideological and discourses that are not, thus retaining the hope of finding a way out of ideology; a hope that Laclau and Mouffe's discourse theory would find naïve.

DIFFERENCES BETWEEN THE APPROACHES

The divergence in the way in which ideology is conceived is just one of the differences between the three approaches. In the following section, we highlight differences between the approaches with respect to, first, the role of discourse in the construction of the world and, second, analytical focus. In both these respects, the differences are matters of degree, and we will position the approaches in relation to each other on two continua to which we will refer throughout the rest of this book.

The Role of Discourse in the Constitution of the World

For all three approaches, the functioning of discourse – discursive practice – is a social practice that shapes the social world. The concept of 'social practice' views actions in terms of a dual perspective: on the one hand, actions are concrete, individual and context bound; but, on the other hand, they are also institutionalised and socially anchored, and because of this tend towards patterns of regularity. Fairclough's critical discourse analysis reserves the concept of discourse for text, talk and other semiological systems (e.g. gestures and fashion) and keeps it distinct from other dimensions of social practice. Discursive practice is viewed as one dimension or *moment* of every social practice in a dialectical relationship with the other moments of a social practice. That means that some aspects of the social world function according to different logics from discourses and should be studied with tools other than those of discourse analysis. For instance, there may be economic logics at play or the institutionalisation of particular forms of social action. Discursive practice reproduces or changes other dimensions of social practice just as other social dimensions shape the discursive dimension. Together, the discursive dimension and the other dimensions of social practice constitute our world.

Laclau and Mouffe's discourse theoretical approach does not distinguish between discursive and non-discursive dimensions of the social – practices are viewed as exclusively discursive. That does not mean that nothing but text and talk exist, but, on the contrary, that discourse itself is material and that entities such as the economy, the infrastructure and institutions are also parts of discourse. Thus, in Laclau and Mouffe's discourse theory there is no dialectical interaction between discourse and something else: discourse itself is fully constitutive of our world.

This difference can be concretised by locating the approaches on a continuum. We have placed in brackets some of the other positions to which we refer in the book. On the left-hand side, discourse is seen as fully constitutive of the social, whereas on the right-hand side discourses are seen as mere reflections of other social mechanisms.

A schematic figure like this has to be approached cautiously since the complexity of the actual theories is bound to be reduced when they are placed on a single line. This is clear, for example, in the case of the positioning of discursive psychology. We have placed discursive psychology somewhat to the left on the continuum, but it is, in fact, difficult to place, as it claims both that discourse is fully constitutive and that it is embedded in historical and social practices, which are not fully discursive.

The approaches on the far right of the continuum are not discourse analytical. If one claims, as they do, that discourse is just a mechanical reproduction of other social practices – that is, discourse is fully determined by something else such as the economy – then there is no point in doing discourse analysis; instead, effort should be invested in economic analysis, for example. We have, therefore, judged the different Marxist positions on the right-hand side of the continuum according to a principle that does not quite do them justice: neither historical materialism nor cultural Marxists such as Gramsci and Althusser, have worked with 'discourse' or 'discourse analysis', so their inclusion is based on both an interpretation and a reduction of their theories. Moreover, both Gramsci

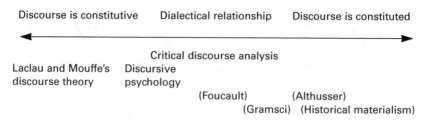

Figure 1.1 *The role of discourse in the constitution of the world*

and Althusser leave a rather large latitude for meaning-making practices that can be interpreted as a discursive dimension. But both of them see the economy as determinant in the 'final instance', and that is why they have ended up so far to the right.

Analytical Focus

Some approaches focus on the fact that discourses are created and changed in everyday discursive practices and therefore stress the need for systematic empirical analyses of people's talk and written language in, for instance, the mass media or research interviews. Other approaches are more concerned with general, overarching patterns and aim at a more abstract mapping of the discourses that circulate in society at a particular moment in time or within a specific social domain.

On a continuum, these differences can be represented as follows:

Figure 1.2 *Analytical Focus*

On this continuum, the focus is on differences of degree rather than qualitative differences. Although discursive psychology focuses on people's everyday practice, it constantly implicates larger societal structures on which people draw, or transform, in discursive practice. And although Laclau and Mouffe's discourse theory is mostly interested in more abstract, 'depersonified' discourses, the idea that these discourses are created, maintained and changed in myriads of everyday practices is implicit in the theory.

But, at the same time, the positions of the different approaches on the continuum reflect differences in theoretical emphasis: discursive psychology is much more interested in people's active and creative use of discourse as a resource for accomplishing social actions in specific contexts of interaction than Laclau and Mouffe's discourse theory, which instead is interested in how discourses, more generally, limit our possibilities for action.

THE ROLE OF THE ANALYST

For the discourse analyst, the purpose of research is not to get 'behind' the discourse, to find out what people *really* mean when they say this or that, or to discover the reality behind the discourse. The starting point is that reality can never be reached outside discourses and so it is discourse itself that has become the object of analysis. In discourse analytical research, the primary exercise is not to sort out which of the statements about the world in the research material are right and which are wrong (although a critical evaluation can be carried out at a later stage in the analysis). On the contrary, the analyst has to work with what has actually been said or written, exploring patterns in and across the statements and identifying the social consequences of different discursive representations of reality.

In working with discourses close to oneself with which one is very familiar, it is particularly difficult to treat them *as* discourses, that is, as socially constructed meaning-systems that could have been different. Because analysts are often part of the culture under study, they share many of the taken-for-granted, common-sense understandings expressed in the material. The difficulty is that it is precisely the common-sense understandings that are to be investigated: analysis focuses on how some statements are accepted as true or 'naturalised', and others are not. Consequently, it is fruitful to try to distance oneself from one's material and, for instance, imagine oneself as an anthropologist who is exploring a foreign universe of meaning in order to find out what makes sense there.

But this suggestion to play anthropologist should just be seen as a useful starting point rather than a full response to the problem of the researcher's role. If the research project is based on a social constructionist perspective, the problem of the researcher's role goes much deeper and needs to be tackled reflexively. If we accept that 'reality' is socially created, that 'truths' are discursively produced effects and that subjects are decentred, what do we do about the 'truth' that we as researcher–subjects produce? This problem is intrinsic to all social constructionist approaches.

Of the approaches that we present, the problem of how to deal with the contingency of truth is most pertinent in Laclau and Mouffe's discourse theory and discursive psychology, and the two approaches solve it in different ways. The problem is largely ignored by Laclau and Mouffe, their theory and analysis being presented as if they were objective descriptions of the world and its mechanisms. In contrast, discursive psychology tries to take account of the role of the analyst through different forms of reflexivity (see Chapters 4 and 6). By comparison with Laclau and Mouffe's discourse theory and discursive psychology, the dilemma does not at first glance seem so urgent in Fairclough's critical discourse analysis because he makes a distinction between ideological and non-ideological discourses: in principle, the researcher ought to be able to produce non-ideological discourses. But the problem re-emerges with the question of *how* to distinguish between what is ideological and what is not, and the question of *who* is sufficiently liberated from the discursive construction of the world to make this distinction.

Philosophically speaking, the problem appears insoluble, if we accept the anti-foundationalist premise, underpinning social constructionism, that it is a condition of all knowledge that it is just one representation of the world among many other possible representations. The researcher always takes a position in relation to the field of study, and that position plays a part in the determination of what he or she can see and can present as results. And there are always other positions in terms of which reality would look different. But that does not mean that all research results are equally good. In Chapter 4, we discuss how, with a social constructionist starting point, research results can be validated and made as transparent as possible for the reader. Generally, theoretical consistency demands that discourse analysts consider and make clear their position in relation to the particular discourses under investigation and that they assess the possible consequences of their contribution to the discursive production of our world.

The relativism inherent in social constructionism does not mean, either, that the analyst cannot be critical. All our approaches regard themselves as critical and in Chapter 6 we discuss at length how it is possible to practise social criticism without being able to make claims to absolute truth.

In brief, our position is that it is the stringent application of theory and method that legitimises scientifically produced knowledge. It is by seeing the world through a particular theory that we can distance ourselves from some of our taken-for-granted understandings and subject our material to other questions than we would be able to do from an everyday perspective. The next three chapters can be seen as different ways to achieve this distance, and in Chapter 6 we contextualise the discussions of scientific knowledge, reflexivity and critique within the wider field of social constructionism.

NOTES

1 However, this field does not cover all uses of the label 'discourse analysis'. The term 'discourse analysis' for example, is used in linguistics to denote the analysis of relations between sentences and statements on the micro level (for example, Brown and Yule 1983). Discourse analysis has also been used to denote the analysis of the ways people use mental schemata to understand narratives (van Dijk and Kintch 1983).

2 For accounts of Foucauldian forms of discourse analysis see, for example, Howarth (2000) and Mills (1997).

3 See Kellner (1995) for a call for 'multiperspectival cultural studies'. And see Chapter 5 in this book for a discussion and illustration of multiperspectival discourse analysis.

4 What we call 'social constructionism' in this text is in many other connections labelled 'social constructivism'. We use the term 'social constructionism' to avoid confusion with Piaget's constructivist theory (see Burr 1995: 2).

5 For discussions of the philosophical foundations of social constructionism see, for example, Collin (1997).

6 The dominance of discourse analysis is manifested in Burr's introduction to social constructionism (Burr 1995), in which her examples of empirical research consist exclusively of forms of discourse analysis, notwithstanding the fact that she emphasises that social constructionists also use other approaches.

7 Here, we draw both on Burr (1995) and Gergen (1985). Burr's account, as noted above, is also based on that of Gergen.

8 As authors, we have collaborated on all of the book's chapters and have developed together many of the ideas and formulations throughout the book. However, main responsibility can be attributed in the following way: Louise Phillips for Chapters 3 and 4, and Marianne Jørgensen for Chapters 2 and 6, while both authors are equally responsible for Chapters 1 and 5.

9 Foucault's own works from the archaeological period include both more abstract presentations of his theory and methodological tools (e.g. Foucault 1972) and empirical analyses (e.g. Foucault 1973, 1977).

2 Laclau and Mouffe's Discourse Theory

In this chapter we present Ernesto Laclau and Chantal Mouffe's discourse theory (sometimes abbreviated to discourse theory). We draw mainly on their principal work, *Hegemony and Socialist Strategy* (1985), supplementing this with a number of texts that Laclau has written alone.

Discourse theory aims at an understanding of the social as a discursive construction whereby, in principle, all social phenomena can be analysed using discourse analytical tools. First, we present the discourse theoretical approach to language, and then extend the theory to cover the entire social field. Because of its broad focus, discourse theory is suitable as a theoretical foundation for different social constructionist approaches to discourse analysis. But since Laclau and Mouffe's texts aim at theory development, they do not include so many practical tools for textually oriented discourse analysis. As a result, it can be fruitful to supplement their theory with methods from other approaches to discourse analysis.

The overall idea of discourse theory is that social phenomena are never finished or total. Meaning can never be ultimately fixed and this opens up the way for constant social struggles about definitions of society and identity, with resulting social effects. The discourse analyst's task is to plot the course of these struggles to fix meaning at all levels of the social.

Laclau and Mouffe have developed their theory through the *deconstruction* of other bodies of theory. Careful reading of other theories, they contend, uncovers their unargued assumptions and internal contradictions. In this way, the ideological content of the other theories is revealed and the contradictions identified can be transformed into tools for further thinking. The deconstructionist method, combined with their writing style, make Laclau and Mouffe rather inaccessible, since they presuppose extensive knowledge of the theories on which they draw.

Our presentation of discourse theory in this chapter both introduces a range of new concepts and gives new content to familiar ones.

TOWARDS A THEORY OF DISCOURSE

Laclau and Mouffe have constructed their theory by combining and modifying two major theoretical traditions, Marxism and structuralism. Marxism provides a starting point for thinking about the social, and structuralism provides a theory of meaning. Laclau and Mouffe fuse these traditions into a single poststructuralist theory in which the whole social field is understood as a web of processes in which meaning is created. First, we will outline their theory of the creation of meaning and their concept of 'discourse'.

In Chapter 1, we outlined Saussure's structural linguistics and the poststructuralist critique of the Saussurian tradition. We suggested that the structuralist view of language can be understood in terms of the metaphor of a fishing-net: all linguistic signs can be thought of as knots in a net, deriving their meaning from their difference from one another, that is, from being situated in particular positions in the net. The post-structuralist objection was that meaning cannot be fixed so unambiguously and definitively. Poststructuralists agree that signs acquire their meanings by being different from each other, but, in ongoing language use, we position the signs in different relations to one another so that they may acquire new meanings. Thus language use is a social phenomenon: it is through conventions, negotiations and conflicts in social contexts that structures of meaning are fixed and challenged.

Laclau and Mouffe take on board the poststructuralist critique of structuralist linguistics, but structuralism can still be used to give an impressionistic idea of Laclau and Mouffe's message. The creation of meaning as a social process is about the fixation of meaning, *as if* a Saussurian structure existed. We constantly strive to fix the meaning of signs by placing them in particular relations to other signs; returning to the metaphor, we try to stretch out the fishing-net so that the meaning of each sign is locked into a specific relationship to the others. The project is ultimately impossible because every concrete fixation of the signs' meaning is *contingent*; it is possible but not necessary. It is precisely those constant attempts that never completely succeed which are the entry point for discourse analysis. The aim of discourse analysis is to map out the processes in which we struggle about the way in which the meaning of signs is to be fixed, and the processes by which some fixations of meaning become so conventionalised that we think of them as natural.[1]

We can now translate this impressionistic picture into Laclau and Mouffe's theoretical concepts:

> [W]e will call *articulation* any practice establishing a relation among elements such that their identity is modified as a result of the articulatory practice. The structured totality resulting from the articulatory practice, we will call *discourse*. The differential positions, insofar as they appear articulated within a discourse, we will call *moments*. By contrast, we will call *element* any difference that is not discursively articulated. (Laclau and Mouffe 1985: 105; italics in original)

Here, Laclau and Mouffe define four important concepts that we will examine below. In the course of this, we will also introduce a number of related concepts: 'nodal points', 'the field of discursivity' and 'closure'.[1]

A discourse is understood as the fixation of meaning within a particular domain. All signs in a discourse are *moments*. They are the knots in the fishing-net, their meaning being fixed through their differences from one another ('differential positions'). Let us take as an example a medical discourse in which the body, illness and treatment are represented in particular ways.[2] All medical research is about dividing the body, illness and treatment into parts and describing the relations between these parts in an unambiguous way. The body is typically seen as split into parts that are to be treated separately and the causes of illnesses are often seen as local. For instance, infection is regarded as caused by a local attack of micro-organisms that should be eliminated by medicine. Medical discourse, then, stretches out a net of interrelated meanings over a domain pertaining to the body and illness. In that sense, we can talk about a discourse: all signs are moments in a system and the meaning of each sign is determined by its relations to the other signs.

A discourse is formed by the partial fixation of meaning around certain *nodal points* (Laclau and Mouffe 1985: 112). A nodal point is a privileged sign around which the other signs are ordered; the other signs acquire their meaning from their relationship to the nodal point. In medical discourses, for example, 'the body' is a nodal point around which many other meanings are crystallised. Signs such as 'symptoms', 'tissue' and 'scalpel' acquire their meaning by being related to 'the body' in particular ways. A nodal point in political discourses is 'democracy' and in national discourses a nodal point is 'the people'.

A discourse is established as a totality in which each sign is fixed as a moment through its relations to other signs (as in a fishing-net). This is done by the *exclusion* of all other possible meanings that the signs could have had: that is, all other possible ways in which the signs could have been related to one another. Thus a discourse is a reduction of possibilities. It is an attempt to stop the sliding of the signs in relation to one another and hence to create a unified system of meaning. All the possibilities that the discourse excludes Laclau and Mouffe call *the field of discursivity* (1985: 111). The field of discursivity is a reservoir for the 'surplus of meaning' produced by the articulatory practice – that is, the meanings that each sign has, or has had, in other discourses, but which are excluded by the specific discourse in order to create a unity of meaning. For instance, medical discourse is constituted through the exclusion of discourses about alternative methods of treatment in which the body, to a greater extent, is seen as a holistic entity pervaded by energy along different paths.

Here we can anticipate a critique of discourse theory to which we will return at the end of this chapter. A discourse is always constituted in relation to what it excludes, that is, in relation to the field of discursivity. But in discourse theory it is not entirely clear if the field of discursivity is a comparatively unstructured mass of all possible constructions of meaning or if it is itself structured by the given competing discourses. In medical discourse, for example, football is not a topic of conversation, but there is nothing to stop elements from a discourse about football from figuring in medical discourse at a given point in time. Does that mean then that football is part of the 'field of discursivity' of medical discourse? Or is it only discourses about, for example, alternative treatment which, to a certain extent, inhabit the same terrain as medical discourse and so constitute the field of discursivity of medical discourse? In Laclau and Mouffe's theory, these two situations are fused in the concept of the field of discursivity. We propose an analytical separation of the two. The field of discursivity would then denote all possible, excluded constructions of meaning (such as football in relation to medical discourse), while 'order of discourse' – a concept from Fairclough's critical discourse analysis – would denote a limited range of discourses which struggle in the same terrain (such as the domain of health and illness).

To return to Laclau and Mouffe's conceptual definitions, the field of discursivity is understood as everything outside the discourse, all that the discourse excludes. But exactly because a discourse is always constituted in relation to an outside, it is always in danger of being undermined by it, that is, its unity of meaning is in danger of being disrupted by other ways of fixing the meaning of the signs. Here, the concept of *element* becomes relevant. Elements are the signs whose meanings have not yet been fixed; signs that have multiple, potential meanings (i.e. they are *polysemic*). Using this concept, we can now reformulate the concept of discourse: a discourse attempts to transform elements into moments by reducing their polysemy to a fully fixed meaning. In the terms of Laclau and Mouffe's discourse theory, the discourse establishes a *closure*, a temporary stop to the fluctuations in the meaning of the signs. But the closure is never definitive: 'The transition from the "elements" to the "moments" is never entirely fulfilled' (Laclau and Mouffe 1985: 110). The discourse can never be so completely fixed that it cannot be undermined and changed by the multiplicity of meaning in the field of discursivity. For instance, in the discourse of Western medicine, the inroads made by acupuncture have led to the modification of the dominant medical understanding of the body in order to accommodate 'networks of energy'.

In Laclau and Mouffe's terms, 'the body' is an element as there are several competing ways of understanding it. In the dominant Western medical discourse, the body can be reduced to a moment by being defined in a specific and unambiguous way, and in the discourse of alternative treatment, the body can correspondingly be defined unambiguously – but in a different way from in the medical discourse. Christian discourse contains yet another way of understanding the body, linking it to the sign 'the soul'. The word 'body', then, does not say so much in itself, it has to be positioned in relation to other signs in order to give meaning. And this happens through *articulation*. In the citation on page 26, Laclau and Mouffe define articulation as every practice that establishes a relation between elements such that the identity of the elements is modified. The word 'body' is in itself polysemic and its identity is therefore decided through being related to other words in an articulation. For instance, the utterance 'body and soul' places 'body' in a religious discourse, whereby some meanings of the word are put forward and others ignored.

Now that we have identified 'the body' both as a nodal point in medical discourse and as an element, a little clarification is appropriate. Nodal points are the privileged signs around which a discourse is organised. But these signs are empty in themselves. As mentioned, the sign 'body' does not acquire detailed meaning until it is inserted in a particular discourse. Therefore, the sign 'body' is also an element. Actually, discourse theory has a term for those elements which are particularly open to different ascriptions of meaning, and that is *floating signifiers* (Laclau 1990: 28, 1993b: 287). Floating signifiers are the signs that different discourses struggle to invest with meaning in their own particular way. Nodal points are floating signifiers, but whereas the term 'nodal point' refers to a point of crystallisation within a specific discourse, the term 'floating signifier' belongs to the ongoing struggle between different discourses to fix the meaning of important signs. Thus 'body' is a nodal point in medical discourse, and a floating signifier in the struggle between medical discourse and alternative treatment discourses.

We can now relate all the terms to one another. Discourse aims to remove ambiguities by turning the elements into moments through closure. But this aim is never completely successful as the possibilities of meaning that the discourse displaces to the field of discursivity always threaten to destabilise the fixity of meaning. Therefore, all moments stay potentially polysemic, which means that the moments are always potentially elements. Specific articulations reproduce or challenge the existing discourses by fixing meaning in particular ways. And because of the perpetual potential polysemy, every verbal or written expression (even every social action, as we will see later on) is also, to some extent, an articulation or innovation; although the expression draws on earlier fixations of meaning – that is, it draws on discourses in which the signs have become moments – the expression is never merely a repetition of something already established (Laclau and Mouffe 1985: 113f). Therefore, every expression is an active reduction of the possibilities of meaning because it positions the signs in relation to one another in only one way, thus excluding alternative forms of organisation.

Discourse, then, can be understood as a type of structure in a Saussurian sense – a fixation of signs in a relational net. But, in contrast to the Saussurian tradition whereby structure covered all signs in a *permanent* closure, discourse, for Laclau and Mouffe, can never be total in the Saussurian sense. There are always other meaning potentials which, when actualised in specific articulations, may challenge and transform the structure of the discourse. Thus the discourse is a *temporary* closure: it fixes meaning in a particular way, but it does not dictate that meaning is to be fixed exactly in that way forever. In Laclau and Mouffe's terms, articulations are contingent interventions in an undecidable terrain. That means that articulations constantly shape and intervene in the structures of meaning in unpredictable ways. Discourses are incomplete structures in the same undecidable terrain that never quite become completely structured. Hence there is always room for *struggles* over what the structure should look like, what discourses should prevail, and how meaning should be ascribed to the individual signs.

Now we have reached a first entry point for concrete discourse analysis. Discourse theory suggests that we focus on the specific expressions in their capacity as articulations: what meanings do they establish by positioning elements in particular relationships with one other, and what meaning potentials do they exclude? The articulations can be investigated in relation to the discourses by addressing the following questions. What discourse or discourses does a specific articulation draw on, what discourses does it reproduce? Or, alternatively, does it challenge and transform an existing discourse by redefining some of its moments? As a starting point for answers to these questions, the nodal points of the specific discourses can be identified: what signs have a privileged status, and how are they defined in relation to the other signs in the discourse? When we have identified the signs that are nodal points, we can then investigate how other discourses define the same signs (floating signifiers) in alternative ways. And by examining the competing ascriptions of content to the floating signifiers, we can begin to identify the struggles taking place over meaning. In that way, we can gradually map the partial structuring by the discourses of specific domains. What signs are the objects of struggle over meaning between competing discourses (floating signifiers); and what signs have relatively fixed and undisputed meanings (moments)?

In contrast to Saussure, who saw the uncovering of the structure as the goal of science, Laclau and Mouffe's discourse theory is interested in analysing *how* the structure, in the form of discourses, is constituted and changed. That is done by looking at how articulations constantly reproduce, challenge or transform discourses. To continue with the medical examples, a specific analysis could explore how, where and when the dominant Western medical discourse and the alternative treatment discourses compete with one another about, for example, the definition of the body, and how medical discourse is transformed in specific articulations, as alternative treatments such as acupuncture become increasingly accepted within medical science.

CRITIQUE OF MARXISM

In Laclau and Mouffe's discourse theory, the discursive processes that we have described above do not only include what we normally regard as systems of signs (language in text and talk, visual communication, and perhaps fashion and architecture); they encompass the entire social field. Laclau and Mouffe's theory of the social is, therefore, an integrated part of their discourse theory. Their theory of the social has been developed through a critical reading of Marxist theory which we will now outline.

To begin with, we will paint a rather caricatured picture of historical materialism.[3] Historical materialism, introduced by Karl Marx, distinguishes between a base and a superstructure in its description of society. Material conditions, the economy and, most importantly, ownership of the means of production, belong to the base. To the superstructure belong the state, the judicial system, the church, mass media and schools, and the entire production of meaning that goes on in society. But the central feature is that the economy is the core in terms of which everything is explained: the base determines the superstructure, and therefore it is the economy that determines what people say and think. It is also the base that keeps history going, because change is understood as caused by changes in the economy.

The base of capitalist society is characterised by the fact that the capitalists own the production apparatus and thereby also the products that are produced. The workers own only their labour which they sell to the capitalists. Thus, in capitalist society, there are two classes which stand in opposition to one another in the sense that the capitalists exploit the workers. The reason that the workers do not immediately rebel is that their consciousness is shaped by the superstructure, which is in turn determined by the base. The superstructure of the capitalist system, then, supports the capitalist economy by producing an ideology that legitimates the system. And because the workers' consciousness is shaped by ideology, they cannot see through it to their true interests – they suffer from 'false consciousness'. The transition to socialism and, later on, communism, will occur when the working class recognises its true interests and engages in revolution.

The main problem with historical materialism is the lack of any explanation for this transformation of consciousness: how will the working class recognise its real position in society and its true interests if its consciousness is determined by capitalist ideology? Different Marxist thinkers throughout the 20th century have tried to solve the problem by pointing out the need for a *political* element in the model.[4] Perhaps the economy does not completely determine the superstructure and people's consciousness; maybe there is room for political struggle at the level of the superstructure which can influence people's consciousness in different directions. By inserting a political element in the base/superstructure model, the determination no longer runs in only one direction: it is no longer the economy that determines everything else. What goes on in the superstructure can now also work back on, and change, the base. The next question is where to set the boundary line between political struggle and economic determination: to what extent does the economy determine and to what extent can superstructural phenomena work back on the base? An important follow-up question has been raised concerning social class. According to historical materialism, the economy determines the division of capitalist society into two objective classes, the ruling class and the working class; these classes exist even if people are not necessarily conscious of their existence. But if one problematises economic determinism, then one can no longer be certain that society consists of two, and specifically these two, classes. One cannot even be certain that classes are the relevant groups into which to divide society.

Antonio Gramsci, who is a major source of inspiration for Laclau and Mouffe, formulated a theory that aimed to solve these questions.[5] He slackened the grip of economic determinism, finding that the position of power of the ruling class could not be explained by an economically determined ideology alone. He applied the concept of *hegemony* to explain the processes in the superstructure that play a part in the creation of people's consciousness:

> Hegemony is best understood as *the organisation of consent* – the processes through which subordinated forms of consciousness are constructed without recourse to violence or coercion. (Barrett 1991: 54, italics in original)

To secure their position, the dominant classes have violence and force at their disposal. But more importantly, the production of meaning is a key instrument for the stabilisation of power relations. Through the production of meaning, power relations can become naturalised and so much part of common-sense that they cannot be questioned. For instance, through a process of nation-building, the people of a particular geographical area may begin to feel that they belong to the same group and share conditions and interests irrespective of class barriers. In Gramsci's theory, hegemony is the term for the social consensus, which masks people's real interests. The hegemonic processes take place in the superstructure and are part of a political field. Their outcome is not directly determined by the economy, and so superstructural processes assume a degree of autonomy and the possibility for working back on the structure of the base. It also means that, through the creation of meaning in the superstructure, people can be mobilised to rebel against existing conditions. This view stands in sharp contrast to the version of historical materialism to which we referred earlier. As already pointed out, historical materialism could not explain where resistance could come from because people's consciousness was completely determined by the economic conditions. With Gramsci, consciousness is determined instead by hegemonic processes in the superstructure; people's consciousness gains a degree of autonomy in relation to the economic conditions, so opening up the possibility for people to envisage alternative ways of organising society. But, according to Gramsci, it is still the economic conditions that control the phenomena of the superstructure *in the final instance* for it is the economy that determines people's true interests and the division of society into classes.

Gramsci's theory of hegemony implies that the processes of meaning creation taking place at the level of the superstructure are worth studying in their own right, unlike in the case of historical materialism, where the only important processes taking place are in the economy. Here, we can begin to discern a link with Laclau and Mouffe's discourse theory – a theory about the creation of meaning. Through his concept of hegemony, Gramsci opens up the political field, but he closes it again when he attributes the division of society into classes to the economy. Classes are, for Gramsci, as for historical materialism, *objective* groups to which people belong whether they know it or not. Laclau and Mouffe radicalise Gramsci's theory by abolishing the objectivism or essentialism that is still to be found here. For Laclau and Mouffe, there are no objective laws that divide society into particular groups; the groups that exist are always created in political, discursive processes. That does not mean that Laclau and Mouffe turn the base/superstructure model of historical materialism on its head and claim that discourses determine the economy. In their theory of the social, they override Marxist essentialism by fusing the two categories – base and superstructure – into one field produced by the same discursive processes.

THEORY OF THE SOCIAL

Once again we will begin with an impressionistic picture of Laclau and Mouffe's theory before we define the specific terms. Laclau and Mouffe's concept of 'discourse' encompasses not only language but all social phenomena. Earlier on, we covered the point that discourses attempt to structure signs, *as if* all signs had a permanently fixed and unambiguous meaning in a total structure. The same logic applies to the whole social field: we act as if the 'reality' around us has a stable and unambiguous structure; as if society, the groups we belong to, and our identity, are objectively given facts. But just as the structure of language is never totally fixed, so are society and identity flexible and changeable entities that can never be completely fixed. The aim of analysis is, therefore, not to uncover the objective reality, for example, to find out what groups society 'really' consists of, but to explore *how* we create this reality so that it appears objective and natural. Where Marxism presumed the existence of an objective social structure that analysis should reveal, the starting point of Laclau and Mouffe's discourse theory is that we construct objectivity through the discursive production of meaning. It is that construction process that should be the target of analysis.

Laclau and Mouffe transform the Marxist tradition in three ways, which we will sketch out in the following sections. First, they abolish the division between base and superstructure and understand all societal formations as products of discursive processes. Second, they dismiss the Marxist conception of society: that society can be described objectively, as a totality constituted by certain classes. According to Laclau and Mouffe, society is never as unambiguous as historical materialism suggests. 'Society', they argue, is our attempt to pin down the meaning of society, not an objectively existing phenomenon. Third, and as a result of this view of the social, Laclau and Mouffe reject the Marxist understanding of identity and group formation. For Marxism, people have an objective (class) identity even if they do not realise it. For Laclau and Mouffe, it cannot be determined beforehand what groups will become politically relevant. People's identities (both collective and individual) are the result of contingent, discursive processes and, as such, are part of the discursive struggle. At the end of this section we will describe how Laclau and Mouffe understand conflict or antagonism and, in relation to this, how they further develop Gramsci's concept of hegemony.[6]

The Primacy of Politics

For historical materialism, the material base was the starting point and the superstructure was determined by the base. Gramsci established a dialectic between base and superstructure: the conditions of the base influence superstructure, but political processes in the superstructure can also act back on the base. For Laclau and Mouffe, it is political processes that are the most important: politics has primacy (Laclau 1990: 33). Political articulations determine how we act and think and thereby how we create society. The more or less determining role of the economy is, then, completely abolished in discourse theory. That does not mean that everything is language or that the material has no significance. That becomes clear when we look at how Laclau and Mouffe understand the two concepts, discourse and politics.

Earlier in this chapter, we presented Laclau and Mouffe's concept of discourse as if discourses were merely linguistic phenomena, but that is not the whole story. Laclau and Mouffe do not distinguish between discursive and non-discursive phenomena. In Chapter 1 we introduced a continuum (Figure 1.1) which contrasted approaches that submit all phenomena to the same discursive logic with approaches that are characterised by a more dialectic view of the relationship between discursive and non-discursive phenomena. Historical materialism lies to the far right on the continuum: all phenomena are organised according to a logic rooted in the non-discursive, in the material; discourses have no autonomy or internal logic. People like Gramsci are situated a little closer to the middle, but still on the right-hand side. Laclau and Mouffe's discourse theory is placed on the far left-hand side, and that has consequences for the choice of analytical tools needed for a study of specific social phenomena. Whereas Fairclough, located in the middle of the continuum, distinguishes between the discursive and non-discursive dimensions of social practice and sees a dialectic relationship between the dimensions, Laclau and Mouffe understand social practices as fully discursive. Consequently, Fairclough needs two sets of theories and analytical tools while Laclau and Mouffe operate with just one. Fairclough uses discourse analysis to analyse linguistic practices and other theories, such as social theories of late modernity, for the analysis of other aspects of social practice, while for Laclau and Mouffe, all social phenomena are understood and analysed using the same concepts: discourse, articulation, closure, and so on.

But, as mentioned, this does not mean that Laclau and Mouffe reduce everything to language because, for them, discourses are *material* (1985: 108). For instance, children in modern societies are seen as a group which in many ways is different from other groups, and this difference is not only established linguistically. Children are also materially constituted as a group in a physical space: they have their own institutions such as nurseries and schools, their own departments in libraries and their own play areas in parks. These institutions and physical features are part of the discourse about children in modern societies.

Some critics have understood Laclau and Mouffe's theory to imply that, since everything is discourse, then reality does not exist.[7] This is a misunderstanding. For Laclau and Mouffe's approach, as for the other discourse analytical approaches, both social and physical objects exist, but our access to them is always mediated by systems of meaning in the form of discourses. Physical objects do not possess meaning in themselves; meaning is something we ascribe to them through discourse. To exemplify this, Laclau and Mouffe point out that a stone does exist independently of social classification systems, but whether it is understood as a projectile or a work of art depends on the discursive context in which it is situated (Laclau and Mouffe 1990: 101). Physical reality is totally superimposed by the social. And in Laclau and Mouffe's discourse theory, all social phenomena are understood as being organised according to the same principle as language. Just as signs in language are relationally defined and therefore acquire their meaning by their difference from one another, so social actions derive their meaning from their relationship to other actions. For instance, a package holiday to Marbella gains its meaning as an act from its difference from a trip to Paris, or from no holiday at all. We interpret this act as a discursive sign, and in the same way as the meaning of linguistic signs is kept in place by closures, although they are constantly in danger of sliding into new articulations, we are forever trying to fix the meanings of other social acts – an attempt which never quite succeeds. All social practices can thus be seen as articulations (Laclau and Mouffe 1985: 113), because they reproduce or change common ascriptions of meaning.

Reproduction and change of meaning ascriptions are, in general terms, political acts. *Politics* in discourse theory is not to be understood narrowly as, for example, party politics; on the contrary, it is a broad concept that refers to the manner in which we constantly constitute the social in ways that exclude other ways. Our actions are contingent articulations, that is, temporary fixations of meaning in an undecidable terrain which reproduce or change the existing discourses and thereby the organisation of society. Laclau and Mouffe understand politics as the organisation of society in a particular way that excludes all other possible ways. Politics, then, is not just a surface that reflects a deeper social reality; rather, it is the social organisation that is the outcome of continuous political processes.

When a struggle takes place between particular discourses, it sometimes becomes clear that different actors are trying to promote different ways of organising society. At other times, our social practices can appear so natural that we can hardly see that there could be alternatives. For instance, we are so used to the understanding and treatment of children as a group with distinctive characteristics that we treat the discourse about children as natural. But just a few hundred years ago, children were, to a much greater degree, seen and treated as 'small adults' (Aries 1962). Those discourses that are so firmly established that their contingency is forgotten are called *objective* in discourse theory (Laclau 1990: 34).[8] That does not mean the reintroduction of the division between the objectively given on the one hand and the play of politics on the other. Objectivity is the historical outcome of political processes and struggles; it is *sedimented* discourse. The boundary between objectivity and the political, or between what seems natural and what is contested, is thus a fluid and historical boundary, and earlier sedimented discourses can, at any time, enter the play of politics and be problematised in new articulations.

The concept of *hegemony* comes between 'objectivity' and 'the political'. Just as the objective can become political again, so manifest conflicts can, in the course of time, disappear and give way to objectivity where one perspective is naturalised and consensus prevails. The development from political conflict to objectivity passes through hegemonic interventions whereby alternative understandings of the world are suppressed, leading to the naturalisation of one single perspective. We will discuss the concept of hegemony in more depth later in this chapter.

Objectivity may, therefore, be said to be the term for what appears as given and unchangeable, for what seemingly does not derive its meaning from its difference from something else. But this is 'seemingly' only, and that is the reason why discourse theory equates objectivity and *ideology* (Laclau 1990: 89ff). All meaning is fluid and all discourses are contingent; it is objectivity that masks contingency and, in so doing, hides the alternative possibilities that otherwise could have presented themselves. Objectivity can therefore be said to be ideological. As we are going to see in the following chapters, critical discourse analysis and discursive psychology define the concept of ideology in such a way that it can be used to identify and criticise unjust power relations. This is not possible in Laclau and Mouffe's discourse theory because a society without ideology is unthinkable in discourse theory since ideology is defined as objectivity. We are always dependent on taking large areas of the social world for granted in our practices – it would be impossible always to question everything. In order not to be confused with a more traditional ideology critique, such as Fairclough's critical discourse analysis, Laclau and Mouffe hardly ever use the concept of ideology, preferring instead the concept of objectivity (for an exception see Laclau 1996a).

The concept of *power* in Laclau and Mouffe's approach is closely connected to their concepts of politics and objectivity (Laclau 1990: 31ff.). It is similar to Foucault's concept of power, outlined in Chapter 1. Power is not understood as something which people possess and exercise over others, but as that which produces the social. It may appear strange to use the word 'power' to denote the force and the processes which create our social world and make it meaningful for us, but the point is that this understanding of power emphasises the contingency of our social world. It is power that creates our knowledge, our identities and how we relate to one another as groups or individuals. And knowledge, identity and social relations are all contingent: at a given time, they all take a particular form, but they could have been – and can become – different. Therefore, power is productive in that it produces the social in particular ways. Power is not something you can make disappear: we are dependent on living in a social order and the social order is always constituted in power. But we are not dependent on living in a *particular* social order, and the exclusion of other social orders is also one of the effects of power. On the one hand, power produces an inhabitable world for us, and, on the other hand, it precludes alternative possibilities.[9]

Objectivity is sedimented power where the traces of power have become effaced, where it has been forgotten that the world is politically constructed (Laclau 1990: 60). Our understanding of Laclau and Mouffe's theory is that power and politics are two sides of the same coin, where power refers to the production of objects such as 'society' and 'identity', while politics refers to the always present contingency of these objects. Objectivity, then, refers to the world we take for granted, a world which we have 'forgotten' is always constituted by power and politics.

By way of summing up these premises, let us briefly discuss *contingency* versus *continuity*. The starting point of the theory is that all articulation, and thus everything social, is contingent – possible but not necessary. This is both the philosophical foundation of the theory and its analytical motor. It is only by constantly looking at those possibilities that are excluded that one can pinpoint the social consequences of particular discursive constructions of the social. But the fact that all social formations could at all times be different does not mean that everything changes all the time, or that the social can be shaped freely. The social is always partly structured in particular ways; discourses have, so to speak, a weightiness and an inertia in which we are more or less caught up, and there is at all times a vast area of objectivity which it is hard to think beyond. People are, like society, fundamentally socially shaped (see pages 40–7 on identity and group formation), and the possibilities we have for reshaping the structures are set by earlier structures. Although the philosophical starting point is that all structures are contingent, our thinking can never transcend all existing structures, for, in giving meaning to the world, we always imply some or other structure. Meanings are never completely fixed, but nor are they ever completely fluid and open (Laclau and Mouffe 1985: 113). Both people and society are understood as historical phenomena that are compelled to work on the basis of the existing structures, presupposing and ensuring continuity in the social.

The Impossible Society

Laclau and Mouffe claim that society is impossible, that it does not exist (1985: 111). By this, they mean that society as an objective entity is never completed or total. Earlier, we explained how the concept of structure in the Saussurian tradition is criticised by poststructuralists on the grounds that Saussurians understand structure as a totality in which all signs relate unambiguously to one another. Laclau and Mouffe replace this concept of structure with the concept of discourse that also refers to a structuring of signs in relation to one another, but which stresses that the structuring never exhausts all the possibilities for the ascription of meaning. A discourse can always be undermined by articulations that place the signs in different relations to one another. According to Laclau and Mouffe's discourse theory, the signs are therefore structured in relation to each other but never in a finished totality. Discourses are always only temporary and partial fixations of meaning in a fundamentally undecidable terrain.

It is the same type of criticism that Laclau and Mouffe direct against Marxism and many other social theories. Historical materialism sees society as an objective totality in which the economy produces demarcated groups (classes) that have fixed relations to one another (on opposite sides of the class struggle). Laclau and Mouffe challenge this view, contending that society does not exist as an objective totality in which everything has a stable position. 'Society' is at all times partly structured, but only partly and temporarily. If, for instance, people identify with different classes, it is not because society is objectively constituted by these classes, but because there has been a temporary *closure* whereby other possibilities for identification, such as gender or ethnicity, are marginalised or excluded.

We continuously produce society and act *as if* it exists as a totality, and we verbalise it as a totality. With words like 'the people' or 'the country' we seek to demarcate a totality by ascribing it an objective content. But the totality remains an imaginary entity. If, for instance, a Labour politician in a British electoral campaign announces that 'we will do the best for the country', and a Conservative politician says the same thing, then it is most probably very different images of the country, and very different plans, they have in mind (cf. Laclau 1993b: 287). 'The country', and all other terms for society as a totality, are floating signifiers; they are invested with a different content by different articulations. Laclau's term for a floating signifier that refers to a totality is *myth*:

> By myth we mean a space of representation which bears no relation of continuity with the dominant 'structural objectivity'. Myth is thus a principle of reading of a given situation, whose terms are external to what is representable in the objective spatiality constituted by the given structure. (Laclau 1990: 61)

This way of thinking parallels the one which we saw in the critique of structuralism: there are only temporary structurings of the social, and any one structure is never final or total. The total structure is, like 'society', something we imagine in order to make our acts meaningful. The social structures, then, are not concordant with the myth. The myth is, on the one hand, a distorted representation of reality, but on the other hand, this distortion is inevitable and constitutive because it establishes a necessary horizon for our acts. Thus the myth, 'the country', makes national politics possible and provides the different politicians with a platform on which they can discuss with one another. At the same time, the choice of myth delimits what it is meaningful to discuss and the manner in which it can be discussed. If 'the country' is the starting point, then 'national economy' is important and local, regional and global economic issues are understood from a national perspective.

One aim of discourse analysis is to pinpoint and analyse the myths of society as objective reality that are implied in talk and other actions. How it is that some myths come to appear objectively true and others as impossible is a central question. And one can analyse how myths as floating signifiers are invested with different contents by different social actors in the struggle to make their particular understanding of 'society' the prevailing one.

IDENTITY AND GROUP FORMATION

How can we conceptualise the actors who participate in the struggles about the definition and shaping of reality? As we mentioned in Chapter 1, all the approaches to discourse analysis are critical of the classical Western understanding of the individual as an autonomous subject. And as we saw in Laclau and Mouffe's critique of Marxist theory, they also reject the position that collective identity (in Marxist theory, primarily classes) is determined by economic and material factors. According to Laclau and Mouffe, individual and collective identity are both organised according to the same principles in the same discursive processes. We begin by presenting their understanding of the subject and individual identity and then move on to cover collective identity and group formation.

Subject Positions

As mentioned in Chapter 1, *interpellation* was Althusser's suggestion for an alternative to the classical Western view of the subject. Individuals are interpellated or placed in certain positions by particular ways of talking. If a child says 'mum' and the adult responds, then the adult has become interpellated with a particular identity – a 'mother' – to which particular expectations about her behaviour are attached. In discourse theoretical terms, the subjects become positions in discourses. By and large, it is this understanding of the subject that Laclau and Mouffe employ in *Hegemony and Socialist Strategy*. However, in Althusser's theory there is still an economic determinism incompatible with discourse theory: Althusser understands the interpellation of the subjects as ideological as it hides the true relations between people. To Laclau and Mouffe, there are no 'true' social relations determined by the economy. But the people are still interpellated by discourses: subjects are to be understood as 'subject positions' within a discursive structure (1985: 115). Discourses always designate positions for people to occupy as subjects. For instance, at a medical consultation the positions of 'doctor' and 'patient' are specified. Corresponding to these positions, there are certain expectations about how to act, what to say and what not to say. For instance, the doctor has the authority to say what is wrong with the patient; the patient can only guess. If the doctor does not believe that the patient is sick, and the patient insists on it, then the patient has exceeded the boundary for what is allowed in the patient position and is branded a hypochondriac.

We have seen that Laclau and Mouffe, in agreement with poststructuralism in general, think that one discourse can never establish itself so firmly that it becomes the only discourse that structures the social. There are always several conflicting discourses at play. As with Althusser, the subject is not understood as sovereign in poststructuralist theory: the subject is not autonomous, but is determined by discourses. In addition, and in contrast to Althusser's theory, the subject is also *fragmented*: it is not positioned in only one way and by only one discourse, but, rather, is ascribed many different positions by different discourses. At elections, the subject is a 'voter', at a dinner party, a 'guest', and perhaps in the family a 'mother', 'wife' and 'daughter'. Often the shifts go unnoticed and the individual does not even realise that he or she occupies several different subject positions throughout each day. But if conflicting discourses strive simultaneously to organise the same social space, the individual is interpellated in different positions at the same time. For instance, on election day, the question may be whether the individual should let herself be interpellated as a feminist, a Christian or a worker. Perhaps all of these possibilities seem attractive, but they point in different directions when it comes to voting. In such cases, the subject is *overdetermined*. That means that he or she is positioned by several conflicting discourses among which a conflict arises. For Laclau and Mouffe, the subject is always overdetermined because the discourses are always contingent; there is no objective logic that points to a single subject position. Subject positions that are not in visible conflict with other positions are the outcome of hegemonic processes (see pages 47–9), whereby alternative possibilities have been excluded and a particular discourse has been naturalised.

Lacan's Theory of the Subject

In texts written since *Hegemony and Socialist Strategy* Laclau has imported Jacques Lacan's theories, via Slavoj Žižek, in order to develop the concept of the subject further. Laclau uses Lacan to give the individual an unconscious, which can explain why people allow themselves to be interpellated by discourses. As we will show, Lacan's theory of the subject parallels Laclau and Mouffe's conceptions of structure and society: Lacan also understands the subject as a perpetually incomplete structure which constantly strives to become a whole.[10]

Lacan's theory begins with the infant. The infant is not aware of itself as a delimited subject but lives in symbiosis with the mother and the world around it. Gradually, the infant becomes detached from the mother but retains the memory of a feeling of completeness. Generally, the condition of the subject is the perpetual striving to become whole again. Through socialisation, the child is presented with discursive images of 'who it is' and what identity it has. The subject comes to know itself as an individual by identifying with *something* outside itself, that is, with the images presented to it. The images are internalised, but the child (and, later on, the adult) constantly feels that he or she does not quite fit the images. So the images are, at one and the same time, the basis of identification and of alienation. The images which come from the outside and are internalised are continuously compared to the infant's feeling of wholeness, but they never quite match it. Therefore, the subject is fundamentally *split*. Lacan speaks of 'the self's radical ex-centricity to itself with which man is confronted' (Lacan 1977a: 171): regardless of where the subject is positioned by the discourses, the feeling of wholeness fails to emerge.

The idea of the true, whole self is a fiction (Lacan 1977b: 2) or, using Laclau's term explained above, a myth. Like the social, the individual is partly structured by discourses, but the structuring is never total. The wholeness is imaginary but it is a necessary horizon within which both the self and the social are created.

By incorporating Lacan's understanding of the subject, discourse theory has provided the subject with a 'driving force' as it constantly tries to 'find itself' through investing in discourses. We will now take a closer look at how the individual is structured discursively. Identity, for Lacan, is equivalent to identification with something. And this 'something' is the subject positions which discourses offer the individual. Lacan speaks of *master signifiers*, which, in Laclau and Mouffe's discourse theoretical terms, we can call the nodal points of identity. 'Man' is an example of a master signifier, and different discourses offer different content to fill this signifier. This takes place through the linking together of signifiers in *chains of equivalence* that establish the identity relationally (Laclau and Mouffe 1985: 127ff.). The discursive construction of 'man' pinpoints what 'man' equals and what it differs from. For instance, a widespread discourse equates 'man' with 'strength', 'reason' and 'football' (and many other things) and contrasts that with 'woman': 'passive', 'passion' and 'cooking'.[11] The discourse thus provides behavioural instructions to people who identify with man and woman respectively which they have to follow in order to be regarded as a (real) man or woman.

It is by being *represented* in this way by a cluster of signifiers with a nodal point at its centre that one acquires an identity. Identities are accepted, refused and negotiated in discursive processes. Identity is thus something entirely social. Laclau and Mouffe, then, have rejected the traditional Western understanding of the individual in which identity is seen as an individual, inner core to be expressed across contexts. Likewise, they have deserted historical materialism with its view of identity as determined by the base, situating identity instead in discursive, and so in political, practices.

The understanding of identity in Laclau and Mouffe's discourse theory can be summarised as follows:

- The subject is fundamentally *split*, it never quite becomes 'itself'.
- It acquires its identity by being *represented* discursively.
- Identity is thus *identification* with a subject position in a discursive structure.
- Identity is discursively constituted through *chains of equivalence* where signs are sorted and linked together in chains in opposition to other chains which thus define how the subject is, and how it is not.
- Identity is always *relationally* organised; the subject is something because it is contrasted with something that it is not.
- Identity is *changeable* just as discourses are.
- The subject is *fragmented* or *decentred*; it has different identities according to those discourses of which it forms part.
- The subject is *overdetermined*; in principle, it always has the possibility to identify differently in specific situations. Therefore, a given identity is *contingent* – that is, possible but not necessary.

Group Formation

For Laclau and Mouffe, as noted earlier, collective identity or group formation is understood according to the same principles as individual identity. The boundary between the two types of identity is fuzzy: there is little difference between identification as a 'man' and identification with the group, 'men'.

As we have seen in their critique of Marxism, Laclau and Mouffe claim that there are no objective conditions that determine into which groups the social space is divided. We have seen that individuals have several identities (decentring) and that they have the possibility of identifying differently in given situations (overdetermination). How are groups to be understood in this chaos? Group formation is to be understood as a reduction of possibilities. People are constituted as groups through a process by which some possibilities of identification are put forward as relevant while others are ignored. This process takes place through the establishment of chains of equivalence. For instance, take the group 'blacks'. In the decades following the Second World War, 'blacks' came to form a group in the UK, among other places. At first it was not necessarily 'blacks' who identified themselves in that way, perhaps preferring to identify themselves as Jamaicans, Pakistanis or Asians – or as women or homosexuals or cab drivers. But in British society, everyone who was not white was, in many situations, equated with one another and identified and treated as 'black'. White Britons constituted a collective identity by contrasting themselves with the group of 'blacks'. In the 1960s, many 'blacks' began to use the label positively; it became 'black is beautiful'. Thus, the already constituted discursive identification was mobilised politically, and used for pointing to, and criticising social conditions experienced by 'black people' in common. This example is taken from an article by Stuart Hall (1991), in which he also considers what the category 'black' can be used for today. Like all other group formations, the category 'black' obscures the differences that exist within the group. Thus for example, one overlooks that 'black' women have, in some cases, more in common with 'white' women than they have with 'black' men. Group formations are always closures in an undecidable terrain, and as with discourse in general, they only work by excluding alternative interpretations.

In discursive group formations, then, 'the other' – that which one identifies oneself is excluded, and the differences within the group are ignored. Thereby all the other ways in which one could have formed groups are also ignored. In this sense, group formation is political.[12]

Such discursive processes can be captured with Laclau and Mouffe's pair of concepts 'the logic of equivalence' and 'the logic of difference' (Laclau and Mouffe 1985: 127ff.). The *logic of equivalence* worked as all non-white people gradually were identified as black: the specificity of all the different colours and origins was subsumed in the one category 'black', and 'black' was defined in opposition to what it was not, that is, as 'non-white'. Thus the social space collapsed into a polar opposition according to which the only identities available were 'black' and 'white'. By contrast, Stuart Hall's intervention promotes *the logic of difference*, as he tries to disperse the polar opposition in a larger number of more specific identities. According to Hall, relevant categories are not only black and white, but also, for instance, gender, and the social space, in his representation, is populated with (at least) four different kinds of identity: black women, black men, white women and white men. The example also shows that, as political projects, neither the logic of equivalence nor the logic of difference can *a priori* be designated the more progressive way to go. Whereas the logic of equivalence provided 'blacks' with a common platform from which to claim equal rights, it also overshadowed internal differences and injustices cross-cutting the black/white distinction. And whereas Hall's logic of difference may shed light on such injustices, it may simultaneously weaken the common ground for 'black' mobilisation.

Representation

An important element in processes of group formation is *representation*. Because groups are not socially predetermined, they do not exist until they are constituted in discourse. And that entails that someone talks about, or on behalf of, the group. Representation basically means that one can be represented by proxy when one is physically absent. For instance, all citizens cannot be present in parliament to discuss political issues, and that is why representative democracy is practical. Citizens elect representatives who can be present on their behalf when they cannot be present themselves. The ideal is that there is agreement between the representative and the group that he or she represents; the representative should personify the will of the group. But, according to Laclau and Mouffe, there are no objective groups since groups are always created through contingent constructions of equivalence among different elements. So it is not the case that the group is formed first and later represented; group and representative are constituted in one movement. It is not until someone speaks of, or to, or on behalf of, a group that it is constituted as a group (Laclau 1993b: 289ff.).

Whenever a group is represented, a whole understanding of society follows with it as the group is constituted in contrast to other groups:

The basic point is this: I cannot assert a differential identity without distinguishing it from a context, and, in the process of making the distinction, I am asserting the context at the same time. (Laclau 1996b: 27)

Group formation thus plays a part in the struggle over how the myth about society is to be filled with meaning. And conversely, different understandings of society divide the social space into different groups. For instance, traditional class struggle implies the idea of the division of society into classes that fight against each other, while a feminist perspective emphasises division by gender. The understanding of society which prevails, and the group division that this implies, have critical consequences for our actions.

Eric Hobsbawm has (from a somewhat more traditional Marxist standpoint) reflected on processes of collective identity in the years before the First World War (Hobsbawm 1990: 122 ff.). At the end of the 19th century, people's sense of belonging to nation states was growing and the division of the world along national lines seemed increasingly natural. At the same time, workers' identification of themselves as workers was also growing and this group formation implied another understanding of the world – one constituted by 'workers' in contrast to 'capitalists' across national borders. This was not a big problem since, as we have seen, the subject is fragmented and constituted in several different subject positions. But in the run-up to the First World War, the two understandings of the world came into conflict with one another. Or, to use a discourse theoretical term that we will introduce in the next section, an antagonism arose. Advocates of people as nations competed for the people's favour with advocates representing people as classes, and, finally, the national articulation prevailed. Hobsbawm interprets this as a contributory factor to the war, which was a war between nation states, and which would have been unthinkable if the group formation principles of the class struggle had been established as objectively true (Hobsbawm 1990: 130).

Hobsbawm does not practise discourse analysis, but, as we have presented it, his analysis still serves as an example of what a discourse analysis of discursive and political processes could look like. This kind of analysis would focus on articulations that constitute particular groups through representation and would explore the understandings of society that are implied. When collective (and individual) identity is investigated by discourse analysis, the starting point is to identify which subject positions – individual or collective – the discursive structures indicate as relevant. That can be done by looking for the nodal point around which identity is organised. It could be 'immigrant', 'housewife' or 'worker'.

Then one can investigate the way in which the nodal point is filled with meaning relationally by being equated with some, and contrasted with other, signifiers. It is important to map how different discourses struggle to divide the social into groups along different lines, and to fill the different master signifiers with different content by equating them with different signifiers. For instance, the introduction of 'the new man' challenged the traditional discourse about masculinity that contrasted 'man' and 'feelings'. The construction of subject positions and hence identities, then, is a battlefield where different constellations of elements struggle to prevail. In the next section, we present in some detail Laclau and Mouffe's theorisation of the struggle.

ANTAGONISM AND HEGEMONY

The *struggle* over the creation of meaning has been an ongoing theme in this chapter, and in the discourse theoretical perspective, conflict and struggle pervade the social, so struggle becomes an important focus in specific analysis. We will now take a closer look at how antagonistic conflicts can be understood theoretically within a discourse theoretical framework.

The starting point of discourse theory is that no discourse can be fully established, it is always in conflict with other discourses that define reality differently and set other guidelines for social action. At particular historical moments, certain discourses can seem natural and be relatively uncontested. That it is to this phenomenon that the concept of objectivity refers. But the naturalised discourses are never definitively established and their moments can again become elements and thus objects for new articulations.

A *social antagonism* occurs when different identities mutually exclude each other. Although a subject has different identities, these do not have to relate antagonistically to one another. The implication of Hobsbawm's example is that one can be a 'worker' and a 'Scot' at the same time. But if the worker identity excludes obligations to the country in war, for instance, or if the national identity summons people to kill those whom they consider to be fellow workers in other countries, then the relationship between the two identities becomes antagonistic. The two identities make contrasting demands in relation to the same actions within a common terrain, and inevitably one blocks the other. The individual discourses, which constitute each of the identities, are part of each other's field of discursivity, and, when an antagonism occurs, everything the individual discourse has excluded threatens to undermine the discourse's existence and fixity of meaning (Laclau 1990: 17). Thus its contingency, and the contingency of the identities it constitutes, become visible.[13]

Thus, antagonisms can be found where discourses collide. Antagonisms may be dissolved through *hegemonic interventions*. A hegemonic intervention is an articulation which by means of force reconstitutes unambiguity (Laclau 1993b: 282f.). Thus, in the First World War the reason why soldiers could be recruited among the 'workers' was that the already established worker identity was suppressed through a hegemonic intervention in favour of a national identity.

'Hegemony' is similar to 'discourse' because both terms denote a fixation of elements in moments. But the hegemonic intervention achieves this fixation across discourses that collide antagonistically. One discourse is undermined from the discursive field from which another discourse overpowers it, or rather dissolves it, by rearticulating its elements. The hegemonic intervention has succeeded if one discourse comes to dominate alone, where before there was conflict, and the antagonism is dissolved. For instance, when people from different nations actually went to war against one another in the First World War, this was a sign that the hegemonic articulation of people as 'Germans' and 'Frenchmen' had succeeded at the expense of the articulation of people as 'workers'. Thus 'hegemonic intervention' is a process that takes place in an antagonistic terrain, and the 'discourse' is the result – the new fixation of meaning.

The establishment of hegemonic discourses as objectivity and their dissolution in new political battlefields is an important aspect of the social processes that discourse analysis investigates. But, according to Laclau, the dissolution of hegemonic discourses is also a fitting description of the practice of discourse analysis itself. Using Jacques Derrida's concept of *deconstruction* to capture such interventions, Laclau describes deconstruction and hegemony as 'the two sides of a single operation' (Laclau 1993b: 281). Hegemony is the contingent articulation of elements in an undecidable terrain and deconstruction is the operation that shows that a hegemonic intervention is contingent – that the elements could have been combined differently (Laclau 1993b: 281f.). Thus, deconstruction reveals the undecidability, while the hegemonic intervention naturalises a particular articulation (cf. Torfing 1999: 103). Discourse analysis aims at the deconstruction of the structures that we take for granted; it tries to show that the given organisation of the world is the result of political processes with social consequences. If, for instance, 'immigrants' in a given discourse are equated with 'crime', then the discourse analyst can show how this coupling has been established discursively and what consequences it has for both 'immigrants' and 'natives'.

But the discourse analyst, like anyone else, does not have access to a privileged standpoint outside the discursive structures, so deconstruction has to take its starting point in the given structures:

> The movements of deconstruction do not destroy structures from the outside. They are not possible and effective, nor can they take accurate aim, except by inhabiting those structures. (Derrida 1998: 24)

The discourse analyst is often anchored in exactly the same discourses as he or she wants to analyse. And, under all circumstances, the discourse analyst is always anchored in some or other discursive structure. Although discourse analysis is about distancing oneself from these discourses and 'showing them as they are', in this kind of theory there is no hope of escaping from the discourses and telling the pure truth, truth in itself being always a discursive construction.

All social constructionist approaches to social and cultural research share this dilemma. But the approaches differ as to the way in which they deal – or fail to deal – with the problem. Laclau and Mouffe briefly acknowledge it in their introduction to *Hegemony and Socialist Strategy* (1985: 3), but they do not specify its consequences for the reliability of their own theory. Other researchers have tried to deal with the problem through *reflexivity* (see Chapters 4 and 6). Under all circumstances, the product of the research – the specific discourse analysis, for example – is a kind of political intervention: a contingent articulation of elements which reproduces or challenges the given discourses in the never-ending struggle to define the world.

USING DISCOURSE THEORY

As we have mentioned, Laclau and Mouffe do not do much detailed analysis of empirical material themselves. And when they do identify specific discourses, they are interested in these as abstract phenomena rather than as resources that people draw upon and transform in the practices of everyday life (see Figure 1.2). But that does not mean that Laclau and Mouffe's theory or their concepts cannot be used in detailed empirical analyses.[14] It just takes a little imagination. Here, we will recapitulate some of Laclau and Mouffe's concepts that we find useful as tools for empirical analysis:

- Nodal points, master signifiers and myths, which can be collectively labelled key signifiers in the organisation of discourse;
- The concept of chains of equivalence which refers to the investment of key signifiers with meaning;
- Concepts concerning identity: group formation, identity and representation; and
- Concepts for conflict analysis: floating signifiers, antagonism and hegemony.

First, the different key signifiers: nodal points, master signifiers and myths. Generally speaking, nodal points organise discourses (for example, 'liberal democracy'), master signifiers organise identity (for example, 'man'), and myths organise a social space (for example, 'the West' or 'society'). All of these concepts refer to key signifiers in the social organisation of meaning. When key signifiers are identified in specific empirical material, the investigation can begin of *how* discourses, identity and the social space respectively are organised discursively. This is done by investigating how the key signifiers are combined with other signs. What the key signifiers have in common is that they are empty signs: that is, they mean almost nothing by themselves until, through chains of equivalence, they are combined with other signs that fill them with meaning. 'Liberal democracy' becomes liberal democracy through its combination with other carriers of meaning such as 'free elections' and 'freedom of speech'. By investigating the chains of meaning that discourses bring together in this way, one can gradually identify discourses (and identities and social spaces). It is important to remember that non-linguistic practices and objects are, according to Laclau and Mouffe, also part of discourses. Therefore electoral observers, ballot boxes and the physical set-up of parliament belong to the discourse of liberal democracy.

Individual and collective identities and maps of the social space can similarly be investigated by following the combinations of meaning in chains of equivalence. A social space such as 'the West' typically links a geographical part of the world to, for instance, 'civilisation', 'white people', 'the Christian church' and 'liberal democratic institutions'. Here we see again that the elements in the chain of equivalence are both linguistic and non-linguistic. And we see how entities (discourses, identities or social space) are always established relationally, in relation to something they are not. The West stands in opposition to the rest of the world which is not automatically accepted as civilised and democratic, but rather defined as 'barbaric' and 'coloured'. Analysis of the 'Other' which is always created together with the creation of 'Us' can give some idea of what a given discourse about ourselves excludes and what social consequences this exclusion has. In the case just mentioned, the rest of the world is excluded from the West – it is completely different and has nothing to do with it. But this construction of the West also excludes the existence of barbarism in the West, because the West is defined by civilisation in contrast to the barbarism of the rest of the world.

However, some people maintain that barbarism also exists in the West, indicating that the understanding of the myth of 'the West' just described is not uncontested. 'The West' is (like 'democracy' and 'man') a floating signifier, and different discourses struggle to fill it with different meanings. Generally speaking, Laclau and Mouffe's theoretical point that discourses are never completely stable and uncontested can be turned into methodological guidelines concerning the location of the lines of conflict in one's empirical material. What different understandings of reality are at stake, where are they in antagonistic opposition to one another? And what are the social consequences if the one or the other wins out and hegemonically pins down the meaning of the floating signifier?

Using these concepts, it is possible to investigate the functioning of discourses in empirical material: how each discourse constitutes knowledge and reality, identities and social relations; where discourses function unobtrusively side by side, and where there are open antagonisms; and which hegemonic interventions are striving to override the conflicts – in which ways and with which consequences.

The following is a brief example of such an analysis focusing on the concepts of 'identity', 'antagonism' and 'hegemony' as analytical tools. Our material consists of two letters: a letter from a 21-year-old woman, 'unhappy', to an agony aunt in a Danish women's magazine and the agony aunt's reply.

Sex and relationships

Love collides with my faith

I am 21 years old and, since I was 11, I have had big psychological problems. Without reason, I turned from being happy and outgoing to being insecure with lots of inferiority complexes. I have no education but now have my own little firm and a nice little apartment. Via my parents I am a member of a particular religious community.

Eight months ago I met my boyfriend who is a complete atheist. At the beginning of our relationship he drank himself out of his senses every weekend when he was off. He came and called me all sorts of bad names, made fun of my faith and threatened me with all sorts of things, but never hit me. When I did not open the door, he would stay and ring the doorbell for hours. He always finished by breaking up with me, but then the next day he would regret it and say that he would pull himself together. Now he rarely gets drunk, but, when he does, he goes crazy again and is nasty. Therefore, I am afraid of letting him out of my sight.

I have dropped my life in my religious community. I did it when I found out that I loved him and because I could not handle two lives. It has been difficult and I actually have no friends anymore, at least not in the same way. It was also difficult for my parents to accept, and relations between us were cold for a while. Luckily, it is now going much better.

We have talked about getting engaged and married and I am not afraid of that. But I am still worried that the parties will end up in drunkenness. I would get very disappointed if it ended up that way. How do you prevent that when he has grown up in a family with drinking and violence, and when his entire family has that tendency? I know now that all my problems are because of myself, that I and my emotional life are the problem. What should I do with my life, how do I control my emotions, whom should I go to?

Unhappy

I don't understand how you can give up your faith for such an awful guy. The first thing you should do is, of course, to find your faith again. You can easily hold on to it without being a member of a religious community.

There must be a reason why you got psychological problems when you were 11. You need to go into therapy to find yourself again and to make your faith work positively for you.

As for your boyfriend, I must strongly dissuade you from getting married and engaged and having children until he has shown you, over a long period of time, that he is stable and capable of not drinking too much. I suggest that you go into therapy for a lengthy period of time.

I do not know any therapists in the area where you live. But you can talk to your doctor or perhaps the local minister about who is usually good at giving psychotherapeutic help in a case like yours.

Birgit Dagmar Johansen

Example 2.1. Sample from a problems page in the Danish women's magazine, *Alt for Damerne*, no. 49/1997, p. 128. Translated from the Danish by the authors.

'Unhappy' has been a member of a religious community which she left after she met her boyfriend. She presents herself as having two identities or subject positions. She has given up one identity, constructed around the master signifier, 'religious' or, 'member of a religious community', to embrace an identity as 'girlfriend'. She points out that she experienced the two identities as contradictory – she could not 'handle two lives'. This is because her identity as 'girlfriend' (at least with this particular man) is equated with 'non-religious' (he 'made fun of my faith'). In terms of Laclau and Mouffe's discourse theory, the two identities were in an antagonistic relationship to each other since they were mutually exclusive: as a girlfriend she could not be religious, and as religious she could not be a girlfriend.

Within the universe that she has constructed, the only solution has been to choose between the two identities. On one side was the life with the boyfriend which was equated with love and atheism; on the other side, the religious community, her parents and her friends. She has made a hegemonic intervention in favour of her identity as girlfriend ('I have dropped my life in my religious community. I did it when I found out that I loved him'), and it is not this decision that she has asked the agony aunt for advice about. What she wants to know is how she can prevent the boyfriend from drinking and how she herself can get to feel better.

From reading the letter, one can come to doubt whether she actually has succeeded in establishing the hegemony that she claims she has. The main part of the letter concerns the conflict between the two identities and her decision to exclude one of them, although this does not have anything to do with her specific question to the problems page. In addition, there is a grammatical slip: 'Via my parents I *am* a member of a particular religious community' (our emphasis) instead of 'I was'.

Clearly the agony aunt, Birgit Dagmar Johansen, bases her answer on this suspicion. She challenges the hegemonic intervention 'Unhappy' has made ('I don't understand how you can give up your faith for such an awful guy') and suggests that her reality be articulated differently. Moreover, her answer identifies an antagonism in the young woman's life – but not so much between 'faith' and 'girlfriend' as between 'girl-friend' and 'psychological well-being' ('As for your boyfriend, I must strongly dissuade you from getting married and engaged and having children until he has shown you, over a long period of time, that he is stable and capable of not drinking too much. I suggest that you go into therapy for a lengthy period of time'). 'Psychological well-being' is also a recurring theme of 'Unhappy's letter, but without being connected with the other parts of the letter ('I know now that all my problems are because of myself, that and my emotional life are the problem'). In contrast, in Johansen's answer 'psychological well-being' is linked together in a chain of equivalence with 'belief', 'therapy' and 'change of boyfriend'. Johansen's answer, then, rearticulates the elements in 'Unhappy's letter, thus constructing her situation and available choices in a new way that points at other actions as the obvious ones. The choice is now between 'faith', 'therapy' and perhaps 'change of boyfriend' on the one side, and 'lack of faith', 'alcoholic boyfriend' and 'psychological misery' on the other. And this articulation points to another hegemonic solution than the one the letter writer has thought out for herself: she should invest in her identity as 'religious' and only begin to consider seri-ously the identity of 'girlfriend' when the man has changed.

In the next two chapters, we will describe how to carry out discourse analysis respectively in critical discourse analysis and discursive psychology – from the formulation of the research questions to the production of empirical material and the analysis and presentation of the research results. Laclau and Mouffe do not provide such an instruction manual, but many of the steps and recommendations belonging to the other approaches can be used in analyses along the lines of Laclau and Mouffe's discourse theory. Conversely, tools belonging to Laclau and Mouffe's approach, such as the ones we have just presented, can be imported into studies employing critical discourse analysis or discursive psychology. Whether one wants to work across the approaches or to use Laclau and Mouffe's discourse analysis alone, the steps and recommendations presented in the next chapters are designed so that one can draw on them to construct a framework that fits one's own project.

CONTINGENCY AND PERMANENCE

By now, it should be clear that the starting point of Laclau and Mouffe's discourse theory is that everything is contingent. All discourses and articulations and therefore all aspects of the social could have been different – and can become different. This basic premise has provoked criticism of Laclau and Mouffe for overestimating the possibility of change (for example Chouliaraki 2002; Chouliaraki and Fairclough 1999; Larrain 1994). Lilie Chouliaraki and Norman Fairclough (1999: 125), for example, claim that Laclau and Mouffe overlook the fact that not all individuals and groups have equal possibilities for rearticulating elements in new ways and so for creating change. They refer, for example, to a situation in which a manufacturer has been obliged by a customer to adhere to certain quality standards which involved the documentation of the work process (1999: 127ff.). At the manufacturer's factory this entails the adoption of certain new practices – both new routines in the organisation of the work and new ways of talking about the work process (how it is divided up, categorised and documented). The manufacturer is forced to live up to the demands of the customer if he wants to keep the contract, and the workers are forced to do the same if they want to keep their jobs. The people in the factory change their discourse so that the elements are articulated in new ways – but not as a result of their own choice. According to Chouliaraki and Fairclough, this example shows that people's discourse is often subjected to constraints that do not emanate from the discursive level but from structural relationships of dependency. Important structural conditions that can limit actors' possibilities include class, ethnicity and gender. Chouliaraki and Fairclough argue that Laclau and Mouffe overlook the structural constraints because they focus so much on contingency: everything is in flux and all possibilities are open. Chouliaraki and Fairclough consider it important to pinpoint a structural domain in which the structures are socially created but inert and hard to change – at least for dominated groups. Besides the structural domain, they suggest a contingent domain for the aspects that can be negotiated and changed.

We agree with Chouliaraki and Fairclough that it is important to include considerations of permanence and constraint in any analysis of the social, and we agree that this aspect is sometimes played down in Laclau and Mouffe's discourse theory, as when, for example, they refer to *'the constant overflowing of every discourse by the infinitude of the field of discursivity'* (1985: 113; italics in original). However, the concern with both permanence and the distribution of possibilities for action is far from absent in discourse theory.[15]

First of all, even if *in principle* everything can be different, it does not mean that everything is in flux or that change is necessarily easy. Laclau and Mouffe distinguish between the objective and the political in order to stress that, although everything is contingent, there is always an objective field of sedimented discourse – a long series of social arrangements that we take for granted and therefore do not question or try to change. Secondly, they recognise that not all actors have equal possibilities for doing and saying things in new ways and for having their rearticulations accepted. In Laclau and Mouffe's approach, actors are understood – whether they are groups or individuals – as subject positions determined by discourses. Everyone does not have equal access to all subject positions, and, in our society, constraints can, for instance, be a function of categories such as class, ethnicity and gender. As we mentioned earlier, there are limits as to what a patient can say at a doctor's consultation (if the patient wants to be taken seriously). And it is part of the task of discourse analysis to investigate how people are categorised and how that affects their possibilities for action. Thus, Laclau and Mouffe's discourse theory does include conceptualisations of permanence and constraint, but we agree with Chouliaraki and Fairclough in so far as Laclau and Mouffe undertheorise this aspect of social practice. Laclau and Mouffe recognise that there are large social areas of stability and permanence, but they do not specify how the fixations can be identified and explored in different social domains.

We suggest that one advance in this direction would be to introduce the concept of 'order of discourse' into Laclau and Mouffe's approach. As we shall see in Chapter 3, critical discourse analysis employs such a concept, although with a slightly different inflection from our present suggestion. Laclau and Mouffe operate with two concepts: 'discourse' and 'the field of discursivity', and while 'discourse' is the term for the partial fixation of meaning, 'the field of discursivity' is more difficult to specify. It is the term for the surplus of meaning, everything that is excluded from the specific discourse. But as we discussed earlier, it is unclear whether the concept refers to any meaning whatsoever outside the specific discourse, or if it more narrowly refers only to *potentially competing* systems and fragments of meaning. In our discussion we asked if football, for instance, belongs to the field of discursivity of traditional Western medical discourse, since football is not included in medical discourse, or whether 'the field of discursivity' should be reserved to cover only potentially threatening meaning within the same sphere, for example alternative treatment discourses in the case of medical discourse. We suggest that these two uses of the concept should be kept apart, and we believe that Laclau and Mouffe, in neglecting to do so, undertheorise the relationship between different discourses, and as a result undertheorise the question of permanence versus change.

In our reformulation 'discourse' still refers to the partial fixation of meaning, while 'the field of discursivity' refers to any actual or potential meaning outside the specific discourse (i.e. football belongs to the medical discourse's field of discursivity). Between the two we suggest the insertion of the concept of 'order of discourse', which would then denote a social space in which different discourses partly cover the same terrain which they compete to fill with meaning each in their own particular way (for example, football does not, at the moment, belong to the same order of discourse as Western medicine).[16] The relationship between a discourse and its exterior can now be formulated using three concepts. 'Discourse' continues to be the term for the structuring of a particular domain in moments. A discourse is always structured by the exclusion of other possible meanings and the term for this general exterior is 'the field of discursivity'. But now 'order of discourse' denotes two or more discourses, each of which strives to establish itself in the same domain. Thus, 'order of discourse' is also the term for a potential or actual area of discursive conflict. The concepts of 'antagonism' and 'hegemony' will, in this construction, belong to the level of 'the order of discourse'; 'antagonism' is open conflict between the different discourses in a particular order of discourse, and 'hegemony' is the dissolution of the conflict through a displacement of the boundaries between the discourses.

'The field of discursivity' is thus understood as the general reservoir of all meaning not included in a specific discourse. The concept is necessary insofar as it emphasises the contingency and the fundamental openness of all social phenomena – for example, football might, at some point, threaten to undermine Western medical discourse. But in a given situation, not all possibilities are equally likely and not all aspects of the social are equally open. Laclau and Mouffe do not distinguish between these two cases, and they, therefore, provide no concept which covers the likelihood that some meanings are more probable than others, that some aspects are the objects of open struggle while others remain unquestioned at a given point in time. But Laclau and Mouffe's distinction between the objective and the political provides an opening for a concept such as 'the order of discourse', and thus for further analysis of the conditions of possibility for permanence and change.

Let us end by exemplifying such an analysis. As mentioned, an order of discourse denotes a group of discourses that operate in the same social terrain – both in conflict and in concordance with one another. For example, the political debate in Denmark about the EU can be understood as an order of discourse in empirical research aiming to reveal the objects of struggle on the one hand and the aspects that are commonly accepted on the other. In the EU debate, it is, for example, taken for granted that Danes relate to the EU from a national perspective. Even though there are different opinions as to what Danishness is, most debaters assume that it exists and is relevant to questions about the EU. In contrast to this, there is a struggle between different discourses about whether Danes have a European identity or not, and what the implications of a European identity are for national identity.[17]

The EU debate indicates that it is more likely for a European identity to emerge than for Danish national identity to vanish. This is because there is an open conflict about European identity, making such an identity a realistic possibility, whereas there is an (almost) uncontested, tacit consensus about the existence of national identity, making it improbable that it should suddenly disappear as a relevant category for identification. But nothing is certain: it is possible that the nation state will cease to be a source of identification, and it is also possible that a European identity will never emerge. This openness of possibilities is what is meant by contingency. But at the moment, the question of national identity belongs to the domain of objectivity – national identity is taken for granted as natural and is therefore not questioned. As opposed to this, the question of European identity belongs to the domain of the political (to use Laclau and Mouffe's definition of politics): it is something that is explicitly discussed and fought over, and consequently it is easier to imagine how it could be changed. This kind of evaluation of constraints versus possibilities for change requires a concept of 'order of discourse' with which the interrelationship between different discourses can be examined. In the next chapter, we describe and discuss the use of the concept of order of discourse as part of our presentation of critical discourse analysis, and we continue our development of the concept in Chapter 5.

NOTES

1 For an explication of the concept of discourse and related concepts in Laclau and Mouffe's discourse theory, see also Torfing (1999: Chapter 4) and Howarth (2000: Chapter 6).

2 Inspiration for the examples of illness and health comes from Johannessen (1994).

3 Laclau and Mouffe's reading of the different Marxist theorists is much more nuanced than the account which we can present in this limited space (1985: Chapters 1 and 2).

4 Laclau and Mouffe (1985: Chapter 1) present a number of theorists' suggestions for solutions.

5 For an account of Gramsci's theory and Laclau and Mouffe's use of his theory, see Laclau and Mouffe (1985: Chapter 2) and Barrett (1991: Chapter 4).

6 As a result of this radical reworking of Marxist theory, it has been questioned whether Laclau and Mouffe can be said to be Marxists at all. We will not go into this discussion here but just mention that they themselves define themselves as post-Marxists with the emphasis both on post- and on Marxism (1985: 4).

7 See Laclau and Mouffe (1990) for a discussion with one of these critics, Norman Geras.

8 They are also called 'the social'. We will not use this label here because our use of 'the social' more loosely refers to all social phenomena.

9 For more about the concept of power in Foucault and in Laclau and Mouffe, see Torfing (1999: Chapter 8), and for a wider discussion of different understandings of power from a discourse theoretical perspective, see Dyrberg (1997).

10 For Laclau's reading of Lacan, see Laclau and Zac (1994: 31ff.).

11 The example is inspired by Bracher (1993: 30), who also writes about master signifiers (p. 22ff.).

12 For more about chains of equivalence and collective identity, see Silverman (1985). Laclau and Mouffe's understanding of identity mirrors that of post-structuralism in general, but some writers are more easily comprehensible than Laclau and Mouffe, see, for example, Hall (1990, 1991 and 1996). A similar understanding of identity that also draws on Hall's thoughts, is presented in Chapter 4.

13 In Laclau (1998) the author distinguishes between 'social antagonism' and 'dislocation'. Dislocation refers to the general condition that all identity is constructed by excluding a constitutive outside, which in turn always threatens to subvert any identity's fixity (p. 39). No discourse can provide a fixed and full structure, and dislocation is the term for the disruption of the structure by forces from the constitutive outside (p. 50). 'Social antagonism' is one way of responding to dislocation. Here the dislocation is projected onto an enemy, whereby one discourse of identity attributes responsibility to 'the other' for its failure to constitute a full and fixed identity.

14 See Howarth et al. (2000) and Norval (1996).

15 See also our discussion of contingency versus continuity in Laclau and Mouffe's discourse theory on page 38.

16 Laclau and Mouffe introduce at one point the concept of 'discursive formation' (1985: 105f.) imported from Foucault (Foucault 1972: Chapter 2). We understand Foucault's concept, 'discursive formation', as a frame for the different and potentially conflicting discourses that operate in the same terrain. This corresponds to what we, using Fairclough's concept, have called an order of discourse. The problem with Laclau and Mouffe is that it remains unclear whether they share this understanding of 'discursive formation'. As we see it, they seem to equate 'discourse' and 'discursive formation'. In any case, they do not actually use the concept of 'discursive formation' – they introduce it and then drop it.

17 See Larsen (1999; forthcoming) for an analysis of how 'Europe' is articulated differently in various discourses in Denmark.

3 Critical Discourse Analysis

Critical discourse analysis (often abbrieviated to CDA) provides theories and methods for the empirical study of the relations between discourse and social and cultural developments in different social domains. Confusingly, the label 'critical discourse analysis' is used in two different ways: Norman Fairclough (1995a, 1995b) uses it both to describe the approach that he has developed *and* as the label for a broader movement within discourse analysis of which several approaches, including his own, are part (Fairclough and Wodak 1997). This broad movement is a rather loose entity and there is no consensus as to who belongs to it.[1] While Fairclough's approach consists of a set of philosophical premises, theoretical methods, methodological guidelines and specific techniques for linguistic analysis, the broader critical discourse analytical movement consists of several approaches among which there are both similarities and differences. Below we will briefly present some key elements shared by all the approaches. In the rest of the chapter, we will present Fairclough's approach since, in our view, that represents, within the critical discourse analytical movement, the most developed theory and method for research in communication, culture and society.

FIVE COMMON FEATURES

Among the different approaches to CDA, five common features can be identified. It is these that make it possible to categorise the approaches as belonging to the same movement. In the following account we draw on Fairclough and Wodak's overview (1997: 271ff.).

1. The Character of Social and Cultural Processes and Structures is Partly Linguistic-Discursive

Discursive practices – through which texts are *produced* (created) and *consumed* (received and interpreted) – are viewed as an important form of social practice which contributes to the *constitution* of the social world including social identities and social relations. It is partly through discursive practices in everyday life (processes of text production and consumption) that social and cultural reproduction and change take place. It follows that some societal phenomena are not of a linguistic-discursive character.

The aim of critical discourse analysis is to shed light on the linguistic-discursive dimension of social and cultural phenomena and processes of change in late modernity. Research in critical discourse analysis has covered areas such as organisational analysis (e.g. Mumby and Clair 1997), pedagogy (Chouliaraki 1998), mass communication and racism, nationalism and identity (e.g. Chouliaraki 1999; van Dijk 1991; Wodak et al. 1999), mass communication and economy (Richardson 1998), the spread of market practices (Fairclough 1993) and mass communication, democracy and politics (Fairclough 1995a, 1995b, 1998, 2000).

Discourse encompasses not only written and spoken language but also visual images. It is commonly accepted that the analysis of texts containing visual images must take account of the special characteristics of visual semiotics and the relationship between language and images. However, within critical discourse analysis (as in discourse analysis in general) there is a tendency to analyse pictures as if they were linguistic texts. An exception to this is social semiotics (e.g. Hodge and Kress 1988; Kress and van Leeuwen 1996, 2001) which is an attempt to develop a theory and method for the analysis of multi-modal texts – that is, texts which make use of different semiotic systems such as written language, visual images and/or sound.

2. Discourse is Both Constitutive and Constituted

For critical discourse analysts, discourse is a form of social practice which both *constitutes* the social world and is *constituted* by other social practices. As social practice, discourse is in a *dialectical* relationship with other social dimensions. It does not just contribute to the shaping and reshaping of social structures but also reflects them. When Fairclough analyses how discursive practices in the media take part in the shaping of new forms of politics, he also takes into account that discursive practices are influenced by societal forces that do not have a solely discursive character (e.g. the structure of the political system and the institutional structure of the media). This conception of 'discourse' distinguishes the approach from more poststructuralist approaches, such as Laclau and Mouffe's discourse theory (see Figure 1.1). In critical discourse analysis, language-as-discourse is *both* a form of action (cf. Austin 1962) through which people can change the world *and* a form of action which is socially and historically situated and in a dialectical relationship with other aspects of the social.

Fairclough (1992b) points to the family as an example of how the social structure influences discursive practices. The relationship between parents and children is partly discursively constituted, he says, but, at the same time, the family is an institution with concrete practices, pre-existing relationships and identities. These practices, relationships and identities were originally discursively constituted, but have become sedimented in institutions and non-discursive practices. The constitutive effects of discourse work together with other practices such as the distribution of household tasks. Furthermore, social structures play an independent role in forming and circumscribing discursive practices in the family:

> [T]he discursive constitution of society does not emanate from a free play of ideas in people's heads but from a social practice which is firmly rooted in and oriented to real, material social structures. (Fairclough 1992b: 66)

Here Fairclough suggests that, if discourse is only seen as constitutive, this corresponds to claiming that social reality emanates only from people's heads. But, as we saw in Chapter 2, there is disagreement among theorists as to whether the view that discourse is fully constitutive amounts to this form of idealism. Laclau and Mouffe, for example, argue strongly against the accusation of idealism on the grounds that the conception of discourse as constitutive does not imply that physical objects do not exist but, rather, that they acquire meaning only through discourse.

3. Language use should be Empirically Analysed within its Social Context

Critical discourse analysis engages in concrete, linguistic textual analysis of language use in social interaction. This distinguishes it from both

Laclau and Mouffe's discourse theory which does not carry out systematic, empirical studies of language use, and from discursive psychology which carries out rhetorical but not linguistic studies of language use (see Figure 1.2). The example presented in the final part of this chapter demonstrates how textual analysis is carried out in critical discourse analysis.

4. Discourse Functions Ideologically

In critical discourse analysis, it is claimed that discursive practices contribute to the creation and reproduction of unequal power relations between social groups – for example, between social classes, women and men, ethnic minorities and the majority. These effects are understood as *ideological* effects.

In contrast to discourse theorists, including Foucault and Laclau and Mouffe, critical discourse analysis does not diverge completely from the Marxist tradition on this point. Some critical discourse analytical approaches do ascribe to a Foucauldian view of power as a force which creates subjects and agents – that is, as a *productive* force – rather than as a property possessed by individuals, which they exert over others (see Chapter 1). But, at the same time, they diverge from Foucault in that they enlist the concept of ideology to theorise the subjugation of one social group to other social groups. The research focus of critical discourse analysis is accordingly *both* the discursive practices which construct representations of the world, social subjects and social relations, including power relations, *and* the role that these discursive practices play in furthering the interests of particular social groups. Fairclough defines critical discourse analysis as an approach which seeks to investigate systematically

> [o]ften opaque relationships of causality and determination between (a) discursive practices, events and texts and (b) broader social and cultural structures, relations and processes [...] how such practices, events and texts arise out of and are ideologically shaped by relations of power and struggles over power [...] how the opacity of these relationships between discourse and society is itself a factor securing power and hegemony. (Fairclough 1993: 135; reprinted in Fairclough 1995a: 132f.)

Critical discourse analysis is 'critical' in the sense that it aims to reveal the role of discursive practice in the maintenance of the social world, including those social relations that involve unequal relations of power.

Its aim is to contribute to social change along the lines of more equal power relations in communication processes and society in general.

5. Critical Research

Critical discourse analysis does not, therefore, understand itself as politically neutral (as objectivist social science does), but as a critical approach which is politically committed to social change. In the name of emancipation, critical discourse analytical approaches take the side of oppressed social groups. Critique aims to uncover the role of discursive practice in the maintenance of unequal power relations, with the overall goal of harnessing the results of critical discourse analysis to the struggle for radical social change.[2] Fairclough's interest in 'explanatory critique' and 'critical language awareness', to which we will return, is directed towards the achievement of this goal.

Differences Between the Approaches

Beyond the identification of these five common features, however, there are large differences between the critical discourse analytical approaches with respect to their theoretical understanding of discourse, ideology and the historical perspective, and also with respect to their methods for the empirical study of language use in social interaction and its ideological effects. For instance, as already mentioned, some critical discourse analytical approaches do not share Foucault's understanding of power as productive. Among these is van Dijk's socio-cognitive approach, which also diverges from most of the others by being cognitivist (see Chapter 4 for a critique of cognitivism from the perspective of discursive psychology). We will return to these differences at the end of this chapter.

FAIRCLOUGH'S CRITICAL DISCOURSE ANALYSIS

Fairclough has constructed a useful framework for the analysis of discourse as social practice, which we will describe in detail. As was also the case with Laclau and Mouffe, we are faced here with an explosion of concepts, as Fairclough's *framework* contains a range of different concepts that are interconnected in a complex three-dimensional model.

Furthermore, the meanings of the concepts vary slightly across Fairclough's different works, the framework being under continuous development. In our presentation of Fairclough's theory, we draw on Fairclough's books, *Discourse and Social Change* (1992b), *Critical Discourse Analysis* (1995a) and *Media Discourse* (1995b) as well as on *Discourse in Late Modernity* co-written with Lilie Chouliaraki (Chouliaraki and Fairclough 1999). In those cases in which conceptual changes are critical to an understanding of the framework, we will draw attention to them. In this first section we present Fairclough's framework through outlining the central concepts and then describing how they are linked to one another. This is followed by one of Fairclough's own empirical examples that illustrates the application of the framework.

As mentioned earlier, an important difference between Fairclough (and critical discourse analysis in general) and poststructuralist discourse theory is that, in the former, discourse is not only seen as constitutive but also as constituted. It is central to Fairclough's approach that discourse is an important form of social practice which both reproduces and changes knowledge, identities and social relations including power relations, and at the same time is also shaped by other social practices and structures. Thus discourse is in a dialectical relationship with other social dimensions. Fairclough understands *social structure* as social relations both in society as a whole and in specific institutions, and as consisting of both discursive and non-discursive elements (Fairclough 1992b: 64). A primarily non-discursive practice is, for example, the physical practice that is involved in the construction of a bridge, whereas practices such as journalism and public relations are primarily discursive (1992b: 66ff.).

At the same time, Fairclough distances himself from structuralism and comes closer to a more poststructuralist position in claiming that discursive practice not only reproduces an already existing discursive structure but also challenges the structure by using words to denote what may lie outside the structure (1992b: 66).[3]

However, he diverges in a significant way from poststructuralist discourse theory in concentrating on building a theoretical model and methodological tools for empirical research in everyday social interaction. In contrast to poststructuralist tendencies, he stresses the importance of doing systematic analyses of spoken and written language in, for example, the mass media and research interviews (Figure 1.2).

Fairclough's approach is a text-oriented form of discourse analysis that tries to unite three traditions (Fairclough 1992b: 72):

- Detailed textual analysis within the field of linguistics (including Michael Halliday's functional grammar).

- Macro-sociological analysis of social practice (including Foucault's theory, which does not provide a methodology for the analysis of specific texts).
- The micro-sociological, interpretative tradition within sociology (including ethnomethodology and conversation analysis), where everyday life is treated as the product of people's actions in which they follow a set of shared 'common-sense' rules and procedures.

Fairclough employs detailed text analysis to gain insight into how discursive processes operate linguistically in specific texts. But he criticises linguistic approaches for concentrating exclusively on textual analysis and for working with a simplistic and superficial understanding of the relationship between text and society. For Fairclough, text analysis alone is not sufficient for discourse analysis, as it does not shed light on the links between texts and societal and cultural processes and structures. An interdisciplinary perspective is needed in which one combines textual and social analysis. The benefit derived from drawing on the macro-sociological tradition is that it takes into account that social practices are shaped by social structures and power relations and that people are often not aware of these processes. The contribution of the interpretative tradition is to provide an understanding of how people actively create a rule-bound world in everyday practices (Fairclough 1992b).

The understanding of discourse as both constitutive and constituted, then, is central to Fairclough's theory. He conceives of the relationship between discursive practice and social structures as complex and variable across time, diverging from approaches to critical discourse analysis which assume a higher degree of stability.

FAIRCLOUGH'S THREE-DIMENSIONAL MODEL

Key Concepts

Fairclough applies the concept of *discourse* in three different ways. In the most abstract sense, discourse refers to *language use as social practice*. Above, we have used the term several times in this way, for example in the statement, 'discourse is both constitutive and constituted'. Secondly, discourse is understood as the *kind of language used within a specific field*, such as political or scientific discourse. And thirdly, in the most concrete usage, discourse is used as a count noun (a discourse, the discourse, the discourses, discourses) referring to *a way of speaking which gives meaning to experiences from a particular perspective.* In this last sense, the concept refers to any discourse that can be distinguished from other discourses such as, for example, a feminist discourse, a neoliberal discourse, a Marxist discourse, a consumer discourse, or an environmentalist discourse (Fairclough 1993: 138; reprinted in Fairclough 1995a: 135). Fairclough confines the term, discourse, to semiotic systems such as language and images in contrast to Laclau and Mouffe, who treat all social practice as discourse. We will return to this aspect of Fairclough's theory at the end of this chapter.

Discourse contributes to the construction of:

- social identities;
- social relations; and
- systems of knowledge and meaning.

Thus discourse has three functions: an identity function, a 'relational' function and an 'ideational' function. Here, Fairclough draws on Halliday's multifunctional approach to language.[4]

In any analysis, two dimensions of discourse are important focal points:

- *the communicative event* – an instance of language use such as a newspaper article, a film, a video, an interview or a political speech (Fairclough 1995b); and
- *the order of discourse* – the configuration of all the *discourse types* which are used within a social institution or a social field. Discourse types consist of discourses and genres (1995b: 66).[5]

A *genre* is a particular usage of language which participates in, and constitutes, part of a particular social practice, for example, an interview genre, a news genre or an advertising genre (1995b: 56). Examples of orders of discourse include the order of discourse of the media, the health service or an individual hospital (1995b: 56; 1998: 145). Within an order of discourse, there are specific discursive practices through which text and talk are produced and consumed or interpreted (Fairclough 1998: 145).

For instance, within a hospital's order of discourse, the discursive practices which take place include doctor–patient consultations, the scientific staff's technical language (both written and spoken) and the public relations officer's spoken and written promotional language. In every discursive practice – that is, in the production and consumption of text and talk – discourse types (discourses and genres) are used in particular ways.

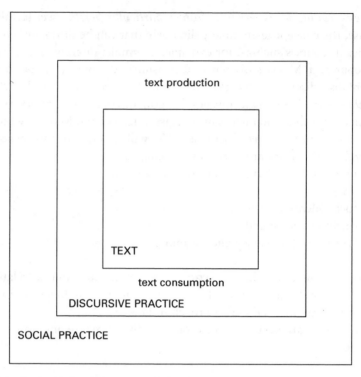

Figure 3.1 *Fairclough's three-dimensional model for critical discourse analysis (1992b: 73)*

Every instance of language use is a communicative event consisting of three dimensions:

- it is a *text* (speech, writing, visual image or a combination of these);
- it is a *discursive practice* which involves the production and consumption of texts; and
- it is a *social practice*.

Fairclough's three-dimensional model is reproduced in Figure 3.1. The model is an analytical framework for empirical research on communication and society. All three dimensions should be covered in a specific discourse analysis of a communicative event. The analysis should focus, then, on (1) the linguistic features of the text (text), (2) processes relating to the production and consumption of the text (discursive practice); and (3) the wider social practice to which the communicative event belongs (social practice).

It is important to be aware that the analysis of the linguistic features of the text inevitably will involve analysis of the discursive practice, and vice versa (Fairclough 1992b: 73). Nevertheless, text and discursive practice represent two different dimensions in Fairclough's model and, consequently, should be separated analytically. Analysis of discursive practice focuses on how authors of texts draw on already existing discourses and genres to create a text, and on how receivers of texts also apply available discourses and genres in the consumption and interpretation of the texts. For instance, TV news is a news genre that can deploy different discourses (e.g. a welfare discourse or a neoliberal discourse) and genres (e.g. a 'hard-news' or a 'soft-news' genre). Viewers' familiarity with TV news as a news genre shapes their interpretation and, later on, in discussion with others of the subjects covered by the news, they may draw on the discourses and genres that were used, perhaps combining them with other discourses and genres in hybrid forms.

Text analysis concentrates on the formal features (such as vocabulary, grammar, syntax and sentence coherence) from which discourses and genres are realised linguistically.

The relationship between texts and social practice[6] is mediated by discursive practice. Hence it is only through discursive practice – whereby people use language to produce and consume texts – that texts shape and are shaped by social practice. At the same time, the text (the formal linguistic features) influences both the production and the consumption process (Fairclough 1992b: 71ff.; 1993: 136; 1995b: 60). Those discourses and genres which are articulated together to produce a text, and which its receivers draw on in interpretation, have a particular linguistic structure that shapes both the production and consumption of the text. The analysis of a communicative event thus includes:

- analysis of the discourses and genres which are articulated in the production and the consumption of the text (the level of discursive practice);
- analysis of the linguistic structure (the level of the text); and
- considerations about whether the discursive practice reproduces or, instead, restructures the existing order of discourse and about what consequences this has for the broader social practice (the level of social practice).

Discourse analysis is not sufficient in itself for analysis of the wider social practice, since the latter encompasses both discursive and non-discursive elements. Social and cultural theory is necessary in addition to discourse analysis. We will return to the implications of this at the end of this chapter. The main aim of critical discourse analysis is to explore the links between language use and social practice. The focus is the role of discursive practices in the maintenance of the social order and in social change. Investigation proceeds by the analysis of specific instances of language use, or to use Fairclough's terminology, the analysis of the communicative event in relation to the order of discourse. Every communicative event functions as a form of social practice in reproducing or challenging the order of discourse. This means that communicative events shape, and are shaped by, the wider social practice through their relationship to the order of discourse. We elaborate on this in the next section.

The general purpose of the three-dimensional model is, then, to provide an analytical framework for discourse analysis. The model is based on, and promotes, the principle that texts can never be understood or analysed in isolation – they can only be understood in relation to webs of other texts and in relation to the social context. In Chouliaraki and Fairclough (1999), the authors replace the three-dimensional model with a conceptualisation of texts and talk as part of a process of articulation (1999: 21, 37f.). For the concept of articulation, they draw partly on Laclau and Mouffe's understanding of social practice as the product of the co-articulation of different elements but differ from them with respect to the nature of the elements articulated: while Laclau and Mouffe see social practices as fully discursive and therefore explain all processes of articulation in terms of a discursive logic, Chouliaraki and Fairclough distinguish between non-discursive and discursive moments of a social practice and propose that these moments adhere to different kinds of logic. To conceptualise the different logics, they draw on critical realism (for example, Bhaskar 1986; Collier 1994), in particular, the theory that social life operates according to a range of mechanisms which each have their own distinctive 'generative effect' on events but which are always mediated by one another in producing the event (Chouliaraki and Fairclough 1999: 19). To conceptualise these mechanisms in terms of moments of social practice, they draw on David Harvey's (1996) theorisation of moments as elements that 'internalise', but cannot be reduced to, one another (Chouliaraki and Fairclough 1999: 21).

For example, going shopping typically involves both verbal communication with the shop assistant and an economic transaction. Talking and paying are thus two moments articulated together in the practice of shopping. If we wanted to analyse shopping using Chouliaraki and Fairclough's concept of articulation, we would analyse the conversation with the shop assistant as discourse using linguistic tools, and to that analysis we would have to add an economic analysis of the exchange of money for goods, drawing on economic theory. Economics and discourse, according to Chouliaraki and Fairclough, are two different kinds of mechanisms, and cannot be analysed using the same theories and tools. In this way, and contrary to Laclau and Mouffe, Chouliaraki and Fairclough maintain the distinction between the discursive and the non-discursive: the discursive is one kind of mechanism working in combination with other mechanisms – e.g. economical, physical, biological and psychological – to constitute a social practice. The mechanisms represent moments of every social practice, which are in a dialectical relationship with each other, but each mechanism has its own logic, and must be analysed in its own terms using appropriate analytical tools. According to Chouliaraki and Fairclough, it is possible to explore empirically the particular configuration of moments in a specific social practice and the relative weightings of each moment in producing that social practice.

By comparison with the three-dimensional model, the new conceptualisation may provide better guidelines for analysis of what is called discursive practice and social practice in the three-dimensional model, since specification of the discursive and non-discursive moments of the social practice under study may provide pointers as to the kinds of theories appropriate for analysis of the different kinds of logic. Nevertheless, in relation to the implications for empirical research, we do not consider the new understanding very different from the three-dimensional model,[7] and we have chosen the three-dimensional model to represent Fairclough's basic framework for discourse analysis on the grounds that it depicts the relationship between text and context in a highly pedagogical way. Moreover, our view is that the new conception suffers from the same weakness as the three-dimensional model: how to go about unpicking and analysing the dialectical relations between the different discursive and non-discursive moments of a social practice is just as unclear as how to go about investigating the dialectical relations between discursive and non-discursive practices. We return to this problem in our concluding critical comments on the approach.

Communicative Events and Discourse Orders

Fairclough understands the relationship between the communicative event and the order of discourse as dialectical. The discourse order is a system, but not a system in a structuralist sense. That is, communicative events not only reproduce orders of discourse, but can also change them through creative language use. For instance, when a public relations officer at a hospital uses a consumer discourse, she draws on a system – an order of discourse – but, in so doing, she also takes part in *constituting* the system. Or, when a journalist draws on a discourse which is routinely used within the media, he or she also plays a part in the reproduction of the media system. The order of discourse is the sum of all the genres and discourses which are in use within a specific social domain. First of all, the order of discourse is a system in the sense that it both shapes and is shaped by specific instances of language use. Thus it is both structure and practice. The use of discourses and genres as resources in communication is controlled by the order of discourse because the order of discourse constitutes the resources (discourses and genres) that are available. It delimits what can be said. But, at the same time, language users can change the order of discourse by using discourses and genres in new ways or by importing discourses and genres from other orders of discourse. Orders of discourse are particularly open to change when discourses and genres from *other* orders of discourse are brought into play.

For instance, certain discourses and genres have been characteristic of the different discursive practices that have made up the order of discourse of the British health service. Welfare discourse has been dominant, but, since the beginning of the 1980s, it has been engaged in a struggle with other discourses, including a neoliberal consumer discourse, which previously was almost exclusively associated with the order of discourse of the market. To a greater extent, public relations officers now use discourses that promote healthcare services as if they were goods and which appeal to patients as consumers rather than fellow citizens. This can be seen as a reflection of, and a driving force in, a change in the wider social practice that Fairclough views in terms of the 'marketisation of discourse' – a societal development in late modernity, whereby market discourses colonise the discursive practices of public institutions (Fairclough 1992b, 1993, 1998).

What is the relationship between the order of discourse and its social context? In his earlier work, Fairclough tended to relate orders of discourses to specific institutions (as in the order of discourse of the university, the order of discourse of the media, etc.) (Fairclough 1995b), while emphasising at the same time that discourses and orders of discourse can operate across institutional boundaries. In his later book with Chouliaraki, the concept of 'order of discourse' is fruitfully coupled with Pierre Bourdieu's concept of 'field' (Chouliaraki and Fairclough 1999: 101ff.). Very briefly put, to Bourdieu a *field* is a relatively autonomous social domain obeying a specific social logic (see Bourdieu and Wacquant 1996: 94ff.). Actors within a specific field, such as the field of sports, politics or the media, struggle to attain the same goal, and they are thus linked to one another in a conflictual way whereby the individual actor's position in the field is decided by his or her relative distance from the goal. For instance, in the political field the different politicians and political parties struggle to gain political power and they are distributed across the field in terms of their relative strength. Society, for Bourdieu, consists of a range of such fields, governed by an overarching 'field of power' and interconnected in a complex network of relations.

Chouliaraki and Fairclough (1999: 114) suggest that we see the order of discourse as the discursive aspect of a field. They criticise Bourdieu for undertheorising and underestimating the role of discourse in the struggles within and between fields, and they offer discourse analysis as a necessary supplement to Bourdieu's theory (Chouliaraki and Fairclough, 1999: 104ff.). But they suggest that Bourdieu can provide critical discourse analysis with a theory that can anchor the order of discourse in an order of social practice, a combination of discursive and non-discursive moments. The order of discourse is reconceptualised as a potentially conflictual configuration of discourses within a given social field, and this reconceptualisation sharpens the concept as an analytical tool. More generally, the import of Bourdieu's theory into critical discourse analysis opens up for discourse analytical investigations of relations within and between different fields.

Intertextuality and Interdiscursivity

Interdiscursivity occurs when different discourses and genres are articulated together in a communicative event. Through new articulations of discourses, the boundaries change, both within the order of discourse and between different orders of discourse. *Creative* discursive practices in which discourse types are combined in new and complex ways – in new 'interdiscursive mixes' – are both a sign of, and a driving force in, discursive and thereby socio-cultural change. On the other hand, discursive practices in which discourses are mixed in *conventional* ways are indications of, and work towards, the stability of the dominant order of discourse and thereby the dominant social order.[8] Discursive reproduction and change can thus be investigated through an analysis of the relations between different discourses within an order of discourse and between different orders of discourse (Fairclough 1995b: 56).

Interdiscursivity is a form of *intertextuality*. Intertextuality refers to the condition whereby all communicative events draw on earlier events. One cannot avoid using words and phrases that others have used before. A particularly pronounced form of intertextuality is *manifest intertextuality*, whereby texts explicitly draw on other texts, for instance, by citing them (Fairclough 1992b: 117).

A text can be seen as a link in an *intertextual chain* (Fairclough 1995b: 77ff.): a series of texts in which each text incorporates elements from another text or other texts. An example is the intertextual chain that binds a scientific report to a media text and to audience texts and talk: the journalist incorporates elements of the scientific report in the production of the media text; and in the consumption process, receivers incorporate elements from the media text in the construction of a new text.

Intertextuality refers to the influence of history on a text and to a text's influence on history, in that the text draws on earlier texts and thereby contributes to historical development and change (Kristeva 1986: 39; quoted in Fairclough 1992b: 102).[9] Whereas some poststructuralists (e.g. Fiske 1987) see intertextuality and interdiscursivity as a manifestation of the extreme instability and changeability of language, Fairclough sees it as a mark of both stability and instability, both continuity and change. Change is created by drawing on existing discourses in new ways, but the possibilities for change are limited by power relations which, among other things, determine the access of different actors to different discourses (see our discussion of hegemony in the next section on pages 75–6).

> [T]he seemingly limitless possibilities of creativity in discursive practice suggested by the concept of interdiscursivity – an endless combination and recombination of genres and discourses – are in practice limited and constrained by the state of hegemonic relations and hegemonic struggle. (Fairclough 1993: 137)

Discursive relations are sites of social struggle and conflict:

> [O]rders of discourse can be seen as one domain of potential cultural hegemony, with dominant groups struggling to assert and maintain particular structuring within and between them. (Fairclough 1995b: 56)

That a society is not controlled by one dominant discourse does not mean that all discourses are equal. For instance, it is obvious that some discourses have a stronger impact on the mass media than others. It is more difficult for a purely academic discourse to be taken up in the media than it is for a hybrid discourse that combines academic discourse (from the order of discourse of the university) and popular discourse (from the order of discourse of everyday life). To understand the relations of power between different discourses and their consequences we will now turn to Fairclough's conceptions of ideology and hegemony.

DISCOURSE, IDEOLOGY AND HEGEMONY

Ideology, for Fairclough, is 'meaning in the service of power' (Fairclough 1995b: 14). More precisely, he understands ideologies as constructions of meaning that contribute to the production, reproduction and transformation of relations of domination (Fairclough 1992b: 87; cf. Chouliaraki and Fairclough 1999: 26f.). Ideologies are created in societies in which relations of domination are based on social structures such as class and gender. According to Fairclough's definition, discourses can be more or less ideological, the ideological discourses being those that contribute to the maintenance and transformation of power relations. Our view is that there is a problem in operationalising this definition. The question is whether there are any discourses which do *not* have consequences for power or dominance relations in society. It is difficult to distinguish between what is ideology and what is not.

Fairclough's understanding of ideology as embedded in discursive practice draws on John Thompson's view of ideology as a practice that operates in processes of meaning production in everyday life, whereby meaning is mobilised in order to maintain relations of power (Thompson 1990). This focus contrasts with the conception of ideology in many Marxist approaches. Many Marxists have not been interested in the structures of particular ideologies, or in how ideologies are articulated in particular social contexts. Instead they have treated ideology as an abstract system of values that works as social cement, binding people together and thus securing the coherence of the social order.[10]

In common with Thompson and many other social and cultural theorists who have formulated approaches to *ideological practice*, Fairclough draws on the work of Althusser and, to a greater extent, Gramsci. As mentioned in Chapter 1, both of these theorists represent important forms of Cultural Marxist perspectives and both of them ascribe to the production of meaning in everyday life an important role in the maintenance of the social order. Fairclough also adheres to the consensus within critical cultural studies in rejecting parts of Althusser's theory on the grounds that Althusser regards people as passive ideological subjects and thus underestimates their possibilities for action. Within communication and cultural studies, there is now a consensus that the meaning of texts is partly created in processes of interpretation. Fairclough shares this consensus position. Texts have several *meaning potentials* that may contradict one another, and are open to several different interpretations.

Resistance is possible even though people are not necessarily aware of the ideological dimensions of their practice:

> [S]ubjects are ideologically positioned, but they are also capable of acting creatively to make their own connections between the diverse practices and ideologies to which they are exposed, and to restructure positioning practices and structures. (Fairclough 1992b: 91)

Fairclough also rejects Althusser's understanding of ideology as a totalising entity. Fairclough believes that people can be positioned within different and competing ideologies, and that this can lead to a sense of uncertainty, the effect of which is to create an awareness of ideological effects (Fairclough 1992b). This standpoint draws on Gramsci's idea that 'common-sense' contains several competing elements that are the result of *negotiations of meaning* in which all social groups participate (Gramsci 1991). Hegemony is not only dominance but also a process of negotiation out of which emerges a consensus concerning meaning. The existence of such competing elements bears the seeds of resistance since elements that challenge the dominant meanings equip people with resources for resistance. As a result, hegemony is never stable but changing and incomplete, and consensus is always a matter of degree only – a 'contradictory and unstable equilibrium' (Fairclough 1992b: 93).

According to Fairclough, the concept of hegemony gives us the means by which to analyse how discursive practice is part of a larger social practice involving power relations: discursive practice can be seen as an aspect of a hegemonic struggle that contributes to the reproduction and transformation of the order of discourse of which it is part (and consequently of the existing power relations). Discursive change takes place when discursive elements are articulated in new ways.

RESEARCH DESIGN AND METHODS

We will now proceed to outline the research methods that Fairclough suggests for the analysis of discourse as text, discursive practice and social practice. It is not necessary to use *all* the methods or to use them in exactly the same way in specific research projects. The selection and application of the tools depend on the research questions and the scope of the project. For the majority of discourse analytical approaches (including those presented by this book) – and for qualitative research in general – there is no fixed procedure for the production of material or for analysis: the research design should be tailored to match the special characteristics of the project.

In the following analysis applying Fairclough's framework, we cover six different phases of research, from the formulation of the problem to the use of the research results. We concentrate on the phase of analysis, structuring it according to Fairclough's three-dimensional model (Figure 3.1). The delineation of the steps and their internal order should be seen as an ideal type: in practice, a study may not follow the framework in a linear way; rather the researcher may move backwards and forwards between the levels a number of times before finding it appropriate to move on.

In our outline of the steps and methodological tools, we draw particularly on Chapter 8 in Fairclough's *Discourse and Social Change* (1992b) which presents a checklist of all the phases, concepts and analytical tools that are introduced earlier in the book. We are not able to cover all the different aspects of the framework, so, before doing critical discourse analysis, it is a good idea to look at Chapter 8 and other texts by Fairclough in addition to our outline.[11]

To provide an illustration of the methodological guidelines we have selected extracts from an analysis that Fairclough himself has made of two job advertisements (1993; reprinted in 1995a). The advertisements are reproduced as Examples 3.2. and 3.3.

I. Choice of Research Problem

As its name indicates, critical discourse analysis is intended to generate *critical* social research, that is research that contributes to the rectification of injustice and inequality in society. Chouliaraki and Fairclough define the aim of critical discourse analysis as *explanatory critique*, importing Roy Bhaskar's concept (Bhaskar 1986, in Chouliaraki and Fairclough 1999: 33; Fairclough 2001: 235–236). Explanatory critique takes its starting point in a problem that the research should help to solve. This can either be a problem identified by individuals or groups in society, perhaps formulating an unmet need, or it can be identified by the researcher who may want to disclose a 'misrepresentation', that is, a mismatch between reality and the view people have of this reality that functions ideologically. The concept of 'misrepresentation' implies that the researcher has access to a more adequate description of reality than the people he or she is studying – without such access, the researcher would not be able to identify descriptions as misrepresentations. Many other social constructionists, including ourselves, would object to this kind of privileging of scientific knowledge, and we go into the discussion in detail in Chapter 6.

On identification of the problem, the whole research design is geared to the analysis of the discursive and other social dimensions of the problem and the obstacles there might be to its solution.[12]

2. Formulation of Research Questions

Fairclough's three-dimensional framework structures all components of the research design including the formulation of the research questions. The governing principle is that discursive practices are in a dialectical relationship with other social practices: discourse is socially embedded. The specific character of a discursive practice depends on the social practice of which it forms part. It is for this reason that we start with the social practice when formulating the research questions. To pin down the social practice and formulate the research questions, it is necessary to draw on the discipline, or disciplines, that studies the social practice of interest. The discipline(s) in question could be, for example, sociology, social psychology, political science or history. By simultaneously drawing on discourse analysis, one engages in an interdisciplinary analysis of the relations between the discursive practice and the social practice. It is one of the main purposes of the analysis to show the links between discursive practices and broader social and cultural developments and structures. The underlying premise is that discursive practice both reflects, and actively contributes to, social and cultural change.

In the sample analysis of the job advertisements, Fairclough explores a discursive practice in a particular institution, the university, in the light of the spread of consumer culture across British society. The spread of consumer culture is, then, the broader social practice that provides the context for the discourse analysis of the actual texts, the job advertisements. More specifically, the example explores how promotional discourses[13] contribute to the spread of consumer culture to the universities – a social domain which was earlier organised according to other principles.

3. Choice of Material

The choice of research material depends on several aspects: the research questions, the researcher's knowledge as to the relevant material within the social domain or institution of interest, and whether, and how, one can gain access to it.

Example 3.2. *Advertisement from Sheffield City Polytechnic. Reproduced from Fairclough 1995a: 143.*

SCHOOL OF ENGINEERING

With our reputation as one of the UK's leading centres of teaching excellence and research innovation, we're making a lasting impact on the next generation of innovators and business leaders in the field of Engineering – and you can help.

With your ambition, energy and expertise, you will be committed to teaching at both undergraduate and post-graduate level, while enjoying the advantage of our close links with Industry and applied research initiatives to add to both your own reputation and ours.

SENIOR ACADEMIC POST
VEHICLE EMISSION TECHNOLOGY

Up to £31,500 p.a. plus substantial enhancement available by negotiation.

The School of Engineering is renowned for its innovative work in the area of Vehicle Emission Technology and is a leader in the field of Automotive Research. A team leader is now required to join this active team to help build on our success.

This leading post requires an outstanding Engineer who can bring expertise in at least one of the following:- Vehicle Pollution, Hybrid Vehicles, Air Quality Systems. You'll also need to be dedicated to progressing research and consultancy whilst lecturing to undergraduate and postgraduate students.

Along with appropriate qualifications, technological expertise and industrial experience, you will need to have energy, enthusiasm and communication skills to motivate your team.

We offer an excellent salary and benefits package, but more importantly the ideal environment and opportunity to really make a contribution to the future of automotive engineering.

You may be awarded the title of Professor if the relevant criteria are met.

For an informal discussion about the post please ring Professor David Tidmarsh, Director of School of Engineering on (0742) 533389.

Application forms and further details are available from the address below. Ref. 40/92.

LECTURERS /SENIOR LECTURERS
PRINCIPAL LECTURERS

£10,949 – £28,851 p.a.

COMPUTER AIDED ENGINEERING

With expertise in one or more of the following: CAD, CAM, FEA, Expert Systems, AMT. Ref. 41/92.

QUALITY SYSTEMS

Applications to both Design and Manufacturing Engineering, offering expertise in one or more of the following areas: TQM, SPC, BS5750, BS7000, Taguchi Methods. A capability to contribute to the teaching of operations management will be an advantage. Ref. 42/92.

MANUFACTURING TECHNOLOGY

With expertise in one or more of the following: Metal and Polymer Forming, Non-conventional Manufacturing, AMT, Environmental Impact of Manufacturing. Ref. 43/92.

OPERATIONS MANAGEMENT

With expertise in one or more of the following: Expert Systems, Database Systems, Simulation, Manufacturing Planning and Control, CIM, CAPP, MRP. Ref. 44/92.

ENVIRONMENTAL ENGINEERING

(Two Posts)

Post 1: With expertise in one or more of the following: The chemistry of air/water pollution, the impact of geology, hydrology and ecology on environmental issues, impact of transport on the environment. Ref. 45/92.

Post 2: With expertise in Electro-hydraulic Control Systems, Automation, PLCs, Environmental Noise, Noise Control, Acoustics, Vibrations. Ref. 46/92.

MATERIALS ENGINEERING : MATERIALS RESEARCH INSTITUTE

An experienced graduate Materials Scientist or Metallurgist, ideally with an appropriate higher degree, to undertake research and development work in the Metals and Ceramics Research Group. The research work will involve the use of extensive SEM/STEM/XRD and surface analysis facilities applied to a range of metallurgical problems with a particular emphasis on surface engineering. Ref. 47/92.

For all the above posts you will ideally have industry-related experience to add to your degree and a record of achievement in research and/or consultancy activities. You will be committed to teaching excellence at both undergraduate and postgraduate levels and also have the enthusiasm and ability to be part of an active group and to initiate and supervise research, consultancy and short course programmes.

If you feel you have the ideas and expertise to make an impact in a dynamic, forward-looking environment, then please send for an application form and further details to the Personnel Department, Floor 3, 5 Storey Block, Pond Street, Sheffield S1 1WB. Telephone (0742) 533950. Closing date 8th June 1992.

We are actively implementing equality of opportunity policies and seek people who share our commitment. Job share applicants welcome. Women are under represented in this area and applications from this group are particularly welcomed.

The University working in partnership with industry and the professions.

MAKE AN IMPACT ON THE NEXT GENERATION

Sheffield
City Polytechnic

Promising Futures

Example 3.3. *Advertisement from University of Newcastle upon Tyne. Reproduced from Fairclough 1995a: 144.*

University of Newcastle upon Tyne

Department of English Literature

LECTURER

Applications are invited for a Lectureship in the Department of English Literature from candidates who have expertise in any Post-Medieval field. The post is available to be filled from 1st October, 1992, or as soon as possible thereafter.

Salary will be at an appropriate point on the Lecturer Grade A scale: £ 12,860 – £ 17,827 p.a. according to qualifications and experience.

Further particulars may be obtained from the Director of Personnel, Registrar's Office, University of Newcastle upon Tyne, 6 Kensington Terrace, Newcastle upon Tyne NE1 7RU, with whom applications (3 copies), together with the names and addresses of three referees, should be lodged not later than 29th May, 1992.

Please quote ref: 0726/THES.
(18704)   B9905

The analysis by Fairclough that we present here uses a wide range of different material, but we limit ourselves to the two job advertisements: an advertisement from an established British university, Newcastle upon Tyne (Example 3.3), and one from a polytechnic, newly granted university status, Sheffield City Polytechnic (Example 3.2).

4. Transcription

There is no transcription in Fairclough's example since his corpus of material does not include interviews or other forms of talk. But if talk is used as material, it needs to be transcribed – or at least parts do. What it is relevant to transcribe has to be decided on the basis of the research goals. It is not only a question of selection, but also of interpretation. As Ochs (1979) points out, transcription is inevitably *theory* because the transcription process involves interpretation of the spoken language (Fairclough 1992b: 229). As an example, let us imagine that three people are talking and that one of them talks 80 per cent of the time. As Fairclough notes, we can present this as a 'conversation' in which everybody takes their turn to talk, or as 'a monologue' with interruptions and interventions from the other speakers. If there is an overlap between speakers, the analyst has to decide who it is that interrupts whom, and if there is silence on the tape she needs to decide to which speaker it should be ascribed (1992b: 229f.).

The discourse analyst has to choose between systems of transcription; no system can show everything. She needs to consider what is required in view of the research questions. It is obvious that if the aim is to do a detailed microlinguistic analysis, it is necessary to use a rather detailed system of transcription such as, for example, Gail Jefferson's system (used, for example, as the standard system of transcription in the introduction to discourse analysis edited by van Dijk, 1997b). But if the plan is to do a less detailed textual analysis, it will be sufficient to employ a system that shows pauses, silent periods and overlaps between speakers – for example, the simpler version of Gail Jefferson's system which is often used in discursive psychology (see, for example, Potter and Wetherell 1987; Wetherell and Potter 1992).

5. Analysis

In his three-dimensional model, Fairclough distinguishes between discursive practice, text and social practice as three levels that can be analytically separated. In this section, we go through what it is the analyst should look for at each of the three levels, using examples from the job advertisements. We treat each level in turn for pedagogical reasons, rather than presenting a combined analysis of all three levels as is usual in accounts of research. It should be noted that Fairclough analyses the Sheffield advertisement in more depth than the Newcastle advertisement.

Discursive Practice

Analysis of the discursive practice focuses on how the text is produced and how it is consumed. There are several ways of approaching this. If the empirical material is newspaper articles, for instance, the researcher can examine newspaper production conditions: what kinds of processes does a text go through before it is printed, and what changes does it undergo during those processes? Perhaps she can trace an *intertextual chain* of texts where the 'same' text can be seen in a range of different versions. When analysing an intertextual chain, one can see how structure and content are transformed, and can start to formulate a hypothesis about the kinds of production conditions to which the different versions are subject (Fairclough 1995b: 77ff.). At the consumption end, audience research can be carried out in order to find out how readers interpret the texts. Unfortunately, very few critical discourse analysts do this.[14] In most of his own analyses, Fairclough does not sociologically examine the ways in which texts are produced or decoded. More often he works from a linguistic starting point in concrete texts, identifying what discourses they draw on (*interdiscursivity*) and how they *intertextually* draw on other texts.

Example

The Sheffield advertisement contains a high degree of interdiscursivity. Different promotional discourses are articulated together with traditional discourses to create a complex interdiscursive mix. One promotional discourse is a 'commodity advertising' discourse. This is, for example, articulated in the headline 'Make an Impact on the Next Generation' and in the personification of both reader and institution (addressed as 'you' and 'we'). By using personification, the advertisement also simulates a conversational discourse.

There are also elements from a 'corporate advertising' discourse apparent in phrases such as 'with our reputation' and in the logo. Additionally, the advertisement draws on a narrative genre when talking about the impact of the institution on the next generation ('With our reputation as one of the UK's leading centres of teaching excellence and research innovation, we're making a lasting impact on the next generation of innovators and business leaders in the field of Engineering').

Other elements in the interdiscursive blend are a personal quality discourse (e.g. 'with your ambition, energy and expertise') and a management discourse ('teaching excellence and research innovation'; 'expertise'; 'research initiatives'). At the same time, the text draws on traditional educational discourses and on elements common to university and similar, institutional advertisements such as 'Application forms and further details are available from the address below'.

In contrast, Newcastle University's advertisement has a low degree of interdiscursivity. With respect to intertextuality, the text draws on traditional academic discourse in every statement, articulating the discourse in conventional ways.

According to Fairclough's theory, a high level of interdiscursivity is associated with change, while a low level of interdiscursivity signals the reproduction of the established order. At this stage in the analysis, we conclude tentatively that the Sheffield advertisement is a manifestation of wider societal change, while the Newcastle advertisement works to maintain the traditional discourse order at the universities.

Text

By detailed analysis of the linguistic characteristics of a text using particular tools, it is possible to cast light on how discourses are activated textually and arrive at, and provide backing for, a particular interpretation.

Fairclough proposes a number of tools for text analysis. Those with a background in linguistics will probably recognise the following selection:

- interactional control – the relationship between speakers, including the question of who sets the conversational agenda (Fairclough 1992b: 152ff.);
- ethos – how identities are constructed through language and aspects of the body (1992b: 166ff.);
- metaphors (1992b: 194ff.);
- wording (1992b: 190);[15] and
- grammar (1992b: 158ff., 169ff.).

All of these give insight into the ways in which texts treat events and social relations and thereby construct particular versions of reality, social identities and social relations.

We will now look more closely at two important grammatical elements, transitivity and modality.[16] When analysing *transitivity* the focus is on how events and processes are connected (or not connected) with subjects and objects. The interest lies in investigating the ideological consequences that different forms can have. In the sentence '50 nurses were sacked yesterday', a passive form is used and consequently the agent is omitted. The dismissal of the nurses is presented as a kind of natural phenomenon – something that just happened without a responsible agent (such as the administrators of the hospital). The sentence structure absolves the agent of responsibility by emphasising the effect and disregarding the action and process that caused it. Another linguistic feature that reduces agency and emphasises the effect is *nominalisation* whereby a noun stands for the process (e.g. 'there were many dismissals at the hospital').

Analyses of *modality* focus on the speaker's degree of affinity with or affiliation to her or his statement. The statements, 'it's cold', 'I think it's cold' and 'perhaps it's a little cold' are different ways of expressing oneself about the temperature; that is, they represent different modalities by which speakers commit themselves to their statements to varying degrees. The chosen modality has consequences for the discursive construction of both social relations and knowledge and meaning systems.

One type of modality is *truth*. The speaker commits herself completely to the statement. For instance, the statement, 'Hardening of the arteries attacks the arteries over almost the whole body',[17] presents a particular knowledge-claim as true and incontrovertible whereas the statement, 'Hardening of the arteries may attack the arteries over almost the whole body' expresses a lower degree of certainty. An example of a modality that constructs social relations in a particular way is *permission*. The speaker puts herself in a position whereby she can give the receiver permission to do something: 'A few weeks after you have got your pacemaker, you do not have to pay much attention to it. You *can* take part in sports, have sex, give birth and go to work'.[18] Modality can also be expressed by intonation (e.g. a hesitant tone can express distance from the statement) or by *hedges*. Speakers hedge when they moderate a sentence's claim and thereby express low affinity, for example, by using 'well' or 'a bit' as in 'the medical establishment got it wrong – well, maybe they did a bit'.

Different discourses use different forms of modality (Fairclough 1992b: 160ff.). For instance, the mass media often present interpretations as if they were facts, partly by using categorical modalities and partly by choosing objective rather than subjective modalities (for example, by saying 'It is dangerous' instead of 'We think it is dangerous'). The media's use of categorical, objective modalities both reflects and reinforces their authority.

Example

In order to analyse the construction of identities and social relations in the job advertisements, Fairclough investigates how the advertisements construct representations of the reader and the institution itself. As an expression of the interdiscursivity of the Sheffield advertisement, the text contains conflicting interpersonal meanings, corresponding to the different discourses that are articulated. But it is the promotional discourses, and, consequently, their construction of identity, which are dominant. The institution is characterised by, for example, the nominalisations, 'teaching excellence and research innovation'; 'expertise'; 'research initiatives'. It is personified, a particular identity being promoted through these nominalisations. At the same time, the advertisement actively constructs a professional identity for the applicant according to which the successful applicant has to have a particular set of personal qualities – e.g. 'with your ambition, energy and expertise, you will be committed to teaching'. In this way, the institution asserts authority over both its own and the applicant's identity ('we' and 'you'), and this applies in relation to personal qualities as well as to working conditions and application procedure. Note how, at the same time, the personification of the institution and the reader simulates a conversation which contributes to the creation of a personal and apparently equal relationship between the two.

There are many subordinate clauses with the modal verb 'will' (e.g. 'you will ideally have industry-related experience'), marking the future and manifesting a high affinity modality, but there are no explicit obligational modalities such as e.g. 'you *should* have industry-related experience'. Sentences of the type 'for the post [...] you *will ideally* have industry-related experience' (our italics) downplay obligations and open up for alternatives. This feature also promotes a personified, equal relationship between institution and applicant.

In contrast to Sheffield Polytechnic's advertisement, the institutional voice in the Newcastle one is impersonal, conservative and distancing. Analysis shows that the traditional structure of advertisements for academic positions is reproduced thus: a title that identifies the institution; a main title that refers to the position; information about the position, salary and application procedure. The institution asserts its authority over the conditions of the job and the application procedure through the many indicative subordinate clauses with high affinity modalities such as 'the post is available' and 'salary will be'. But the institution does not claim authority over the reader's identity and there is, therefore, no attempt to create a specific professional identity for the applicant.

With respect to transitivity, there are two elements in the Newcastle advert that contribute to the promotion of an impersonal relationship between the university and the applicant: passive tenses and nominalisation. In 'Applications are invited for a Lectureship' (instead of 'We invite you to apply for a lectureship') we find a passive verb without an agent. Nor is the institution explicitly mentioned. The nominalisation, 'applications', also lacks an agent and this means that the potential applicant is absent. The choice of words is formal and slightly old fashioned, so contributing to the impersonal, distanced, institutional identity that is typical of the discourses of old universities.

In analysis of the text dimension, it has become clear that the texts represent two different discourses, each with their own linguistic features, which construct the social relations between institution and applicant in different ways. The Sheffield advert actively constructs particular identities for both institution and applicant, and simultaneously implies that the two parties have an equal and personal relationship in which they can talk about things. In contrast, the Newcastle advert drily presents the conditions that the applicant must live up to in order to be accepted and otherwise does not intervene in how the applicant's identity should be.

Social Practice

Now that we have analysed the text as text and as discursive practice, our focus turns to the broader social practice of which these dimensions are part. There are two aspects to this contextualisation. First, the relationship between the discursive practice and its order of discourse is to be explored (Fairclough 1992b: 237). To what kind of network of discourses does the discursive practice belong? How are the discourses distributed and regulated across texts? Second, the aim is to map the partly non-discursive, social and cultural relations and structures that constitute the wider context of the discursive practice – *the social matrix of discourse*, in Fairclough's terms (Fairclough 1992b: 237). For instance, to what kind of institutional and economic conditions is the discursive practice subject? Such questions cannot be answered by discourse analysis, as Fairclough defines it; it is necessary to draw on other theories – for example, social or cultural theory – that shed light upon the social practice in question.

Doing critical discourse analysis will, then, always involve the transdisciplinary integration of different theories within a multiperspectival research framework – linguistic theory and analysis can never suffice to account for the non-discursive aspects of the phenomenon in question. Chouliaraki and Fairclough (1999) outline ways in which social analysis and discourse analysis can fruitfully cross-fertilise one another and give pointers as to the forms of non-discourse analytical theory that it may be appropriate to import into a discourse analytical framework. The different discourse analytical and non-discourse analytical theories one uses in order to carry out a specific project need to be translated into an integrated theoretical and analytical framework, where they are adapted to one another and to the aim of the research project (Chouliaraki and Fairclough 1999: 112ff.). In Chapter 5 we will discuss in more detail the problems and potential gains of multiperspectival discourse analysis.

It is in the analysis of the relationship between discursive practice and the broader social practice that the study arrives at its final conclusions. It is here that questions relating to change and ideological consequences are addressed. Does the discursive practice reproduce the order of discourse and thus contribute to the maintenance of the status quo in the social practice? Or has the order of discourse been transformed, thereby contributing to social change? What are the ideological, political and social consequences of the discursive practice? Does the discursive practice conceal and strengthen unequal power relations in society, or does it challenge power positions by representing reality and social relations in a new way? Through drawing such conclusions, the research project is rendered political and critical. We will return to this aspect in the section headed 'Results'.

Example

The interdiscursive blend of promotional and traditional university discourses that we have identified in the Sheffield advert can be understood as a product of the blurring of boundaries between two orders of discourse – the orders of discourse of higher education and of the business sector. Traditional university discourses are mixed together with the business world's promotional discourses. The spread of promotional discourses across orders of discourse is a driving force in the wider societal development which Fairclough has dubbed the 'marketisation of discourse'.

If the Sheffield advert's interplay with other social practices in the UK is analysed, its use of promotional discourse can be understood in the light of Thatcherism's hegemonic project, where a neoliberal consumer discourse (together with a traditional Conservative discourse and a populist discourse) had spread across social and political domains, thereby contributing to social, cultural and political change in the UK.

In order to cast light on the wider social processes, which also include non-discursive forces, Fairclough draws on theories of late modernity. For instance, he uses Anthony Giddens' theory of post-traditional society, which claims that people's social relations and identities are no longer based on stable social positions, but are rather created through negotiations in everyday interaction (Giddens 1991). In the light of this theory, the Sheffield advert can be understood as a reflection of, and a driving force for, processes of change towards a post-traditional society, whereas the Newcastle advert becomes an example of the continued reproduction of traditional university discourses. Fairclough also applies theories of consumer culture (e.g. Featherstone 1991; Wernick 1991) to gain insight into the role of the expansion of promotional discourses in the spread of consumer culture and the restructuring of the economy from a focus on production to a focus on consumption.

When put into a broader social context, the two adverts together indicate that there is an ongoing struggle about how universities are to function and to be understood in late modern Britain. On one side are forces that press for a redefinition of the universities in which they become, to a larger extent, institutions in which products are bought, sold and negotiated. That it is the new university, Sheffield City Polytechnic, which is representative of this side of the struggle can partly be understood in the light of the strong historical links between the poly-technic institutions and the business sector, where these institutions have been oriented towards vocational qualifications to a greater extent than have the traditional universities. On the other side is positioned an old university like Newcastle upon Tyne that maintains the boundary between university and corporate sector and consequently reproduces a more traditional definition of what universities are and should be.

6. Results

According to Fairclough, discourse analysts should consider certain ethical questions regarding the public use of their research results. The researcher needs to recognise that there is a risk that the results may be used as a resource in social engineering. Fairclough sees this kind of use of the results as a manifestation of the 'technologisation of discourse' (1992b: 221f.) whereby discourse research is employed to alter discur-sive practices and also to train people to use new forms of discursive practice, for example, to train managers of businesses.

As we mentioned earlier, the aim of critical discourse analysis as explanatory critique is to promote more egalitarian and liberal dis-courses and thereby to further democratisation. A step in this direction is to make people aware that discourse functions as a form of social prac-tice which reflects and takes part in the reinforcement of unequal power relations. The researcher can apply a technique for this purpose that Fairclough labels *critical language awareness*.[19] Critical language aware-ness should give people insight into the discursive practice in which they participate when they use language and consume texts and also into the social structures and power relations that discursive practice is shaped by and takes part in shaping and changing. Through training in critical lan-guage awareness, people can become more aware of the constraints on their practice and of the possibilities for resistance and change (Fairclough 1992b: 239).

If the researcher seeks to promote this sort of development, it is impor-tant to convey the results in such a way that they are accessible for the people on which the research has focused. If the project shows that a particular group of people controls communication processes, other groups might be able to use the research results to develop forms of communication that involve a more equal distribution of power.[20]

SOME CRITICAL COMMENTS

In conclusion, we will present some critical comments on critical discourse analysis, primarily directed towards Fairclough's approach but also relating to critical discourse analysis in general.

Among the different approaches to critical discourse analysis, Fairclough has, in our view, constructed the most sophisticated framework for analysis of the relationship between language use and societal practices in general. The main problem with his approach is that the consequences for empirical research of the theoretical distinction between the discursive and the non-discursive remain unclear. How can one demonstrate empirically that something is in a dialectical relationship with something else? Where does one locate the line of demarcation between two or more things that are in dialectical interplay? And how can one show exactly *where* and *how* the non-discursive moments influence and change the discursive moment – and vice versa? In specific studies, the problem often manifests itself in the presentation of the broader social practices as the *background* for the discursive practices. For instance, the analysis of City job advertisements presented in this chapter can be criticised on the grounds that it installs a post-traditional consumer society as the objective social reality which different discursive practices then more or less reflect. Consequently, Sheffield Polytechnic's profile as a promotional discursive practice is in line with the times, whereas the Newcastle advert represents something antiquated which is on its way out. The analysis of the job advertisements in itself does not generate any new knowledge or new hypotheses about the larger societal structures. The overall account leaves little space for the possibility that the struggle is not yet over and that the discursive practices can still work to change the social order. And this is in spite of the fact that Fairclough stresses that discourses shape the social world. One source of the problem is probably that his analysis is limited to single texts. It is easier to show how dynamic discursive practices take part in constituting and changing the social world when analysing the reproduction and transformation of discourses across a range of texts (cf. Chouliaraki and Fairclough 1999: 51).

One way to solve the theoretical problem of the distinction between the discursive and the non-discursive is to treat it as an *analytical* distinction rather than an empirical one. As Laclau and Mouffe argue, it is difficult to point to the precise dividing line between the discursive and the non-discursive. To take the economy as an example: should the economy be seen as a non-discursive system obeying its own logic, different from the logic of meaning-making, or should it rather be conceptualised as an infinite number of specific choices people make on the basis of meaning-ascription, together making up 'the economy'? In the second understanding, economy could be analysed as a discursive practice, whereas the first understanding would lead to a different kind of analysis of the economy as a non-discursive system. One problem is, therefore, where to differentiate between the discursive and the non-discursive, and another problem is how we, as researchers, could ever hope to analyse what is (at least partly) outside of discourse. Lilie Chouliaraki (2002) suggests that even if we can only know about social reality through representation, we can still analyse it *as if* social reality is more than meaning-making. This implies that what the researcher points to as non-discursive logics, and where she draws the boundary between the discursive and the non-discursive, is more a result of a theoretical and analytical choice. In this way, a critical discourse analysis is able to draw on a number of social theories to map out other parts of the domain under study than those covered by the specific discourse analysis, without installing an essentialist boundary between the discursive and the non-discursive.[21]

A shortcoming that Fairclough shares with other types of critical discourse analysis is a theoretically weak understanding of processes of group formation, the subject and agency, including questions regarding subjectification and subjectivity and how much control people have over their language use. In so far as Fairclough stresses that discourses take part in constructing social identities and social relations (in addition to knowledge and meaning-systems), he cannot be said to have entirely neglected these social psychological aspects, but they are the weakest element of his theory.[22] This deficiency on the part of Fairclough and the other forms of critical discourse analysis is accompanied by a corresponding dearth of empirical research into the consumption of texts (notwithstanding their view that people are active in interpretation processes and that texts are polysemic). For the most part, their studies consist of textual analyses, in spite of Fairclough's insistence that textual analysis should be combined with analysis of text production and text consumption practices (Fairclough 1995b: 33).

In contrast to critical discourse analysis' neglect of social psychological aspects, Laclau and Mouffe's discourse theory provides insight into the discursive construction of groups. And discursive psychology has developed a sophisticated theory about the individual and the social world and carries out empirical studies into people's language use as a dynamic discursive practice (see Chapter 4 on discursive psychology and Chapter 5 for ideas on how to build a framework for concrete discourse analysis that combines elements from discourse theory, discursive psychology and critical discourse analysis).

At the outset, we described critical discourse analysis as one school, but it is, of course, important to be aware of the differences between the various approaches within critical discourse analysis, for example, if one would like to draw on more than one of them. An important difference between Fairclough and the other critical discourse analytical approaches is his more poststructuralist understanding of discourse and the social. The conception of discourse as partly constitutive underpins his empirical interest in the dynamic role of discourse in social and cultural *change*. Against this, the other approaches have a tendency to regard discourse as a reflection of an underlying structure and also to focus empirically on the role of discourse in *social reproduction*.

The major differences within critical discourse analysis are illustrated by the fact that Teun van Dijk's discourse analytical approach is also understood as part of the school. In contrast to the majority of the other approaches, van Dijk's socio-cognitive approach (e.g. 1991, 1993, 1997a) understands *cognitive structures* as mediating social and discursive practices (see the critique of cognitivism in the next chapter). Furthermore, van Dijk does not understand power in Foucault's sense as *productive*, but as *abuse*. Power is always oppressive, it is used by certain interest groups and imposed on passive subjects. This conception of power stands in contrast to both the poststructuralist understanding of power as productive as well as oppressive (based on Foucault's view), and to Gramsci's concept of hegemony on which Fairclough draws (in which power is seen as 'negotiated', in the sense that people can, to a certain extent, act as agents with possibilities for resistance). As a consequence of his understanding of power, van Dijk has a tendency to neglect people's possibilities for resistance. And although he follows today's consensus about active interpreters and polysemic texts, he is disposed to take the ideological effects of texts for granted (for example, to take for granted that people will accept racist messages).

Most of the critical discourse analytical approaches, however, do have important features in common. Fairclough's approach, French structuralist discourse analysis, social semiotics, reading analysis and the Duisburg school all draw on Foucault's discourse theory (as Laclau and Mouffe also do). They see discourse as partly constitutive of knowledge, subjects and social relations. At the same time, they try to do a discourse analysis which is *text oriented*, that is, they try systematically to analyse language use as social practice – *actual instances of language use* – in relation to the wider social practice of which the discursive practice is part. Here they differ from Foucault and from Laclau and Mouffe's more abstract discourse analysis. And this is one of the most important reasons why the latter approaches are not covered by the critical discourse analytical umbrella.

But discursive psychology, the subject of the next chapter, also involves close textual analysis, and in general has much in common with critical discourse analysis, without being regarded as such. If we go by Fairclough and Wodak's description of the defining characteristics of critical discourse analysis (1997), it is clear that discursive psychology also has the necessary qualifications for membership of the club, though discursive psychology practises rhetorical, rather than linguistic, analysis.[23] That discursive psychologists are not considered as members of the club may have something to do with disciplinary allegiance. Critical discourse analysis has roots in linguistics, whereas discursive psychology stems from social psychology. As suggested in Chapter 1, we can understand discourse analysis itself as an order of discourse in which different approaches represent different discourses about language, discourse and society, and in which some discourses are stronger than others. The disciplinary boundaries have become looser, but they have not vanished, and they play a role in relation to the power and impact an approach can have.

NOTES

1 In a survey of the field of critical discourse analysis, Fairclough and Wodak identify the following approaches as members of the broad critical discourse analytical movement: French structuralist discourse analysis (e.g. Pecheux 1982); critical linguistics (e.g. Fowler et al. 1979; Fowler 1991); social semiotics (e.g. Hodge and Kress 1988; Kress and van Leeuwen 1996; Kress, Leite-Garcia and van Leeuwen 1997)); Fairclough's critical discourse analysis (e.g. Fairclough 1989, 1992b, 1995a, 1995b); socio-cognitive analysis (e.g. van Dijk 1991, 1993); discourse historical method (e.g. Wodak 1991; Wodak and Menz 1990); reading analysis (e.g. Maas 1989) and the Duisburg School (e.g. Jäger 1993; Jäger and Jäger 1992). It is worth noting that only three of

these approaches – besides Fairclough's own – have been described as critical discourse analysis by their àdherents: the socio-cognitive, the social semiotic and the discourse historical approach.

2 The nature and consequences of critical work today are the objects of extensive debate within many movements across the social sciences including post-Marxism, poststructuralism, feminism and postmodernism. For a good discussion of critical social studies, see for example, Calhoun (1995). For a good discussion of critical cultural studies, see Kellner (1989, 1995). We will develop the discussion of critical social research in Chapter 6.

3 However, Fairclough does not explicitly mention poststructuralism here.

4 See Halliday (1994) for an account of systemic linguistics. For a description of how Fairclough draws on Halliday's approach, see Fairclough (1992b: Chapter 6). See also Fowler et al. (1979) and Fowler (1991) for examples of another approach within critical discourse analysis – critical linguistics – which like Fairclough draws on Halliday's systemic linguistics including Halliday's systemic grammar that is used for textual analysis. Fairclough draws on critical linguistics in his methods for textual analysis (see the section on methods), while rejecting some of its assumptions, such as the tendency to take the ideological consequences of texts for granted.

5 In his earlier work, Fairclough identifies other discourse types – 'activity type' and 'style' (Fairclough 1992a: 124ff.). In his later work, he distinguishes mainly between 'discourse', 'discourse type' and 'genre' – sometimes with analytical gains, but sometimes more at random (see Fairclough 1995b). In this presentation, we mostly use the term, discourse, to cover all three discourse types.

6 In Fairclough (1995b), 'social practice' has been replaced by 'sociocultural practice'.

7 And the basic idea of the three-dimensional model also appears to survive in the new understanding (cf. Chouliaraki and Fairclough 1999: 113).

8 Fairclough (1992b, 1992c) points out that the 'discursive creativity' that underpins interdiscursivity occurs in social conditions that promote change; thus it is not merely a product of individuals with creative abilities.

9 Besides Kristeva, another important source of inspiration for Fairclough (and for others who work with the concept of intertextuality) is Bakhtin, see e.g. Bakhtin (1981, 1986).

10 For a critique of this perspective and a presentation of his own perspective, see Thompson (1984, 1990).

11 See also Fairclough (2001) for a presentation of research steps and tools based on the more recent version of Fairclough's framework.

12 For a five-step research plan for explanatory critique, see Chouliaraki and Fairclough (1999: 59ff.).

13 As mentioned, Fairclough distinguishes between discourses, discourse types and genres. In this example he uses both terms, discourse and genre. But in our presentation of his analysis, we take the liberty of abbreviating his terminology and mostly use the term, 'discourse', to cover all three concepts.

14 For a critique of CDA for not carrying out empirical analyses of reception, see Schrøder (1998). For examples of the few audience studies that draw on CDA, see Chouliaraki (1998), Phillips (2000a, 2000b) and Richardson (1998).

15 A hegemonic struggle may be taking place over the meanings of the key words. To analyse this, Laclau and Mouffe's concept, 'floating signifiers', could be imported. See also Phillips (1996, 1998) for an analysis of how key words and formulaic phrases contributed to the construction and transformation of the discourse of Thatcherism.

16 To analyse transitivity and modality, Fairclough draws on critical linguistics (e.g. Fowler 1991; Fowler et al. 1979). However, he rejects critical linguistics' tendency to assume that audiences are passive and to take texts' ideological effects for granted. Pragmatics can also be drawn on for this type of analysis (see e.g. Leech 1983; Mey 1993).

17 This example is taken from *Længe leve livet: en håndbog om dit hjerte og kredsløb*, Hjerteforeningen 1994 [*Long may you live: a handbook about your heart and circulation* The Heart Association]. The translations and the italics in the last citation are ours.

18 Also from "Længe leve livet: en håndbog om dit hjerte og kredsløb" see footnote 17.

19 For illustrations of how to use critical language awareness for educational purposes, see Fairclough (1992a, 1995a: Chapters 9 and 10). For a brief outline of the purpose of critical language awareness in media teaching, see Fairclough (1995b: Chapter 10) about critical media 'literacy'. See Kellner (1995) for a discussion of critical media pedagogy from a cultural studies perspective.

20 Fairclough's book on the language of New Labour (2000) is directed at an audience outside, as well as within, academic circles and can thus be seen as an attempt to spread critical awareness of the workings of contemporary language and rhetoric in the political field.

21 In Chapter 5, we present an example of research based partly on critical discourse analysis in which an analytical rather than an ontological distinction is made between the discursive and the non-discursive and different social theories are imported to cast light on the wider social practice.

22 For a description of Fairclough's understanding of the role of discour⌐
the construction of identities and social relations, see Fairclough (1992a:
Chapter 5). See also Chouliaraki and Fairclough (1999: Chapter 6) for
an attempt to develop a deeper understanding of the subject by use of the
concepts of habitus and voice.

23 Fairclough and Wodak note that another non-linguistic approach, critical
feminist studies, belongs to critical discourse analysis, but that they do not
have space to cover it (1997: 281).

iscursive Psychology

Traditionally, the field of social psychology has been dominated by the cognitivist paradigm which explains social psychological phenomena in terms of *cognitive processes* – thinking, perception and reasoning. Using predominantly experimental methods, research aims at identification of universal, cognitive processes as the causes of social action. The interest is in social cognition, understood as the mental processing of information about the social world. In this chapter we deal with the social constructionist forms of discourse analysis that have been developed in the field of social psychology as a critique of, and challenge to, cognitivism (see for example, Edwards 1996; Edwards and Potter 1992; Gergen 1985, 1994a, 1994b; Potter and Wetherell 1987). Discourse analysis has become one of the most important social constructionist approaches within social psychology (in the following, we use *discursive psychology* as an umbrella term for this approach). In cognitivist approaches to language, written and spoken language are seen as a reflection of an external world or a product of underlying mental representations of this world (Edwards and Potter 1992: 2). In contrast to cognitivism, discursive psychology treats written and spoken language as constructions of the world oriented towards social action.[1]

All social constructionist approaches share the structuralist and post-structuralist premise, mentioned in Chapter 1, that language is a dynamic form of social practice which shapes the social world including identities, social relations and understandings of the world. This premise entails the view of mental processes and categories as constituted through social, discursive activities rather than as 'internal', as in cognitive psychology and psychoanalysis (Edwards 1996; Edwards and Potter 1992). Here, discursive psychology draws partly on Ludwig Wittgenstein's later philosophy in which it is emphasised that claims about psychological states should be treated as *social activities* instead of as manifestations of deeper 'essences' behind the words (Wittgenstein 1953; see, for example, Edwards 1996; Potter 2001).[2] Utterances are oriented towards action in specific social contexts, and their meanings are therefore dependent on the particular use to which they are put. Thus language use is context-bound or *occasioned*. It is language use in this sense that discursive psychologists define as *discourse*.

In analysing discourse empirically as situated language use, discursive psychology differs both from the approaches within cognitive psychology that focus on abstract structures of language (including Chomsky's approach) and from structuralist and poststructuralist discourse theories (including Foucault's and Laclau and Mouffe's discourse theories) that do not focus on specific instances of social interaction.

In this chapter we will describe the main elements of discursive psychology as a theory and method for research on communications, culture and society. First we describe its roots in a challenge to cognitive social psychology. We do not give a detailed account of cognitive social psychology but, rather, a brief outline of key aspects of the approach and of discursive psychology's critique of these aspects. The purpose is to give an introductory impression of discursive psychology by tracing its origins in a paradigmatic challenge to cognitivism. The aspects of cognitive social psychology which we have selected are its conception of the self and mental processes and two of its main areas of research – research on attitudes and on group conflicts. We have selected these focal points since they are central to social psychology and relevant for social research in general. Second, we present the social constructionist premises underpinning discursive psychology, and we outline and compare three different strands of discursive psychology. Following this, we expand on the view of the self and identity within discursive psychology, and its stance towards reflexivity in relation to the research process and knowledge production. Finally, we outline methods for empirical research and give some examples of the empirical application of two approaches to discursive psychology.

We draw heavily on Jonathan Potter and Margaret Wetherell's work in relation to theory, method and empirical research since their work has played a central role in the development of discursive psychology and since it provides some useful research tools. In particular, Potter and Wetherell's book *Discourse and Social Psychology* (1987) was central in the emergence of discursive psychology as a challenge to cognitive psychology, and their book, *Mapping the Language of Racism* (Wetherell and Potter, 1992) gives an account of one of the most extensive studies within discursive psychology. In our account of discursive psychology we will refer repeatedly to this study. The subject of the study is the discourses of *Pākehā* (white New Zealanders) about Māori culture and the social consequences of these discursive constructions.

DISCURSIVE PSYCHOLOGY AS A CHALLENGE TO COGNITIVE PSYCHOLOGY

The Self and Mental Processes

Cognitive psychology ascribes to the modern conception of the individual as an autonomous, delimited agent with a set of authentic characteristics. The individual and society are regarded as separate entities, thus implying the existence of a *dualism* between the individual and society. The social world is treated as information to be processed, and people are understood as isolated information processors who, by way of cognitive processes, observe the world and thus accumulate knowledge structures and experience that govern their perception of the world. A main premise in cognitive psychology is that the individual handles the mass of information about the world through use of cognitive processes which categorise the world in particular ways. The assumption underpinning this premise is that the world contains so much information that the individual is unable to create meaning out of the chaos unless he or she uses categories. Categories are seen as mental structures that control our actions (Condor and Antaki 1997). This perspective builds on *perceptualism*, that is, the idea that categorisation is based on direct, empirical experience (Edwards and Potter 1992).[3] We observe the world directly and, on the basis of our perception, we construct mental structures or representations which we then employ to categorise the information about the world. Two of the mental representations that cognitivist research has identified are *schemata* such as *scripts*. Scripts contain sketches of routine situations and the corresponding appropriate behaviour (Condor and Antaki 1997: 326). For instance, students have a script about what happens at a seminar: you come in and sit down, listen, perhaps ask a question and pretend not to have fallen asleep. This script, then, provides the student with guidelines for action.

'Consistency theories' represent a perspective on cognitive processing which was extremely influential until the beginning of the 1980s, and of which discursive psychology has mounted a critique. These theories are based on the assumption that people strive for consistency in their thinking. They include the 'theory of cognitive dissonance' formulated by Louis Festinger (1957). On the basis of a number of experiments, Festinger concluded that if someone experiences dissonance – that is, inconsistency between two or more of their cognitions – they enter into an uncomfortable state of psychological tension and become motivated to reduce the tension by changing their cognitions so that they return to being consistent. For instance, if someone is badly paid for a job, it can be rationalised afterwards as a very rewarding experience. This will reduce the dissonance. According to this perspective, variations between attitudes and actions are not seen as something common or natural, but as psychologically uncomfortable states. In relation to planned communication, for example, the theory of cognitive dissonance would assume that if audience members or readers do not experience that a communicated opinion is in line with their other opinions, the sender will have difficulty in getting it accepted (Cheesman and Mortensen 1991: 91).

According to social constructionists, theorists of cognitive consistency, in common with other cognitivists, underestimate the *social* origin of psychological states by basing their explanations on hypotheses about universal processes. Michael Billig (1982: 141) notes, for example, that the theorists took the universality of the processes for granted instead of demonstrating it through intercultural studies. In discursive psychology, it is argued that our ways of understanding and categorising the world are not universal, but historically and socially specific and consequently contingent. Furthermore, discursive psychologists draw attention to studies that challenge the findings of 'cognitive consistency'. These studies demonstrate that *variations* in people's talk, whereby people contradict themselves, are very frequent and that the attempts at making one's opinions cohere (that is, eliminate the variation) are relatively rare (Potter and Wetherell 1987: 38). Whether something is understood as consistent or inconsistent depends on the social situation and on the individual. Consistency and inconsistency are themselves variable conditions and one of the aspects in which discursive psychology has special interest is how consistency and inconsistency are used as rhetorical strategies in situated language use (Potter and Wetherell 1987: 38). The assumption that it is universal, individual cognitive processes that underpin individual and collective action is integral to the cognitivist view of the individual as an isolated, autonomous agent. The difference between this view and the social constructionist conception of the self is, as we will see later on, crucial for the differences between the two research traditions.

Attitude Research

Based on cognitivism, attitude research views attitudes as controlling people's actions through the production of ongoing mental evaluations of the world. An important goal of the research is to enhance the capacity of planned communication such as information campaigns to change attitudes and behaviour. Realisation of this goal is hindered by the 'attitude/behaviour problem' – namely, that a particular attitude does not necessarily lead to behaviour in line with that attitude. In attitude research, several studies have been carried out that show that there is a low degree of correspondence between people's expressed attitudes and their actions.[4]

In attitude research, the theory of 'planned action' (Azjen 1988; Fishbein and Azjen 1975) represents an attempt to improve the ability of attitude measurement to predict actions. Intentions to behave in particular ways (for example, to buy organic food) are seen as a result of three factors: the person's attitude towards the object of the action (for instance, organic food), his or her impression of what significant others such as friends or family think about the action (the normative dimension), and his or her control over the action (for example, whether or not he or she can afford to buy organic food or whether or not the local shops stock it). The model predicts actions much better than earlier models, but the fact that one has to take such a wide range of complex, circumstantial and normative factors into account reduces the usability of the concept of attitude (Potter 1996a).[5]

From the perspective of discursive psychology, attitude research suffers from a number of general problems. For instance, attitude researchers treat every attitude as an isolated entity and not as a part of a larger system of meaning, and no theory has been formulated to account for the ways in which an individual's different attitudes are connected to one another. In a critique along these lines, Potter depicts this problem aptly by way of the following metaphor: attitude research treats attitudes as entities which are dispersed in the brain like raisins in a fruit cake (1996a: 135). A related problem that Potter points out is that attitude research neglects how attitudes are constructed through social interaction between people in everyday life. And perhaps the most important point is that the variations that characterise people's talk are hard to reconcile with the idea that attitudes merely reflect underlying cognitive processes and stable structures (Billig 1991; Edwards and Potter 1992). Thus social constructionists criticise the basic premise of attitude research – that attitudes should be sought after in individual cognitive structures. They believe, in contrast, that attitude formation is constituted through *social activities*.[6]

Group Conflicts

Cognitivist approaches to stereotypes and group conflicts attempt to understand the typical social psychological processes that create conflicts between groups. One of the central ideas is that, when people become members of a group, they begin to identify with that group and view social reality from its perspective. They come to regard members of their own group as better than members of other groups. Racism and ethnocentrism, then, are understood as results of group membership. This perspective implies that, as a consequence of universal mental processes, everybody more or less functions identically. It also contains an element of *perceptualism* as it is assumed that change in stereotypes takes place only when new information contradicting the stereotypes is received. This implies that if the victims of the stereotypes were to act differently, people would treat the new information in a non-stereotypical way. Consequently, the victims of stereotypes are considered to be the *causes* of prejudices, and people's prejudices are treated as inevitable *effects* of information processing strategies (Wetherell 1996a).

Within discursive psychology, *social identity theory* is regarded as the most fruitful of the cognitivist approaches.[7] Social identity theory differs from other cognitivist approaches in emphasising that conflict between groups has roots in particular social and historical contexts. However, it retains a cognitivist aspect in that it sees categorisation as a psychological process. The aim is to determine what happens to people's identity and their evaluations, perceptions and motivations when they interact within groups. The main point is that people's cognitive processes change since self-categorisation as a group member leads to the expression of a social identity rather than a personal identity; when expressing a social identity, stereotypes are deployed. One's sense of self becomes based on shared ideas regarding the group (for example, about what it means to be a student, a Christian or a European). According to social identity theory, people's self-esteem is intertwined with the group. In order to feel good about oneself, the individual has to feel good about the group. The result is that people favourise their own group ('in-group favouritism') and discriminate against other groups ('out-group discrimination'). It is in this way that conflicts arise between groups.

Discursive psychologists have launched some of the same points of criticism against social identity theory as they have against the other cognitivist approaches. They question the assumption that there is a universal psychological process that causes group conflict. As in the case of the theories of cognitive consistency, social identity theory does not provide evidence from intercultural research. On the contrary, intercultural studies show that children with other cultural backgrounds do not discriminate between groups in the same way as British and Northern American children, for example do (Wetherell 1982, 1996). The results of the studies are in line with the social constructionist assumption that the processes of identification and categorisation underpinning social identity are historically and socially specific. The results indicate that group members' discrimination of other groups is not due to an automatic, psychological connection between group identification and competition between groups but to the interpretation of group relations on the basis of cultural frameworks of understanding; it is this culturally relative process of interpretation that determines whether group identification leads to 'in-group favouritism' and 'out-group discrimination' or has another outcome altogether.

The Position of Discursive Psychology: Summary

In contrast to cognitivism, social constructionism – including discursive psychology – argues for the *social construction* of attitudes, social groups and identities. Social constructionism rejects the cognitivist attempt to explain attitudes and behaviour in terms of underlying mental states or processes. Instead of understanding psychological processes – including processes of social categorisation – as private, mental activities produced by individual information processing, social constructionists understand them as social activities. Furthermore, they do not view attitudes as stable, mental dispositions (that the individual 'owns') but as products of social interaction.

According to discursive psychology, language does not merely express experiences; rather, language also constitutes experiences and the subjective, psychological reality (Potter and Wetherell 1987; Shotter 1993; Wetherell 1995). In the next section we discuss in depth discursive psychology's social constructionist perspective and its understanding of self and identity.

SOCIAL CONSTRUCTIONISM AND DISCURSIVE PSYCHOLOGY

As mentioned in Chapter 1, social constructionists propose that the ways in which we understand and categorise in everyday life are not transparent reflections of a world 'out there', but a product of historically and culturally specific understandings of the world and therefore contingent. These understandings of the world are created and maintained through social interaction between people in their everyday lives. This viewpoint is based on *anti-essentialism*: that the social world is constructed socially implies that its character is not pre-determined or pre-given, and that people do not have inner 'essences' – a set of genuine, authentic and immutable characteristics.[8]

According to discursive psychology, discourses do not describe an external world 'out there' as schemata and stereotypes do according to cognitivist approaches. Rather, discourses *create* a world that looks real or true for the speaker. As mentioned in Chapter 1, this point of view is poststructuralist. Language is not seen as a channel that transparently communicates a pre-existing psychological reality which is the basis of experience; rather, subjective psychological realities are *constituted* through *discourse*, defined as *situated language use* or *language use in everyday texts and talk* (Shotter 1993; Wetherell and Potter 1992). Claims about psychological states should be treated as social, discursive activities rather than as expressions of deeper 'essences' beneath the words (Wittgenstein 1953). We give meaning to experiences by virtue of the words which are available, and the resulting meanings contribute to producing the experience rather than being merely a description of the experience or an 'after-the-event' occurrence. As Potter, Stringer and Wetherell claim, discourse can be said to 'construct' our lived reality (Potter et al. 1984).

The idea that our lived reality is constituted discursively does not mean that discursive psychology argues that social phenomena do not have material aspects, or that there does not exist a physical reality outside discourse. In line with Laclau and Mouffe, the point is that phenomena only gain meaning through discourses, and that the investment of phenomena with meaning contributes to the creation of objects and subjects. Wetherell and Potter stress this point in their study of discursive practice in New Zealand:

> New Zealand is no less real for being constituted discursively – you still die if your plane crashes into a hill whether you think that the hill is the product of a volcanic eruption or the solidified form of a mythical whale. However, material reality is no less discursive for being able to get into the way of planes. How those deaths are understood [...] and what caused them is constituted through our systems of discourses. (Wetherell and Potter 1992: 65)

In contrast to Laclau and Mouffe, most discursive psychologists contend that social events, relations and structures have conditions of existence that lie outside the realm of discourse. For instance, it is argued, nationalism is not only constituted through discourses but also through state violence and material force, while, at the same time, being constructed as something *meaningful* within discourse (Wetherell and Potter 1992). Discursive psychology thus locates certain social practices outside discourse, although it does not distinguish as sharply between discursive and non-discursive practices as does critical discourse analysis.

Discursive psychology also differs from Laclau and Mouffe's discourse theory in rejecting a tendency within poststructuralism to analyse discourses as abstract phenomena, not as situated and 'occasioned' social practices:

> The study of discourse can [...] become something very like the geology of plate tectonics—a patchwork of plates/discourses are understood to be grinding violently together, causing earthquakes and volcanoes, or sometimes sliding silently one underneath the other. Discourses become seen as potent causal agents in their own right, with the processes of interest being the work of one (abstract) discourse on another (abstract) discourse, or the propositions or 'statements' of that discourse working smoothly and automatically to produce objects and subjects. (Wetherell and Potter 1992: 90)[9]

Discursive psychology draws on the poststructuralist understanding of the self as a discursive subject but only in modified form since it also subscribes to the interactionist position that people use discourses actively as resources and consequently stresses that people are producers as well as products of discourses.

DIFFERENT STRANDS OF DISCURSIVE PSYCHOLOGY

Even though discursive psychologists on the whole distance themselves from the very abstract conception of discourse in, for instance, Laclau and Mouffe's approach, in favour of a more interactionist position, discursive psychologists disagree as to how to balance between the larger circulation of patterns of meaning in society on the one hand, and the meaning production occuring in specific contexts on the other. We will distinguish between three different strands of discursive psychology, and in this section we will outline their contours as distinctive approaches to both theory and empirical research within the field of discursive psychology. In short, the three strands can be described as follows:

- A poststructuralist perspective that builds on Foucauldian theory on discourse, power and the subject.
- An interactionist perspective that builds on conversation analysis and ethnomethodology.
- A synthetic perspective that unites the two first perspectives.

The differences between the three strands can be illustrated by way of the continuum that we drew in Chapter 1 (Figure 1.2). On the right-hand side lie the approaches in which the researcher identifies abstract discourses without examining in detail their use across different social contexts. On the left-hand side are the approaches in which the researcher investigates details in language use as activities in social interaction without systematically analysing the links between the details and broader social and cultural processes and structures. The first perspective belongs to the right-hand side, the second perspective to the left-hand side, and the third to the middle position.

The focus in the first perspective, closest to the more abstract conception of discourse, then, is on how people's understandings of the world and identities are created and changed in specific discourses and on the social consequences of these discursive constructions.[10] The second perspective concentrates on the analysis of the action orientation of text and talk in social interaction. Drawing on conversation analysis and ethnomethodology, the focus is on how social organisation is produced through speech and interaction. The researcher analyses people's conversations as manifestations of a world that the participants create themselves. The aim of the researcher is to keep her/his own theoretical perspective on this world out of the analysis, and it is considered to be an assault on the empirical material to apply frames of understanding and explanation not thematised by the informants themselves.[11]

In the third perspective, a poststructuralist interest in how specific discourses constitute subjects and objects is combined with an interactionist interest in the ways in which people's discourse is oriented towards social action in specific contexts of interaction.[12] Equal stress is placed on what people do with their text and talk and on the discursive resources they deploy in these practices. The concept of *interpretative repertoire* is often used instead of discourse to emphasise that discourses are drawn on in social interaction as flexible resources. Proponents of this synthetic perspective distance themselves from both poststructuralist discourse analysis and conversation analysis in their unadulterated forms. On the one hand, they criticise poststructuralist discourse analysis for *reifying* discourses – treating them as things out there in the world – and for neglecting people's situated language use (for example, Wetherell 1998). In poststructuralist discourse analyses of a particular domain (such as the domain of sexuality, politics or the media), it is argued, discourses are viewed as monolithic structures to which people are subjected, and insufficient account is taken of the ways in which people's talk is shaped and changed by the specific contexts of interaction in which the talk is situated and to which it is oriented.[13] On the other hand, they argue that conversation analysis as practised both in the field of conversation analysis itself and in the purely interactionist perspective in discursive psychology[14] neglects the wider social and ideological consequences of language use (for example, Billig 1999a, b;[15] Wetherell 1998). These consequences, it is proposed by followers of the synthetic perspective such as Wetherell (1998) and Billig (1999b), can – and should – be explored through application of social theory in addition to conversation analysis or discourse analysis.

This option is ruled out by conversation analysts on the grounds that the proper object of analysis is the participants' own meaning-making through talk-in-interaction and not the analysts' interpretations of that talk in terms of the wider social patterning of talk. But this claim to produce an analysis of participants' own understandings free from the 'pollution' of analytical assumptions is an expression of epistemological naïvity as well as being undesirable from the perspective of critical research, according to Billig (1999b). All analysis of the world, Billig points out, is based on particular assumptions and it is therefore impossible to fully understand people's talk purely in their own terms. In addition, one should draw on systematised theory about the social (as well as implicit assumptions) in order to carry out critical research on the role of everyday talk in relation to wider questions of social practice and power – the type of research attempted within the synthetic perspective (Billig 1999b; Wetherell 1998).[16]

Although we will refer to the first two strands in cases of disagreement between the three strands of discursive psychology, in most of this chapter we concentrate mainly on the third perspective, focusing on the work of Potter and Wetherell, since their approach has been central for the development of discursive psychology in general and provides particularly useful and widely used tools for research in communication, culture and language. Below, we outline their view of discourses as 'interpretative repertoires'. And towards the end of the chapter, we present both an example from Wetherell and Potter's empirical analysis of *Pākehā's* (white New Zealanders) discourse about Māori culture (1992), and an example of empirical work that belongs to the perspective which draws heavily on conversation analysis and ethnomethology.

Interpretative Repertoires

Central to Potter and Wetherell's model is the view of discourses as 'interpretative repertoires' that are used as flexible resources in social interaction. The purpose is to gain insight into questions about communication, social action and the construction of the self, the Other and the world. Potter and Wetherell analyse how discourse is constructed in relation to social action, how people construct their understandings of the world in social interaction, and how these understandings work ideologically to support forms of social organisation based on unequal relations of power.

Potter and Wetherell define discourse in several ways: as all types of verbal interactions and written texts (Potter and Wetherell 1987: 7) and as meanings, conversations, narratives, explanations, accounts and anecdotes (Wetherell and Potter 1992: 3). In their empirical investigation of *Pākehā* discourse in New Zealand they use the expression 'interpretative repertoire' instead of discourse in order to emphasise that language use in everyday life is flexible and dynamic. An interpretative repertoire consists of 'a limited number of terms that are used in a particular stylistic and grammatical way' (Wetherell and Potter 1988: 172), or as they wrote later:

> By interpretative repertoire, we mean broadly discernible clusters of terms, descriptions and figures of speech often assembled around metaphors or vivid images. (Wetherell and Potter 1992: 90)

Each repertoire provides resources that people can use to construct versions of reality. While Wetherell and Potter emphasise that the term 'discourse' can be used to describe the same process – and do it themselves now and again in their analysis – they prefer to use the concept 'interpretative repertoire'. This is in order to distance themselves from the view of discourses as abstract, reified phenomena mentioned on p. 104 and 105 and to emphasise instead that discourses are used by people actively as flexible resources for accomplishing forms of social action in texts and talk. As flexible resources, interpretative repertoires are, at one and the same time, identifiable entities that represent distinct ways of giving meaning to the world *and* malleable forms that undergo transformations on being put to rhetorical use:

> One of the advantages of considering constructions like culture-as-heritage as interpretative repertoires is that it suggests that there is an available choreography of interpretative moves – like the moves of an icedancer, say – from which particular ones can be selected in a way that fits most effectively in the context. This emphasises both the flexibility of ordinary language use and the way that interpretative resources are organised together in developed ways. It shows the way the tectonic image breaks down in studies that focus on discourse use in practice. (Wetherell and Potter 1992: 92)

The aim of the analysis is *not* to categorise people (for example, as nationalists, racists or 'green' consumers) but to identify the discursive practices through which the categories are constructed. People cannot be expected to be consistent; rather, it is to be expected that their texts and talk *vary* as they draw on different discourses in different contexts. Thus the analysis also places emphasis on the content of discourse in social interaction as something important in itself, not just a reflection of underlying psychological processes. This perspective, as noted earlier, combines a poststructuralist focus on the ways in which specific discourses (conceived as 'interpretative repertoires') constitute subjects and objects with an interactionist focus on the ways in which people's discourse is oriented towards social action in specific contexts.

With their starting point in Foucault's genealogical approach, Wetherell and Potter are not interested in finding out if an interpretative repertoire is a true or false reflection of the world but in analysing the practices through which the repertoires are constructed to appear as true or false. They analyse how people's accounts of themselves, experiences and events are established as solid, real and stable (1992: 95) and how competing accounts are exposed as false and biased (Potter 1996b). But in contrast to Foucault – and in common with critical discourse analysis – they are interested in the ideological effects of people's accounts. They define *ideology* as discourses that categorise the world in ways that legitimate and maintain social patterns. They reject an understanding of ideology as 'false consciousness' and the understanding of power as the property of particular individuals or groups. As in critical discourse analysis, they understand ideology as a practice and its power as diffuse and discursively organised. The ideological content of a discourse can be judged by its *effects*. The aim is to demonstrate that the effect of certain discourses is to further a group's interests at another group's expense.

MINDS, SELVES AND IDENTITIES

Discursive psychology, as already noted, is based on the social constructionist premise that the individual self is not an isolated, autonomous entity but, rather, is in constant, dynamic interaction with the social world.[17] Minds, selves and identities are formed, negotiated and reshaped in social interaction.[18] Drawing partly on the work of Bakhtin, Mead and Vygotsky, discursive psychologists view minds and selves as constructed through the internalisation of social dialogues. According to Michael Billig's rhetorical psychology, for example, every opinion is a position in an argument rather than an isolated, individual evaluation (for example, Billig 1991, 1996). This is based on a rhetorical model of the mind inspired, in particular, by Mikhail Bakhtin. Bakhtin proposed that thought is internal dialogue, resulting from the internalisation of public debate (Bakhtin 1981). The social dialogues that form the basis for the self are made up of cultural narratives and discourses which position individuals in particular social categories such as gender (see for example, Gergen 1994a). Children develop their sense of self by internalising their positioning in categories within different narratives and discourses. By listening to accounts of the world, children learn appropriate modes of talking about themselves and others, including about thoughts and emotions. And through the stories that they tell themselves, children represent, try out and negotiate aspects of the self (Wetherell and Maybin 1996). Far from being formed once and for all in childhood, the individual self is in an ongoing process of construction throughout the individual's life through participation in narrative and discursive practices in social interaction. With this understanding of the self, the distinction between an external world outside the individual and an internal psychological world is softened. The self is understood as relational or 'distributed':

> The person, consciousness, mind and the self are seen as social through and through. As a consequence, it makes little sense to ask what is determined from the 'inside' and what is determined from the 'outside'. [...] The self, in this approach, is not an object to be described once and for all but is taken to be a continuously changing and fluid history of relationships (Gergen 1991, 1994). Jerome Bruner captures this point nicely when he argues that the self has to be seen as *distributed*, not localised as in the snooker ball but continually spreading, changing, grouping and regrouping across a relational and social field. (Wetherell and Maybin 1996: 222; italics in original)

As mentioned earlier, discursive psychology rejects the modernist idea that the individual self consists of a single, stable identity, and instead conceives of the self as made up of multiple, discursively constituted identities.[19] It is important to point out, though, that while discursive psychologists share the view that identities are formed through the ways in which people *position* themselves in texts and talk in everyday life, they vary as to their specific understanding of the discursive construction of identity. The differences have their basis in the three main strands of discursive psychology, which we described earlier on p. 104–6.

In the interactionist perspective, identities are theorised and empirically explored as resources that people enlist to accomplish the business of talk (for example, Antaki and Widdicombe 1998). The focus is on the ways in which particular identities are used in talk in a specific context to perform social actions such as legitimising a particular attitude. In contrast to this perspective, the two other strands of discursive psychology – the strict poststructuralist perspective and the perspective which combines the interactionist and the poststructuralist perspectives – define and analyse the particular ways of talking in which identities are embedded as *discourses* that structure and circumscribe talk across contexts of interaction. The poststructuralist, Foucauldian perspective views identities as the products of subject positions within discourses (for example, Hollway 1989; Parker 1992). One of the adherents of this perspective within sociology, Stuart Hall, on whom many discursive psychologists draw, describes this conception of identity in the following way:

> I use 'identity' to refer to the meeting point [...] between on the one hand the discourses and practices which attempt to 'interpellate', speak to us or hail us into place as the social subjects of particular discourses, and on the other hand, the processes which produce subjectivities which construct us as subjects which can be 'spoken'. Identities are thus points of temporary attachment to the subject positions which discursive practices construct for us. (Hall 1996: 5f)

The third strand, that embraces poststructuralism but combines it with interactionism, treats identity both as a product of specific discourses *and* as a resource for accomplishing social actions in talk-in-interaction. Within this strand, the concept of positioning has been developed by theorists such as Davies, Harré and Langenhove (for example, Davies and Harré 1990; Harré and van Langenhove 1999). Positioning is viewed as an integral part of the processes by which people construct accounts of themselves in interaction with others. These processes are understood as processes of negotiation as people actively take up positions within different, and sometimes competing, discourses. People are treated as *both* products of specific discourses *and* producers of talk in specific contexts; as such, they are both subjects of discourse *and* agents in social and cultural reproduction and change. They are limited by the words which exist as resources for talk but use them as flexible resources in arguing and, by combining them in new ways, can contribute to change.

Both the poststructuralist perspective and the perspective that combines poststructuralism and interactionism stress that identities have become additionally fragmented and unstable in late modernity as they are constructed across a number of contradictory and often antagonistic discourses (Hall 1996: 6).[20] Where dimensions such as nation, class, gender and family earlier functioned as central categories, shaping all the other identities, there is now a wide range of centres that produce contradictory identities. An identity as a Christian, for example, can challenge an identity as a feminist or as a worker. Or a person's identity as a consumer can conflict with an identity as environmentally aware. As a consumer, the person may have a subject position in a consumerist discourse that advocates individual freedom of choice and the principle that the quality should match the price, but this subject position may be in conflict with an environmentalist discourse that conceives of shopping as a means to preserve a collective good, the environment. The identity of 'green consumer' may emerge from the individual's positioning within a hybrid discourse in that the consumerist and the environmentalist discourses are articulated together. This can be understood as part of 'identity politics' where traditional and stable relations based, for example, on class, family or nation have been replaced by new, unstable identifications partly created through consumption.[21] Power operates discursively through the individual's positioning of herself and others within particular discursive categories – for example, in the category of member of the 'civilised' West or of the 'barbaric' Islamic world within a discourse of Orientalism.

The poststructuralist approach can cast light on these discursive patterns, focusing on the relationships between the different discourses and the subject positions and power relations they construct, while the approach which combines poststructuralism and interactionism can give insight into the ways in which people, through use of the available discourses as flexible resources in talk, position themselves and others in ways that support each others' accounts, creating a consensus of meaning, or challenge each others' accounts, leading to a negotiation of meaning. As illustrations of this type of analysis, we summarise elements of Wetherell and Potter's analysis of Pākehā talk later in this chapter and also present an analysis from a study of environmental discourse (Phillips 2000a, 2000b) in Chapter 5.

Across all three strands of discursive psychology, the dominant view is that identities are constructed on the basis of different, shifting discursive resource and are thus relational, incomplete and unstable, but not completely open. In Hall's terms, we form a 'sense of self' by choosing one version of the self out of all the possible versions of 'me'. This is a *closure* which is, however, only temporary:

> But doesn't the acceptance of the fictional or narrative status of identity in relation to the world also require as a necessity, its opposite – the moment of arbitrary closure? Potentially discourse is endless: the infinite semiosis of meaning. But to say anything at all in particular, you do have to stop talking. Of course every full stop is provisional. So what is this 'ending'? [...] It's a kind of stake, a kind of wager: It says: 'I need to say something, something ... just now'. It is not forever, not totally universally true [...]. But just now, this is what I mean; this is who I am. At a certain point, in a certain discourse, we call these unfinished closures:

'the self', 'society', 'politics' etc. Full stop. OK. There really (as they say) is no full stop of that kind. (Hall 1993: 136–137)

The production of meaning, and hence identity construction, are constrained by the range of discursive resources which are available to individuals by virtue of their social and cultural position and status. It is easier for some individuals to adopt, and be ascribed, certain identities such as the identity of 'civilised' Westerner within an Orientalist discourse or the identity of 'expert' within a scientific discourse. Moreover, the changeable, contingent nature of identity does not mean that people start all over again with new identities every single time they speak. The identity that is articulated at a given time can be understood as the sedimentation of earlier discursive practices (Wetherell and Potter 1992: 78). One factor responsible for continuity is that the individual has to present herself in a way which is acceptable and recognisable both to herself and to the people with whom she interacts.

The fact that people create their identities through temporary 'closures' opens up for the possibility of creating collective identities, *imagined communities* (Anderson 1983), which are based on an idea of a common identity – for example, as a woman or as a Dane. At the same time, these communities cannot be taken for granted since the closure that creates the identification with, and consequently constructs, the community is only temporary. Because subjectivity is fragmented, people do not necessarily experience that they share interests with, or feel affiliated to, the same groups permanently. At one point, people can have a politically motivated affiliation to a group, while later on they may relate antagonistically to some of the group's members. For instance, a female Kenyan engineer living in England can, in different situations, position herself as, respectively, a member of the dominant class, a member of a dominated group, 'women', and a member of the oppressed minority of non-native British. Closure entails that a person temporarily fixes on one identity – you have to stop talking, as Hall says. But in principle, the identity is always open to change, and, consequently, the community can be dissolved and new ones can be created.

The conception of minds, selves and identities as products of social interaction shared by all three strands of discursive psychology leads to analysis of the *rhetorical* organisation of text and talk – that is, how text and talk are oriented towards social action – rather than the linguistic organisation of text and talk as in critical discourse analysis. The interest is in how people use discourses actively as resources in talk-in-interaction. Utterances are viewed as context-bound or 'occasioned', their meanings being dependent on their rhetorical context, such as their deployment in an argument to justify an action. A point stressed particularly in the strands of discursive psychology adhering to the interactionist perspective (either solely or in combination with poststructuralism) is that people in social interaction treat each other as agents who can profit from – and therefore have a stake in – their actions (Potter 1996b). Thus everyday language use involves *dilemmas of stake* as people struggle to establish their accounts as factual and stable representations of the world and to deconstruct other accounts as the product of personal or group interests (Potter 1996b).[22]

Here, discursive psychology draws partly on ethnomethodology and conversation analysis and partly on rhetoric. While ethnomethodology and conversation analysis cast light on the rules that people follow and the techniques they apply to accomplish the business of talk, rhetoric gives insight into how people's constructions of the world are designed to counter potential or actual challenges and to undermine alternative versions.[23]

Psychological Investment

Discourse analysis, then, tells us that people form identities through their positioning within discourses on which they draw in everyday text and talk, but discourse analysis by itself cannot account for why people position themselves within, or *invest* in, particular discourses. Why is it that people identify with some discourses and not others? As we saw in Chapter 2, Laclau and Mouffe enlist Lacan's psychoanalytical theory to provide an account of the psychological mechanisms responsible for people's investments in discourses. Several discursive psychologists have also sought insight from different forms of psychoanalysis in an effort to cast light on the question of psychological investment. In this section we evaluate, respectively, the attempts of Hollway and Billig to combine discourse analysis and psychoanalysis.

Wendy Hollway (1984, 1989, 1995) works with a combination of Foucauldian discourse theory, object relations theory and Lacanian theory in order to cast light on questions of sexuality and heterosexuality.[24] Her aim in drawing on this mix of theories is to theorise gender, power, subjectivity *and* discourse without treating subjectivity as solely 'the sum of positions in discourses' (1995: 91). Object relations theory proposes that subjectivity is formed by experiences in the 'pre-oedipal phase' in which the child shifts from being at one with the mother to being separate. In the beginning, the child does not have a self-understanding that is independent of the mother – its self-knowledge is 'non-differentiated'.

It is through social interaction that the child becomes 'differentiated' from the mother, and, when it is approximately six months old, it starts seeing itself and the mother as separate individuals. Object relations theorists consider this process of differentiation to be central to the development of the individual's self-knowledge and self-confidence and his or her sense of ontological security (Wetherell 1995). The theory implies that boys have a particular problem as they need to reject the mother more than girls since their creation of a gender identity entails the casting-off of the feminine dimension. Hollway (1984) argues, for instance, that men resist their desire for intimacy with the Other because intimacy would make them too vulnerable. To hold intimacy at bay, men project their desire for mutual self-affirmation onto women. According to Hollway, this provides an explanation as to why men invest in discourses that construct women as vulnerable and emotional and men as strong and rational. A bridge between the discursive perspective and object relations theory is provided by Lacanian theory which represents a constructionist understanding of the relationship between mother and child and the resulting production of self. As outlined in Chapter 2, Lacan claims that the child first goes through an imaginary stage in which it is given a sense of completeness through its relationship with its mother. Then, on becoming a subject of language, it loses this sense of completeness but constantly strives to return to the state of wholeness. It is this desire for wholeness which underpins the individual's investment in different discourses.

Another part of object relations theory proposes that certain psychological forces create a universal desire for security (Hollway and Jefferson 1997). It is in order to satisfy this desire that people invest in certain discourses. For instance, people can draw on a particular discourse about the spread of crime in order to cope with the proliferation of risks in late modernity. They choose this discourse instead of other discourses because, in contrast to discourses such as those about global environmental catastrophes, it provides them with a risk that has a clear source (a criminal), and suggests a course of action in which they themselves can engage (such as buying a burglar alarm).

At first glance, object relations theory appears to be in conflict with discourse analysis since it points to universal, internal, mental processes as the cause of specific investments. But Hollway and Jefferson try to reconcile the approaches by claiming that while the desire for safety and completeness emanates from deep-rooted psychological forces and universal anxiety, it is manifested in different ways as a function of the different meanings ascribed to experience by different people and in different historical periods and social contexts. But although Hollway and

Jefferson draw on Lacanian theory in order to take into account that experiences are constructed in meaning in discourses, their use of object relations theory leads to the ascription of too much importance to individual, unconscious, psychological forces and very early, direct experiences. By stressing the effects of direct experiences that took place in the distant past, object relations theory conflicts with the discourse analytical premise that psychological categories are open to change through the individual's participation in discursive practices, experiences being constituted through discourse. We think that if the aim is to combine the approaches, then object relations theory needs to be 'translated' into discourse analytical terms to a greater extent than is the case here (see the next chapter for a general discussion of the issue of 'translation').

In another attempt to combine psychoanalytic theory and discursive psychology, Michael Billig has done more 'translation' work (Billig 1997). Billig chooses Freudian rather than Lacanian theory, since he considers the latter to be based on an understanding of language as detached from everyday language use. According to Billig, psychoanalysis and discourse analysis can be linked together through the concept of 'the dialogic unconscious'. The dialogic unconscious consists of statements that have been repressed in specific social contexts. While Freud viewed social activities including language use as manifestations of unconscious internal motivations, Billig conceives of the unconscious as the product of dialogue with, and in, the social world. The idea is that it is through dialogue that people repress things and, at a more general level, acquire the ability to repress. The role of language in processes of repression can be investigated through discourse analysis. Some ways of talking make certain themes possible and make others taboo, so that statements do not only express things but also take part in repression. Taboos about certain subjects lead the speaker to choose between the different discourses available and invest in one particular discourse. Thus, in furthering certain understandings of the world and excluding others, repression has ideological consequences.

Billig gives an illustration from his study of English families' talk about the British royal family (1992). The informants discuss whether the British crown prince should be allowed to marry a non-white woman. The informants say that they are not themselves racists and personally would have nothing against such a match and do not suppose that it would be a problem for the royal family either. But notwithstanding this, they do not think that the heir to the throne would be able to choose a non-white woman since the 'general public' is racist and would therefore never condone it. According to Billig, what is happening here is that speakers are projecting their own repressed racism onto others, by ascribing to the general public their own repressed disapproval of such a marriage.

Billig's theory of the dialogic unconscious provides us with a method for 'reading between the lines' and identifying the unsaid. But not all silences are repressions. The discourse analytical point of departure is that statements are always historically and socially contingent, and, if something is not said, it may be because it would not make sense in the social and historical context in question. When, for example, people did not talk about national identity in pre-modern societies, it was because the national discourse was not yet available. In our view, a problem with Billig's theory is that he does not combine the term of repression with an analysis of the range of discourses that are available in a given socially and historically specific situation. In Chapter 5 we suggest the use of the concept 'order of discourse' in order to chart which discourses are available, and to whom, in particular social domains. On obtaining an overview of the order of discourse, one can go on to analyse the rhetorical means by which taboos and the repression of utterances are established within the field of possible statements.

However, caution is imperative when combining psychoanalysis and discourse analysis since the two approaches rest on different premises. It is necessary to think about the relations between the two approaches on the basis of a reflexive understanding of their contrasting theoretical premises and the type of (contingent and delimited) knowledge produced within each approach.

REFLEXIVITY

Many social constructionists, including discursive psychologists, view their own studies as discursive constructions that do not provide the only possible representation of the world but, rather, just one version which is part of the discursive struggle within the research field in question. Scientific knowledge is seen as *productive*. As with all other discourses, scientific discourse produces knowledge, social relations and identities. This understanding of knowledge production stands in contrast to the objectivist view of science to be found in positivism, whereby knowledge is seen as a reflection of reality. As a result of their distinctive understanding of knowledge, social constructionists often emphasise *reflexivity* – that is, they attempt to apply their theories to their own research practice (Burr 1995: 180).

An important question which the reflexivity debate raises has to do with discourse analysis' relativism. Discursive psychology challenged cognitive psychology by revealing that its claims to universal truth were merely one possible version of the world. But how can researchers know that their versions are better than other versions and how can they provide backing for these claims? We are faced with a problem if one wants to defend or privilege one viewpoint over others (Parker and Burman 1993). For instance, how is it possible to give academic support to one particular political position (for example, an egalitarian, antiracist or feminist position)?

According to Wetherell and Potter (1992) and Edwards et al. (1995), relativism does not reduce the academic value or the political significance of the research. With regards to academic standards, the researcher's claims can be supported by evaluating the *validity* of the research. Although discourse analysis does not accept objectivism's scientific demands of reliability and validity, this does not mean that all demands for validity are dismissed (we return to this on p. 125). With respect to political significance, the researcher can judge her/his own and others' research in terms of the role that the research plays in the maintenance of, or challenge to, power relations in society, that is, in relation to the ideological implications of the research. For example, Wetherell and Potter argue that their study of racism and discourse in New Zealand challenges power relations by revealing the role of discourse in the maintenance of discrimination against the Maoris. This contrasts with cognitive approaches to racism such as research on stereotypes that maintain existing power relations by claiming that stereotypes are inevitable. But the acceptance of relativism is also challenged *within* discursive psychology by theorists such as Parker (1992) and Willig (1999b). Their position is that the relativism of social constructionism leads to a levelling of all statements of the world as 'equally good' and that this makes critical research impossible. Therefore, they advocate the combination of social constructionism with the ontology of critical realism.

Another aspect of the debate about reflexivity involves considerations about the power relations between researcher and informants. Traditional reseach is criticised for having illegitimately privileged its own knowledge as the only objective knowledge of the world. To overcome this, the researcher can put herself and her own accounts on the same plane as her respondents and their accounts (Burr 1995). The respondents' comments on the researcher's use of their accounts and on her interpretations can be incorporated into the study. Obviously this does not guarantee that the inequality in the power relations between researcher and respondents is eliminated. The researcher can still place more emphasis on her own interpretations. As a result, reflexivity can give a false impression of democratisation and hide the power relations (Burr 1995). However, it can be argued that the researcher ought to privilege her own reading since she produces another – and valuable – form of knowledge through the usage of particular theories and methods. Irrespective of the position one takes in relation to this, considerations based on reflexivity compel the researcher to take into account her own role as a researcher and to justify the choices that are made in the research. In Chapter 6 we return to the discussion of the role of the researcher and questions of relativism and knowledge production.

SUMMARY

Key points common to all strands of discursive psychology can, in simplified form, be summarised in the following way:

- Discourse – defined as language use in everyday text and talk – is a dynamic form of social practice which constructs the social world, individual selves and identity. The self is constructed through the internalisation of social dialogues. People have several, flexible identities which are constructed on the basis of different discourses. Power functions through the individual's positioning in particular discursive categories. Discourse does not give expression to pre-constituted psychological states; rather, subjective psychological realities are constituted in discourse. Individuals' claims about psychological states should be treated as social, discursive activities instead of as expressions of deeper 'essences' behind the words.
- Discourse is best viewed not as an abstract system (the tendency in structuralist and poststructuralist theories of discourse) but as 'situated' language use in the contexts in which it takes place.
- People use discourse rhetorically in order to accomplish forms of social action in particular contexts of interaction. Language use is, in this sense, 'occasioned'. The focus of analysis, then, is not on the linguistic organisation of text and talk as in critical discourse analysis but on the rhetorical organisation of text and talk. The following questions are asked. What do people do with their text and talk? How are accounts established as solid, real and stable representations of the world? How are people's constructions of the world designed

so that they appear as stable facts, and how do they undermine alternative versions ('dilemmas of stake')?

- Language constitutes the unconscious as well as consciousness. Psychoanalytical theory can be combined with discourse analysis in order to account for the psychological mechanisms underpinning the 'unsaid' and people's selective investment in particular discourses from the range of available discourses.
- The understanding of the contingent nature of research knowledge leads to reflexive consideration of issues relating to relativism and the role of the researcher in knowledge production.

RESEARCH DESIGN AND METHODS

What are the consequences of these theoretical and methodological considerations for empirical research into the opinions expressed by people in, for example, research interviews, media texts, audience studies and political speeches? Before presenting examples of empirical analyses, we will outline the research methods shared by approaches within discursive psychology, charting the research process across ten steps. These ten steps have been specified by Potter and Wetherell (1987: 160–175), and we draw on their presentation of them here. It is important to mention that discursive psychology deploys many of the same methods as other qualitative approaches and we will draw attention to important overlaps.

1. Research Questions

As in other qualitative approaches, research questions in discursive psychology point in the direction of analyses of the production of meaning. But discursive psychology differs from other qualitative approaches in being interested in how meanings are produced within the discourses or repertoires that people draw on as resources in order to talk about aspects of the world. Thus the questions asked lead up to study of how people, through discursive practice, create constructions of the world, groups and identities. If, for instance, the general topic of study is whether the new electronic media make possible new forms of social relations, the focus of research could be on people's discursive constructions of the new media and their use of the media.

2. Choice of Sample

Discourse analysis takes a long time. In addition to the time spent on systematic analysis, much time has to be spent on reading and rereading texts. With respect to size of sample, it is often sufficient to use a sample of just a few texts (for example, under ten interviews) (Potter and Wetherell, 1987: 161). The reasons for this are that the focus of interest is language use rather than the individual, and that discursive patterns can be created and maintained by just a few people (Potter and Wetherell 1987: 161). Sometimes more interviews can create work without enriching the analysis. How large the sample needs to be depends on the research questions (Potter and Wetherell, 1987: 161). Many analyses (e.g. Woolgar 1980) have focused on one single text and its significance in a particular social domain. Other analyses have larger samples because the researchers have wanted access to different and varied discursive practices, and because they have been interested in finding out whether a discourse is dominant within a field. Basically there is no correct, natural limit; what is important is that researchers clearly describe their chosen sample and justify their choice on the basis of the research questions and methodology (Potter and Wetherell 1987: 162).

3. Production of Naturally Occurring Material

Often discursive psychologists use 'naturally occurring' material instead of, or in combination with, material that the researcher creates through contact with respondents (for example, in research interviews) (Potter and Wetherell 1987: 162; see also Potter 1997). Examples of naturally occurring material include transcriptions of everyday conversations, scientific texts and media texts. Advantages are that the researcher does not influence the material and the type of material collected opens up for an analysis of variation across social contexts. For instance, an individual can give one version of the world in an interview and another in a conversation with friends or in something he or she writes (Potter and Wetherell 1987: 162). A practical problem is that natural conversations often take a long time to transcribe. And for ethical reasons, the researcher has to gain permission to follow and use the conversation (Potter and Wetherell 1987: 163; Potter 1997).

One possibility is to study intertextual chains (see Chapter 3) where different types of text are collected: for example, a report on water pollution from the Department of the Environment, a press statement regarding the report, news coverage of the report as well as interviews with newspaper readers and TV viewers about news broadcasts and newspaper articles. The production and transformation of discourse across these domains can then be charted.[25]

4. Production of Material Through Interviews

In this section we compare discursive psychology first with the survey method and then with other qualitative approaches.

Discursive Psychology Versus Survey Methodology

Within discursive psychology semi-structured and unstructured interviews are the dominant methods of producing material as opposed to questionnaires or structured interviews.[26] Participants can potentially influence the agenda and produce longer accounts, and the researcher can analyse the discursive patterns that are created when the participants use specific discursive resources in their argumentation. In unstructured interviews the respondent controls the direction of the interview, while in semi-structured interviews the researcher makes sure that all the themes on the interview schedule are covered albeit not necessarily in the same order or with the same formulations.

The survey method's questionnaires are not suited to discourse analysis since they contain isolated questions and statements on which the respondent has to take a stance. This makes it difficult to gain access to the discourses on which the respondents draw in their answers. Consequently, it becomes very difficult to make an analysis of people's discursive practice including the relations between the different discourses. Furthermore, the questions are formulated within a specific discourse and this can influence the answers (O'Shea 1984; Phillips 1998). Alan O'Shea (1984: 35) gives an example of a question from a questionnaire, 'Who would be the right person to protect the British taxpayer?' According to O'Shea the term 'British taxpayer' – rather than the term 'British citizen' – constructs a subject position for the individual that belongs to the discourse of Thatcherism. And this influences the answers. O'Shea concludes that opinion polls do not enable the researcher to investigate questions about the relations between different discourses – in this case, for example, the question of whether the discourse of Thatcherism dominates in the discursive struggle for hegemony.

Another problem is that questionnaires presuppose that people's attitudes are stable mental dispositions. As mentioned earlier, this view towards attitudes is challenged by the variation which has been found in people's answers in interviews and questionnaires in opinion polls. Several studies show that small changes in the formulation of the questions lead to major differences in the answers (Potter and Wetherell 1987: 40). Potter and Wetherell note how self-contradictory answers within survey research often are regarded as threats to the reliability of the study rather than as signs of variation in the use of language. In opposition to this, variation and self-contradictory answers are taken for granted in discursive psychology and such variations are seen as signs of the use of several discourses.

Evaluated in terms of the premises of discursive psychology, survey research is not suited to the investigation of meaning systems and identities as opinion polls treat individual opinions as if they were isolated, stable and static cognitive entities – like 'raisins in a fruit cake' (Potter 1996a: 135). In contrast to survey research, the focus in discursive psychology is on the dynamic (discursive) practices through which representations are created and changed in different social contexts:

> The montage [of incoherently related themes] needs to be studied as it unfolds in discourse rather than assembled from responses to questionnaires which resemble series of static photographs in comparison. (Wetherell, Stiven and Potter 1987: 60)

Exploring how discourses containing particular vocabularies are used in social interaction, discursive psychology diverges sharply from the method of 'content analysis', which identifies certain words, codes them on the basis of different categories and counts them.[27] Wetherell and Potter note that the fact that people use the word 'nation' three times does not necessarily tell us anything about people's racism (1992: 93). They emphasise that quantitative methods should not be excluded for theoretical reasons, but that the ways in which they have been used until now are not in line with the perspective of discourse analysis.

Discursive Psychology Versus Other Qualitative Methods

Discursive psychology makes use of many of the same methods as other qualitative methodologies. As with other qualitative methods, discursive psychology rejects the positivist epistemology that underpins much opinion poll research and some sociological schools.[28]

In positivist epistemology, it is important that interviews produce clear and consistent answers that enable the researcher to draw conclusions about underlying opinions or prior actions (e.g. consumption practic Interviews based on a positivist epistemology are usually structured. Standard questions are asked without deviating from the pre-prepared formulations and order. Researchers within this tradition try to minimise the effects of the social interaction between interviewer and respondent. For instance, they insist that the interviewer should stick to the questions. If the interviewer deviates from the formulations in the interview schedule, this threatens the reliability of the study. The formulations are evaluated on the basis of whether the questions will produce the type of information that is needed. Threats to the collection of the desired information include unclear formulations, 'leading' questions and double questions (where two questions are asked at the same time). If the questions are not posed properly, it is less probable that the respondent will understand them as they were meant and will consequently answer 'incorrectly'. Incorrect answers undermine the validity of the research since the questions do not measure what they were intended to measure.

In qualitative methodologies that reject positivist epistemology, the interview is regarded as a form of social interaction which both researcher and respondent contribute to shape. The interviewer is much more active and intervenes more than in the structured interviews. Accordingly, in the analysis, both interviewer and respondent(s) are regarded as equal.[29] The interview is seen as a way of investigating the meanings that all participants create in social interaction.[30] Here, language is both a tool for analysis and an object of analysis (Jensen and Jankowski 1991: 32).

Although qualitative methods treat the interview as a form of social interaction created by both parties, there are still some researchers who consider 'leading' questions to be a problem.[31] But much qualitative research – including all forms of discourse analysis – do not see 'leading' questions as a problem, but rather as inherent to the interview as interaction. However, it is crucial that the researcher takes into account how the questions are formulated when analysing the interview. Furthermore, in the planning of the interview, it is necessary to consider both aspects relating to content (the thematic dimension) and aspects relating to interaction (the dynamic dimension) (Kvale 1996). According to Steiner Kvale (1996), a good interview question should contribute thematically to the creation of knowledge and dynamically to the creation of a good interaction. The researcher should think up good, open questions, follow-up questions and structuring questions.[32]

The biggest difference between discursive psychology and many other qualitative perspectives is that discursive psychology has another view of the relations between language, meaning and people's psychological

to discursive psychology, meaning is embedded in
s therefore necessary to investigate language in order to
gs. Other approaches such as phenomenological psycho-
pondents' language as a reflection of a deeper psychologi-

5. Transcription

In studies based on discursive psychology the same considerations about transcription apply as in critical discourse analysis presented in Chapter 3. What we will particularly stress here are the implications of discursive psychology's treatment of the interview as social interaction. It is important to choose a transcription system that enables the researcher to analyse the interview as social interaction. Potter and Wetherell (e.g. Potter and Wetherell 1987; Wetherell and Potter 1992) use a simpler version than the system (Jefferson's system) which is frequently used in critical discourse analysis. If an interview is regarded as social interaction, both questions and answers should be transcribed and analysed. A good transcription, state Wetherell and Potter, can show how a respondent's answer is, in part, a result of the interviewer's evaluation of the respondent (Wetherell and Potter 1992).

6. Coding

How then, does the researcher handle the enormous amount of material that has been produced through, for example, interviews? As with other qualitative methods of analysis, there is no clear-cut procedure or recipe as in the natural sciences or in social scientific approaches that imitate the natural sciences. But, for discursive psychology as for other qualitative methods, coding is usually the first step.[34]

The way to start is to read and reread the transcriptions in order to identify *themes*. It is a form of coding where text fragments are placed in categories. The aim is not only to identify themes that derive from the theoretical frame but also to be open for new themes that can be found during the interviews or during the reading of them. The interview excerpts can be copied onto different subject files and when an understanding of a theme develops, it is possible to go back to the material and look for more examples. In the process some themes are rejected and new ones are created (Potter and Wetherell 1987: 167).

A technique which can be used to get the analysis going is to look for *crisis points*: signs indicating that something has gone wrong in the interaction. These signs can reflect conflicts between different discourses. A sign could be that one of the participants tries to save a situation by e.g. repeating a statement, or it could be 'disfluency' where the participant hesitates or repeats utterances, silence or sudden change in style (Fairclough 1992a). Another technique is to look at *pronouns*. A shift in pronouns (for example, from 'I' to 'we') can indicate a shift from a subject position within one discourse to a subject position within another.

7. Analysis

The different types of discursive psychology have different ways of approaching discourse analysis. The choice of analytical techniques depends on the theoretical frame and method. Later on in the chapter on p. 126–132, we give a short sketch of two examples of discourse psychological analysis.

8. Determination of validity

A common critique of qualitative research from the perspective of quantitative research is that qualitative research is less stringent and hence less valid. This is not necessarily true. Of course it is not certain that the criteria used to validate qualitative research can always determine whether the research is valid. But this also applies to validation techniques within the natural sciences (Potter and Wetherell 1987).

One way in which the validity of a discourse analysis can be determined is by focusing on *coherence*. Analytical claims are supposed to form a coherent discourse; the presence of aspects of the analysis that are not in line with the discourse analytical account reduces the likelihood that readers will accept the analysis (Potter and Wetherell 1987: 170). Another way of determining validity is to evaluate the *fruitfulness* of the analysis (Potter and Wetherell 1987: 171–172). This method has been applied traditionally across scientific paradigms. In evaluating the fruitfulness of the analysis, the focus is on the explanatory potential of the analytical framework including its ability to provide new explanations (1987: 171).[35]

9. The Research Report

The report is not only the presentation of the research results; it is also part of the validation (Potter and Wetherell 1987: 172). The researcher has to present analysis and conclusions in a form that enables the reader to judge the researcher's interpretations (Potter and Wetherell, 1987: 172). Here, *transparency* is crucial. The report should contain representative examples from the empirical material plus detailed accounts of the interpretation that connects analytical claims with specific text extracts. This is how the analytical steps from discursive data to researcher's conclusions are documented. Readers should be given the possibility of evaluating every step of the process and form their own impression. A large part of the report consists of extracts of the transcription and detailed interpretations which identify patterns in the material. When researchers make their own interpretations, problems often become apparent. A discursive pattern which they thought was obvious may crumble, and it becomes necessary to return to coding or indeed, to the transcriptions (Potter and Wetherell 1987: 173–174).

10. Applying Research Results

The communication of discourse analytical insights to people outside the research field is an important challenge. The researcher needs to choose whether the target group for the research results should be the scientific community, the people the investigation concerned (for example, the people that were interviewed), the group to which these people belonged (for example, a particular subculture) and/or people in general. One possibility is to choose the mass media as a medium. Another possibility is to create a dialogue with the people that were studied (Potter and Wetherell 1987: 175) (see the discusion of dialogical research Chapter 6 pages 198–200). Here the concept of 'critical language awareness' that Fairclough has taken part in developing can be applied (see Chapter 3).

EXAMPLES

In the following sections we present examples of empirical uses of two discourse analytical approaches in order to give an impression of the implications of the distinctive features of each approach for the type of discourse analysis carried out. In doing this, we hope to provide some ideas for how to apply theory and method in other research projects. The first example is from Wetherell and Potter's (1992) study of discourse in New Zealand. In the study they combine a poststructuralist focus on how particular discourses construct objects and subjects in particular ways with an ethnomethodological focus on how people's statements in interactions function as social actions.[36] The other example is from Sue Widdicombe and Rob Wooffitt's (1995) discourse analysis of the discursive construction of cultural identities. As mentioned earlier, they draw to a greater extent on ethnomethodology and conversation analysis than do Wetherell and Potter. Consequently, their analysis focuses on people's speech and does not encompass broader social and discursive patterns or political perspectives on the ideological effects of the discourses. The study concentrates on how people's verbalisation of identities is directed towards the context of the interaction.

Wetherell and Potter: 'Culture' as a Discursive Construction

Wetherell and Potter's study deals with *Pākehās* (white New Zealanders') use of particular discourses or interpretative repertoires in which 'culture', 'race' and 'nation' are constructed in particular ways. Potter and Wetherell understand categorisation – how people categorise themselves in relation to a group and how they categorise others – as a discursive practice. The goals of the analysis are critical in the sense that the authors aim to show the social significance and the social consequences of particular interpretative repertoires. Their conclusion is that apparent 'egalitarian' and 'liberal' discourses contribute to the strengthening of racism and discrimination. For instance they show that particular ways of understanding culture – that is particular discursive constructions of culture – contribute to the legitimation of discrimination of the Māoris in New Zealand.

Potter and Wetherell do not believe that racism is merely a question of language, they say that the focus should also be on institutional practices and social structures that are only partly discursive. But they argue that discourse is an important form of social action which has an impact on the ways in which the Māoris are treated in many different social contexts and therefore is not 'just talk'. Some of the texts they analyse are as follows (words in brackets are the interviewer's responses).

Example 1 Wetherell and Potter (1992: 120)

Knight: The Māoris seem more advanced than the Aboriginals.

Example 2 Wetherell and Potter (1992: 120)

Davison: The Māori on the whole isn't a leader, uh, I think that the Māori that is leading in this way probably has a lot of *Pākehā* blood. Cause there are no pure-bred Māoris in New Zealand and that probably, you know, that's the reason why.

Example 3 Wetherell and Potter (1992: 91 and 129)

Shell: I'm quite, I'm certainly in favour of a bit of Māoritanga it is something uniquely New Zealand, and I guess I'm very conservation minded (yes) and in the same way as I don't like seeing a species go out of existence I don't like seeing (yes) a culture and a language (yes) and everything else fade out.

Example 4 Wetherell and Potter (1992: 129)

Williamson: I think it's important they hang on to their culture (yeah) because if I try to think about it, the *Pākehā* New Zealander hasn't got a culture (yeah). I, as far as I know he hasn't got one (yeah) unless it's rugby, racing and beer, that would be his lot! (yes) But the Māoris have definitely got something, you know, some definite things that they do and (yeah). No, I say hang onto their culture.

Example 5 Wetherell and Potter (1992: 132)

Broadman: Uh you know the rootless young Polynesian is perhaps a little more obvious than the rootless young European although there's quite a few of those, and for the same reasons surprisingly, is still very visible in the streets (mmmhm). Um, and part of the recent upsurge in Māoritanga has been to encourage many of them to go back and find their roots, and that's exactly what they needed (yes).

The first two examples are accounts that refer to 'race' but they are not totally racist. They do not talk directly about superiority and inferiority but they both draw on a *race repertoire* (Wetherell and Potter 1992: 120). Although the accounts praise the Māoris, they are based on racist premises because 'race' as a category treats people as biological objects: group membership is a question of biological roots (Wetherell and Potter 1992: 122). In the race repertoire, group characteristics determine individual characteristics. Racial groups are seen as organised in hierarchies. In example 1, Māoris are placed higher in the hierarchy than other 'races' such as aboriginals. In example 2 'pure-bred' is inferior to those with 'mixed' blood and they are not as good as the whites (Wetherell and Potter 1992: 122). The social and ideological consequences of this discourse are clear: from the perspective of this discourse, social change is impossible (Wetherell and Potter 1992: 122).

While there were many examples of race-based explanations like these, Potter and Wetherell found that there has been a general discursive shift from the race discourse of the 1970s to today's culture discourse or *culture repertoire* (Wetherell and Potter 1992: 128). The focus is no longer on biological differences but on cultural differences. Wetherell and Potter identified two interpretative repertoires that categorise 'culture' in different ways: culture as heritage (cultural heritage/valuable tradition) and culture as therapy.

'Culture as heritage' (Examples 3 and 4) is a discursive construction of culture as something traditional and unchangeable in contrast to a conception of culture as a dynamic process. The Māoris are constructed as museum custodians that have a duty to maintain their culture for their own sake (Wetherell and Potter 1992: 129). Wetherell and Potter think that this interpretative repertoire has an ideological effect because it separates culture and politics so that problems involving the oppression of minorities do not become an issue. Social and political problems are understood as cultural problems. The more recent social practices of the Māoris are not identified as cultural strategies but rather as degenerated forms of activity that pollute the clean culture of the Māoris. Culture is equated with traditional culture, and contact with modern society is seen as dangerous for those whose roots are in an 'ancient' culture; if they adapt to modern society, they can 'lose their culture' and this leads to 'cultural conflict' and 'culture shock' (Wetherell and Potter 1992: 130).

In the other interpretative repertoire, 'culture as therapy' (Example 5), it is assumed that, if only the Māoris felt good about themselves, the social problems would disappear (Wetherell and Potter 1992: 131). Having roots in a traditional culture is healthy, it creates pride and a sense of self-confidence that is based on recognition of cultural differences. This discourse constructs the Māoris' protests and 'anti-social' behaviour as a result of psychological problems from which the Māoris suffer when they lose their culture rather than as a result of social problems such as their position at the bottom of society (as members of the underclass in capitalist society). If Māoris lose their cultural identity, they do not automatically become *Pākehā* – a white New Zealander-or civilised; rather, they become 'rootless' (Wetherell and Potter: 131). According to Wetherell and Potter, it is this way of using the discourse about culture that is ideological.

Which identities then does the culture discourse construct for white New Zealanders? It constructs them as progressive, liberal, egalitarian people who are interested in, and open to, other cultures. While culture is constructed as a duty for Māoris, it is a playground for *Pākehā* (Wetherell and Potter 1992: 134). They can learn the Māori language and traditions in the same way as they learn to play a musical instrument (Wetherell and Potter 1992: 134). This leads to the maintenance of the status quo. While the Māoris have culture, the whites have civilisation, the opinions of the modern world – in other words, common-sense (Wetherell and Potter 1992: 135). In this discourse, the Māoris become exotic and the white majority becomes 'the normal mode'. It is the Māoris that represent 'difference'; the broader *Pākehā* society surrounds the Māori culture and determines its limits (Wetherell and Potter 1992: 136).

An important factor to mention in relation to this study is that the same person can very well draw on both forms of culture discourse at different points in an interview. Wetherell and Potter found, for example, that respondents frequently drew on the culture as heritage repertoire when talking about Māori language, while they talked in terms of the 'culture as therapy' repertoire when discussing the problems of crime and academic failure amongst young Māoris (Wetherell and Potter 1992: 91). And people can also draw on a race discourse in addition to a culture discourse. The point is that people draw on different discourses in different contexts. Discourses function as resources that are used in argumentation, and in different arguments people draw on different discourses and hence express different identities.

Widdicombe and Wooffitt: Subcultural Identities

Widdicombe and Wooffitt (1995) focus on how people draw on a particular identity as a resource in the account of a given action. In common with other social constructionists, Widdicombe and Wooffitt do not view identities as fixed and determined by the individual's inner essence but rather as products of social interaction which are open to change. Identities are, they say, oriented towards action, and analysis aims to identify the precise ways in which identities are constructed and negotiated in talk. Below we present an extract from an interview with a punk (MR) who describes a violent clash between punks and the police after a concert (FR is the interviewer):

MR: and the police were all outside there (ehr) at the concert there wasn't a bit of trouble part from inside one or two wee scraps you know?
MR: But that happens every one – every gig
FR: There's a scrap?
MR: that's all, somebody doesn't like somebody else
FR: mm
MR: doesn't matter what it is is always happening y' know you cannot stop that
MR: we go outside and there they are
MR: fucking eight hundred old bill
MR: just waiting for the chance
MR: riot shields, truncheons and you're not doing nothing, you're only trying to get down to the tube and go home so what do they do? You're walking by and they're pushing you with truncheons and they start hatting the odd punk here and there
MR: and what happens? The punks rebe-rebel, they don't want to get hit in the face with a truncheon. Nobody does. So what do you do – push your copper back and then what happens? Ten or twelve of them are beating the pure hell out of some poor bastard who's only tried to keep somebody off his back
MR: now that started a riot.[37]

Much of MR's account is designed to construct the punks' actions as completely ordinary – everybody would have reacted in the same way in that situation. The first reference to the punks' actions is a minimal account of what they did after the concert: 'And we go outside'. This implies that their actions were not out of the ordinary. The other reference to their actions also gives this impression: 'doing nothing', just 'going home'. By using the pronoun 'you', instead of 'I' or 'we', it is implied that their action was not specific to a particular group but general (something everybody would do in that kind of situation). The use of 'extreme case formulations' ('*every* gig', '*always* somebody', '*always* happening') gives the impression that these things are general, they are not exclusive to punk concerts. In the statement 'There's always somebody that doesn't like somebody else' violence is presented as a product of interpersonal conflict independent of group membership. 'It's always happening' emphasises that conflicts are a natural part of human existence and that they are not specific to certain groups.[38] MR does not express an identity as a punk but as an ordinary person. Throughout the text it is stressed that punks are ordinary people who only did what everybody else would have done.

In the account of the violence, MR does not say that it was the punks that participated. The punks are constructed as passive victims of violence and when they do engage in violence it is in self-defence. The focus is on how the punks' behaviour is ordinary while the police's behaviour is aggressive and extraordinary. MR builds a series of *contrasts* between the punks' and the police's behaviour: the police are waiting with 'riot shields, truncheons' while the punks are 'only trying to get down to the tube and go home'. The punks are described as 'walking by' while the police are described as 'pushing you with truncheons'. All of this indicates that the respondent takes account of the negative assumptions about punks that are widespread in the media. His descriptions are constructed in order to minimise the possibility that the listener forms the impression that the punks were responsible for the violence. He constructs his description in this way by underlining the *routine* character of the punks' actions: he emphasises that their actions were something that *everybody* does, not just punks.

FINAL REMARKS

In conclusion, we will discuss some criticisms which have been mounted against discursive psychology. We start with the two central strands of discursive psychology represented and illustrated respectively by Wetherell and Potter's, and Widdicombe and Wooffitt's studies. Following this, we mention Serge Moscovici's attempt to develop and expand the social constructionist perspective by incorporating a partly cognitivist perspective.

Through systematic use of conversation analysis techniques, Widdicombe and Wooffitt demonstrate how people draw on discursive resources – including social identities – to construct particular stories. However, discourse analysts in this school are not interested in investigating how particular discourses that circulate in society construct subjects and objects in ways that have social or ideological consequences. They do not try to identify the content of the discourses, the relations between different discourses and their social consequences. The result is that they do not shed light upon the role of discursive practice in the maintenance of a particular social order that is characterised by particular power relations and excludes alternative forms of social organisation. We will return to this problem in Chapter 5 in discussion across the three approaches: Laclau and Mouffe's discourse theory, critical discourse analysis and discursive psychology.

The other type of discursive psychology on which we have focused (using Wetherell and Potter as an example) shares Widdicombe and Wooffitt's interest in rhetorical strategies, and neither do Potter and

Wetherell do close linguistic analysis. Wetherell and Potter (1992) say that they are interested in the content of the interviews and not in their linguistic structure. In some cases this is a problem. Potter and Wetherell identify certain interpretative repertoires in a series of interviews and argue that these repertoires contribute to the maintenance of a particular social order. Nevertheless, they do not give sufficient documentation of the existence of these repertoires. Such empirical support could, for instance, be produced through linguistic analysis (see also Chapter 5).

From a cognitivist point of view, method is one of the main problems of discursive psychology. Cognitivist critics do not consider the methods stringent enough to produce valid results on the grounds that they do not include techniques that are based on positivist epistemology including random samples, 'inter-coder reliability tests' and quantitative data analysis (Potter 1996a: 167). The argument is that, without these techniques, all sorts of subjective interpretations have free rein and there are no criteria for distinguishing the good from the bad and the valid from the invalid.

Cognitive psychologists also refuse – not surprisingly – to accept that it is better to treat and study psychological phenomena as social, discursive activities rather than as internal processes and states. Whether or not one subscribes to the cognitivist or the social constructionist position depends to a large extent on one's understanding of the self – that is, on whether one understands the self as integrated and autonomous and thus distinct from the social, or as relational and distributed and therefore social through and through. With the adoption of a relational view of the self, the research focus is moved from isolated individuals and groups of individuals to processes of meaning production in social interaction. Discursive psychologists argue that the variations in both understandings and identities that are routinely found in people's speech in empirical studies are in line with the social constructionist view of the self. In contrast, cognitivists argue that communication in social interaction involves and presupposes more than just linguistic operations. For instance Moscovici (1994) claims that communication is partly based on representations of the world ('social representations') that are not directly communicated – that is, they are types of presuppositions that make the communication possible but are not expressed linguistically. They shape social actions without being part of the actions themselves (Potter 1996a).

Moscovici is the founder of an approach – social representation theory – that can be seen as a fusion or hybrid of cognitivism and social constructionism as he combines elements from both perspectives. This means that both communication processes in social interaction and cognitive processes are the focus of analysis. Social representation theory is one of the few attempts to combine the perspectives.[39] In the next chapter, we continue investigation of how discourse analysis can be combined with other theoretical perspectives.

NOTES

1 Central studies within discursive psychology include the following: Billig (1992), Edwards and Potter (1992), Potter and Wetherell (1987), Shotter and Gergen (1989), Wetherell and Potter (1992) and Widdicombe and Wooffitt (1995).

2 For examples of this use of Wittgenstein's philosophy, see Edwards and Potter (1992), Shotter (1993) and Billig (1997).

3 For a clear description of perceptualism, see Edwards and Potter (1992: Chapter 1).

4 For a critical overview of this field of research, see Potter (1996a). Within communication planning, opinion research is used in KAP studies ('Knowledge, Attitudes, Practices') or KAB studies ('Knowledge, Attitudes, Behaviour').

5 For a detailed account of these problems, see Potter (1996a).

6 See, for example, Middleton and Edwards (1990) for how 'remembering' can be understood and investigated as a social activity.

7 Tajfel (1981) contains many key texts about social identity theory. See also Abrams and Hogg (1990) for an overview and Wetherell (1996b) for a critical reading.

8 For a comparison between essentialist and non-essentialist perspectives on identity, see Woodward (1997: 11f.).

9 See also Potter (1996b: 87).

10 See, for example, Hollway (1984, 1989) and Parker (1992).

11 See, for example, Antaki (1994), Antaki and Widdicombe (1998), Widdicombe and Wooffitt (1995). For a brief introduction to ethnomethodology and to conversation analysis see, respectively, Watson (1997) and Heritage (1997, 2000). For an overview of ethnomethodology see Heritage (1984) and for descriptions of conversation analysis see for example, Atkinson and Heritage (1984), Sacks (1992), Ten Have (1999) and Wooffatt (2001).

12 For instance Potter and Wetherell (1987), Wetherell and Potter (1992), Phillips (2000a, 2000b) and Potter and Reicher (1987).

13 For a critique of poststructuralist discourse analysis from a conversation analytical position, see Schegloff (1997).

14 Note that this critique is directed at the field of conversation analysis rather than at its use in the purely interactionist perspective within discursive psychology. Our view is that the critique also applies to the interactionist perspective within discursive psychology. See, for example, our discussion of Widdicombe and Wooffitt (1995) later in the chapter.

15 Billig's texts (1999a, 1999b) form part of a critical dialogue with the conversation analyst Emanuel Schegloff. Billig (1999a) presents a critical commentary on Schegloff's critique of poststructuralist discourse analysis (Schegloff, 1997). See Schegloff (1999a, 1999b) for his rejoinders to Billig.

16 See Chapter 6 for a broader discussion of different social constructionist positions in relation to critical research.

17 For an overview of social constructionist approaches to the self, see Wetherell and Maybin (1996). Central approaches are presented in Gergen (e.g. 1991, 1994a, 1994b), Harré (e.g. 1983) and Harré and Gillett (1994).

18 Brundson (1991) and Walkerdine (1990, 1993) have, for example, investigated the social construction of gender.

19 As we mentioned in Chapter 2, Laclau and Mouffe also subscribe to this view on identity, which can be identified as poststructuralist.

20 Fundamentally, the self is seen as ontologically unstable and fragmented, but these characteristics have been intensified in the late modern period.

21 For a good overview of research on identity politics, see Woodward (1997, especially Chapters 1 and 6).

22 See Potter (1996b) for an in-depth account of these processes.

23 Although all strands of discursive psychology focus on the action orientation of talk, there are, as already noted, differences relating to the extent to which, and ways in which, ethnomethodology and conversation analysis are employed as methods, the poststructuralist approach making least use of these methods. The differences are illustrated later in the chapter.

24 See also Henriques et al. (1984) and Butler (1990) for more examples of the joint application of Foucauldian discourse theory and psychodynamic theory.

25 See Phillips (1993, 1996, 1998) for an example of an analysis of discursive production and transformation across political speeches at, respectively, the

British Conservative Party Conference and Labour Party Conference, news coverage of the speeches and interviews with grassroot members of both parties.

26 Group interviews including focus groups are particularly suited to discourse analysis because group processes play a central role in the dynamics of social interaction. For overviews of the focus group as a reseach method, see Lunt and Livingstone (1996).

27 For examples of texts on content analysis, see Berelson (1971), Berger (1991), Fiske (1982), Holsti (1969), Krippendorff (1980) and Rosengren (1981).

28 Mishler (1986) gives a good critique of the positivist-inspired interview approach.

29 For more about interviews in qualitative research, see Kvale (1996) and Mishler (1986).

30 See Condor (1997: 116–117) however, for a critique of the semistructured interview as conducted in discursive psychology on the grounds that researchers do not engage in a dialogical exchange of knowledge with informants but, rather, ask questions which the informants dutifully answer. In additon Condov argues, those answers tend to be analysed in isolation from the questions and thus are cut off from the dialogical context in which they were produced.

31 See for example, Fielding (1993: 141) and Smith (1995: 13). Kvale (1996) suggests that this view on leading questions is based on the naïve empirical assumption that the researcher neutrally can observe an external world (if she asks neutral questions). He provocatively claims that leading questions probably are not used *enough* in qualitative research interviews.

32 For a more detailed account and examples, see Kvale (1996: Chapter 7).

33 For more about the phenomenological perspective, see Kvale (1996: especially Chapters 3, 11 and 12), Smith (1995) and Taylor and Bogdan (1984).

34 It is important to distinguish between this form of coding and the form of coding that is done in research (both quantitative and qualitative) based on positivist epistemology. In positivist research it is important that the coding is as standardised as possible. Big differences in different coders' ways of coding challenge the reliability. 'Inter-coderreliability tests' are carried out to check if the different coders' codings look enough like each other. In discourse analysis these tests are criticised for not recognising that the coding process is not only a question of the use of a set of pre-constructed categories, but also that the coder draws on his or her own discursive impressions of the interview as social interaction in order to understand the interview.

35 See Potter and Wetherell (1987: 170f.) for more ways of evaluating the validity of an analysis, and see also Chapter 5 in this book for a brief discussion of validity.

36 In the part of their investigation we refer to, Potter and Wetherell primarily use poststructuralist strategies for analysis.

37 Widdicombe and Wooffitt's (1995: 126) transcription reproduces the Glaswegian dialect while we decided not to because it can disturb the reader's understanding and is not directly relevant for the analysis.

38 Pomerantz (1986) has identified the use of 'extreme case formulations' in the situations where there is a possibility that the listener will not accept a story or assertion.

39 For an overview of the debate between discursive psychology and social representation theories, see de Rosa (1994). For theoretical assumptions in the theory about social representations, see Moscovici (1984, 1988). For accounts of empirical investigations, see Breakwell and Canter (1993) and Jodelet (1991). And for points of critique against social representation theory from a discourse psychological point of view, see Potter and Wetherell (1987) and Potter (1996a).

5 Across the Approaches

The three previous chapters were organised around the presentation of three distinct approaches to discourse analysis. In this chapter, our principle of organisation is different as we now concentrate on issues concerning the construction of empirical research projects. Central questions include how to build a theoretical framework for discourse analysis, how to get the analysis going, how to integrate perspectives other than discourse analytical ones in the research, and how to validate the results. As we propose the combination of different approaches in specific projects, taking advantage of their respective strengths, these questions will be discussed across different discourse analytical and non- discourse analytical approaches.

In the first part of the chapter, we propose ways in which elements from the three approaches presented in the previous three chapters can be combined with one another in order to construct a theoretical framework for research. Our proposal gives priority to Fairclough's concept of 'order of discourse', on which we elaborate by discussing, first, the relationship between structure, practice and change, and then the distinction between 'discourse' and 'order of discourse'. We also discuss how to delimit discourses in specific projects, and what to look for in the analysis of empirical texts. Thus, having zoomed in on text analysis, we suggest four strategies for implementing textual analysis and gaining an overall understanding of the empirical material. Following that, we broaden our perspective again to cover the integration of different discourse analytical and non-discourse analytical approaches in a multiperspectival framework for social research. Here, we first discuss problems and issues related to the combination of approaches and then we present an empirical example to illustrate the construction of such a framework and its application in analysis of empirical material. Finally, we discuss the question of validity in discourse analysis, and point out some criteria that can help to ensure the quality of the research results.

DISCOURSE AS STRUCTURE AND PRACTICE

Structuralism has often been criticised for being unable to account for change. Stereotypical structuralists may map the structure at a given time and again at another point in time and find out that the structure has changed in the meantime, but they do not have any tools to explain that change. This is because their object of study in the sphere of language is restricted to *langue*, the underlying structure, whereas *parole*, the practice of langue, is neglected. If practice is not investigated, it is hard to explain where the structure comes from and what can change it.

Discourse analysis, although indebted to structuralism, has striven not to inherit this problem. Poststructuralism takes account of change by virtue of its premise that the structure is never fixed as meanings can only be pinned down partially and temporarily; the structure is continuously dependent on how it is crystallised in practice. In this way, poststructuralism tries to fuse the two levels, *langue* and *parole*, structure and practice, into a single process, whereby the structure, rather than being an underlying entity, exists only in the discursive practices that reproduce or transform it.

Among our approaches, Laclau and Mouffe's discourse theory is the most thoroughly poststructuralist, but the other approaches also have a dualist view of discursive practice. They all recognise that in every discursive practice, it is necessary to draw on earlier productions of meaning in order to be understood, but that some elements may also be put together in a new way, bringing about a change in the discursive structures.

Fairclough's key concepts for analysis of these processes are 'intertextuality' and 'interdiscursivity'. By looking at how specific texts draw on earlier meaning formations and how they mix different discourses, he investigates how discourses are reproduced and – his top priority – how they are changed. Among other things, he investigates how different discourses are articulated together in one particular text and whether the same discourses are articulated together across a series of texts or whether different discourses are combined in new articulations. Interdiscursivity is both a sign and a driving force of social and cultural change. By analysing intertextuality and interdiscursivity, it is possible to gain insight into the role of discourse in processes of social change. When studying processes of change from the perspective of critical discourse analysis, it is important to bear in mind that discursive practices always function in a dialectical interplay with other dimensions of social practices, and that the other dimensions can set structural limitations to the ways in which the discourses can be used and changed.

Among the chosen approaches, it is Fairclough's critical discourse analysis that is the most explicitly interested in studying change. In his analysis of the university job advertisements that we summarised in Chapter 3, we pointed to his focus on how a consumer discourse gained a foothold at the universities and went on to transform the traditional discourse. But the other approaches can also be used to study the transformation, as well as the reproduction, of discourses, since they share the view of discursive practice as potentially able to destabilise the prevailing discursive structures. The concept of 'articulation' in Laclau and Mouffe's discourse theory has, by and large, the same theoretical effect as Fairclough's concept of intertextuality. An articulation is a combination of elements that gives them a new identity, Laclau and Mouffe propose. Articulation, then, conceptualises change. But it conceptualises reproduction as well. Every discursive practice is an articulation since no practice is an exact repetition of earlier structures. Every apparent reproduction involves an element of change, however minimal. Like Fairclough's concepts of intertextuality and interdiscursivity, 'articulation' encapsulates the point that discursive practice both draws on, and destabilises, earlier patterns.

Discursive psychology emphasises the unstable relations between discourses. Discursive psychologists analyse how people selectively draw on different discursive resources in different social contexts. Again, the focus is the way in which prevailing structures both provide a basis for, *and* are challenged and transformed in, language use.

At the theoretical level, then, all approaches dissolve structuralism's sharp division between structure and practice, viewing the two levels as unified in one process. But it can be argued that, in empirical study, an analytical distinction has to be made between structure and practice, and that most of the approaches actually do make this analytical distinction. A single study analyses a limited number of discursive utterances, and in order to say something meaningful about them, for example, whether they contribute to reproduction or to change, it is necessary to set them against some kind of background. It is essential to have an idea of what it is, the practice reproduces or changes – that is, one needs to have an understanding of the kind of structure in relation to which it should be analysed.

Fairclough is the most explicit in this respect. He proposes that the researcher should analyse two dimensions: the communicative event and the order of discourse; the practice should be analysed in the light of the structure to which it relates. Laclau and Mouffe operate with a similar distinction, namely between articulation and discourse. Here, the discourse is the more abstract fixation of meaning, and articulation is the specific action that draws on or transforms the discourse.

Discursive psychologists assume a similar duality. They analyse how people draw on specific discursive resources in social interaction, thus presupposing that certain discourses prevail in the background. But some discursive psychologists can be criticised for not operating explicitly with a level comparable to the order of discourse. The order of discourse exists only by implication in their analyses. It seems as if some discursive psychologists approach the opposite extreme in order to avoid seeing discourses as reified and impersonal phenomena where people's agency vanishes – that is, in order to avoid Foucault's and Laclau and Mouffe's forms of analysis. Thus they tend to neglect that discourses and orders of discourse impose limits on people's talk in social interaction.

But how is it possible to investigate the order of discourse as the background for the analysis of language use? Here, it can be fruitful to draw on existing studies to gain an idea of the patterns that prevail in the social domain under analysis. The results of one's own analysis may then contribute to a more general understanding of the order of discourse, although only an extremely large study would enable the researcher to map an entire order of discourse.

DISCOURSE AND ORDER OF DISCOURSE

A discourse analytical framework for empirical research can be constructed in a number of different ways, depending on the research questions as well as on the researcher's theoretical perspective. Here, we will develop the idea, already introduced in earlier chapters, of using the concept of the 'order of discourse' as a main pillar of such an analytical framework. In all three approaches, discourse is defined, in general terms, as the fixation of meaning within a particular domain. But in addition to this, there is a need for a conceptualisation of the different discourses that compete in the same domain, and this can be provided by the concept of order of discourse formulated within critical discourse analysis. An order of discourse is defined as a complex configuration of discourses and genres within the same social field or institution (see Chapter 3). Thus the order of discourse can be taken to denote different discourses that partly cover the same terrain, a terrain which each discourse competes to fill with meaning in its own way.

Whether the theory applied in discourse analytical research distinguishes sharply between the discursive and non-discursive dimensions of social practice (as critical discourse analysis does) or does not (as in Laclau and Mouffe's discourse theory and discursive psychology), it is important to take account of the material and institutional anchoring of the order of discourse as, according to all of the approaches, text and talk are embedded in the wider social practice.

A common way of delimiting research is to focus on a single order of discourse. By concentrating on the different, competing discourses within the same domain, it is possible to investigate where a particular discourse is dominant, where there is a struggle between different discourses, and which common-sense assumptions are shared by all the prevailing discourses. As we discussed at the end of Chapter 2, the relationship between contingency and permanence within a particular domain can be explored by studying an order of discourse: areas where all discourses share the same common-sense assumptions are less open to change and more likely to remain stable, whereas areas where different discourses struggle to fix meaning in competing ways are unstable and more open to change.

Framing the study in terms of an order of discourse, moreover, enables an analysis of the *distribution* of discourses in a certain domain. Moreover, the distribution of access to various discourses within the order of discourses is also an important focal point. Everyone does not have equal access to all discourses. For instance, television news reports often incorporate comments from non-journalists, but some commentators are accorded 'expert' status and make statements with authority that clearly embody truth-claims. Others are positioned as 'ordinary people', their comments framed as 'opinions', not truths.

Many discursive psychologists tend to ignore that there can be power imbalances between different discourses and that people can have differential access to discourses. We believe that an analysis of the order of discourse is useful in that, by identifying the relationship between the discourses within a certain domain, it can explicate why people draw on some discourses rather than others in specific situations.

Although it is often appropriate for researchers to focus on a single order of discourse in individual research projects, they should not forget the relationship between different orders of discourse. Fairclough points out that change occurs especially when discourses are transported interdiscursively *between* orders of discourse, as in his example where the universities incorporate discourses from the order of discourse of the market. Therefore, if one's research is limited to a single order of discourse, it is important to be on the lookout for discourses that emanate from other orders of discourse. One can focus, in particular, on which actors implement the 'foreign' discourses, which discourses the new discourses displace and what the consequences are.

Delimiting Discourses

The question still remains as to how to delimit a discourse and an order of discourse. How does the researcher decide where one discourse stops and another begins? The approaches have given somewhat different definitions of the term 'discourse', but as a common denominator, discourses can be seen as fixations of meaning that have unstable relations to one another. A discourse is a particular *way* of representing the world (or parts of the world). On the basis of this definition, it can be said that the limits of the discourse are where the elements are articulated in a way that is no longer compatible with the terms of the discourse. But this does not solve the problem. One may ask, for example, if it makes sense to talk about a 'medical discourse'. It probably does if it is contrasted with an 'alternative treatment discourse', but when one takes a closer look at the 'medical discourse', one notices many disagreements and struggles about the ascription of meaning (in research publications, treatment practices and so on). And if one takes an even closer look, the material may well dissolve into a myriad of even smaller discourses (cf. Burr 1995: 175). If one only analyses texts (and not the consumption of them) the problem is multiplied, because all the approaches agree that the receivers of texts are active in the consumption process; what is unambiguous for one reader might be considered by another as contradictory.

This is a practical problem in empirical research, as the analyst needs to start out from some kind of idea of how to identify the boundary between one discourse and another. But it is also a theoretical problem to which none of the approaches provides a clear answer. Sometimes it seems as if anything at any level can be a discourse. For instance, in a particular analysis, Fairclough identifies not only a 'military discourse' but also a 'discourse of military attack' which is again divided into an 'official discourse of military attack' and a 'fictive discourse of military attack' (Fairclough 1995b: 95). Notwithstanding this, all the approaches present the concept 'discourse' more or less as if it refers to entities that can actually be found in reality.

We suggest that we treat discourse to a greater extent as an analytical concept, that is, as an entity that the researcher projects onto the reality in order to create a framework for study. This means that the question of delimitation is determined strategically in relation to the research aims. Thus the research aims determine the 'distance' the researcher assumes in relation to the material and hence to what can be treated as a single discourse. For instance, if the researcher is interested in investigating the clash between established medicine and alternative treatment discursively, it may make sense to treat them each as discourses – that is, as homogeneous fixations of meaning. However, if the researcher is interested only in the field of established medicine, it may make more sense to divide the discourse of established medicine into different discourses such as the 'discourse of medical practitioners' and the 'discourse of medical theorists'.

Treating the delimitation of discourses as an analytical exercise entails understanding discourses as objects that the researcher constructs rather than as objects that exist in a delimited form in reality, ready to be identified and mapped. But this does not mean that anything at all can be called a discourse. Researchers have to establish in their reports that the delimitation they have made is reasonable. Delimitation can begin with the aid of secondary literature that identifies particular discourses, but obviously the work continues in the analysis of the material. In analysis it may transpire that the discourses articulated are quite different than originally envisaged. We will return on p. 147–8 to the question of how to provide empirical support for the delimitation of discourses.

An order of discourse, consisting in a range of different discourses, is established at the same time and in the same way as discourses. If the research focus is the relationship between established medicine and alternative treatment, the 'treatment of illnesses' could be chosen as the order of discourse within which the discourses of 'medicine' and 'alternative treatment' operate. And if, for example, the interest is rather in how medical truths are produced within medical science, 'medical science' can be used as the order of discourse in which different discourses struggle to monopolise the production of truth.

The Content of Discourses

We have now presented a particular way of conceptualising discourses and orders of discourse with a view to their operationalisation in empirical analysis: the order of discourse is the common platform of different discourses, and the discourses are the patterns of meaning within the order of discourse. Using this framework, the researcher can delineate the different discourses, focusing on the following:

- the aspects of the world to which the discourses ascribe meaning;
- the particular ways in which each of the discourses ascribes meaning;
- the points on which there is an open struggle between different representations; and
- any understandings naturalised in all of the discourses as common-sense.

Within this framework, emphasis can be placed on discursive change over time (as in Fairclough's work), or – as in approaches to discursive psychology – on how people use discursive resources rhetorically in social interaction.

The content of the discourses depends, of course, on the nature of the discourses under study. But basically the aim is to find out how the world (or aspects of it) is ascribed meaning discursively and what social consequences this has. The starting point is that the discourses, by representing reality in one particular way rather than in other possible ways, constitute subjects and objects in particular ways, create boundaries between the true and the false, and make certain types of action relevant and others unthinkable. It is in this sense that discourse is constitutive of the social. Although Fairclough argues that discourses work together with other non-discursive dynamics in the constitution of the social, whereas the other approaches do not distinguish between the discursive and the non-discursive, all the approaches agree that discursive accounts of reality are important and have social consequences.

Those discursive psychologists who are most influenced by conversation analysis are not particularly interested in analysing how certain discourses circulating in society construct subjects and objects in particular ways and thus work to constitute particular forms of social organisation. Discourses are treated as resources that are freely available for use by people in constructing identities rather than as socially sedimented constraints on the construction of identity. Differences among social groups with respect to access to discourses are also underplayed. In order to take account of the discursive constraints on identity formation in one's analysis, it is necessary to combine this approach with other approaches that take more account of the discursive constitution of the social and its effects – such as Laclau and Mouffe's discourse theory or critical discourse analysis.

If, as we have suggested, one takes one's starting point in an order of discourse rather than in a single discourse, the interplay *between* the discourses in the order of discourse becomes an important focal point in the analysis. This is an advantage as it is in this interplay that the social consequences become most apparent: when two or more discourses in the same area present different understandings of the world, the researcher can begin to ask what consequences it would have if one understanding were to be accepted instead of the other.

Throughout this book, a central point has been the constitution of subjects and identities as one aspect of the constitution of reality in discourses. Fairclough points this out as an aspect that should be investigated (Fairclough 1992b: Chapter 7), but, by comparison with the other approaches, we think that critical discourse analysis has the least developed understanding of self and identity. The conception of subjects and identities adhered to in discursive psychology and Laclau and Mouffe's discourse theory are very alike, both building on poststructuralist theory. The difference between the two approaches in this respect lies to a large extent in their analytical focus and this is an important difference: discursive psychology makes a particular contribution at the empirical level to the understanding of the subject as an agent in dynamic discursive processes in social interaction; and discourse theory is theoretically strong when it comes to analysis of group formation and collective identity.

If the chosen analytical framework is Fairclough's theory, it is maybe an advantage to include the other approaches in relation to the question of the constitution of opinions, the self and groups. They can provide useful tools for casting light on the links between broader cultural and social developments on the one hand and the opinions and actions of individuals and groups on the other.

Analytical Tools

The content of discourses can be investigated using many different tools and in the previous three chapters we have presented some of the tools provided by the three approaches. Fairclough is an adherent of systematic linguistic analysis, and, using his toolbox, it will always be possible to find a way of beginning the analysis, and many features can be identified in the texts that would go unnoticed in an ordinary reading. Furthermore, through systematic linguistic analysis, researchers can provide solid backing for the claims that they make concerning the texts, and can document how they have reached the results of the analysis. The latter, in particular, is important: in the presentation of the analysis, the researcher should ensure that the reader can follow the steps that have been taken in order to reach the result, thus giving the reader the opportunity to make his or her own evaluations. Backing and documentation can also be provided by methods other than the linguistic – for instance, discursive psychology draws on conversation analysis and rhetoric in textual analysis.

Among the presented approaches, Laclau and Mouffe's discourse theory provides the fewest tools for analysis. Therefore, in some cases it may be advisable to start off with Fairclough's linguistics or the rhetorical method of discursive psychology or to combine one (or both) of them with discourse theory. The disadvantage of Fairclough's method is that, with the level of detail he demands, there is often only time for analysis of a small number of texts. Consequently, the method demands that the researcher strategically selects the texts for analysis. To be able to make a strategic selection, likely discourses and orders of discourse need to be identified through an initial survey of relevant texts, including existing research on the topic.

But not everybody conceives of discourse analysis as involving very detailed treatment of only very few texts. Some discourse analysts work with larger numbers of texts, but, unfortunately, they rarely give an account of what tools they have used in the analysis. To gain an impression of the form such a study can take and to gain ideas for one's own research project, it is necessary to read examples of other studies, such as Laclau and Mouffe (1985: Chapter 4) and Foucault's empirical works (e.g. 1973, 1977, 1979).

In earlier chapters, we have given examples of how to analyse different discursive contents applying the tools offered by the different approaches. In conclusion, we will now look at how the tools can also be used to provide empirical support for the discourses and orders of discourse the researcher constructs. Earlier on page 143–4, we claimed that a discourse is not something that the researcher finds in reality, rather, it is constructed analytically with a point of departure in the research questions. It is always necessary to justify one's demarcation of a particular discourse and its boundaries, and the same applies to the orders of discourse one constructs.

In Chapter 4 we identified a problem in Potter and Wetherell's discursive psychology in relation to this issue. In our view, they do not provide enough empirical support for the 'interpretative repertoires' (or discourses) which they claim that people draw on. Fairclough's tools could be used to rectify this deficiency. According to Fairclough, content (for example, how Māori culture is constructed as therapy) cannot be analysed without analysing the linguistic form (vocabulary, grammatical structure, metaphors, etc.). The reason is that the content is always organised in certain forms, the form also being part of the content (Fairclough 1992b). To demonstrate the linguistic form that particular repertoires take, the methods for textual analysis that Fairclough suggests can be deployed. Although Wetherell and Potter's discourse analysis emphasises both what people do with their spoken and written language *and* their interpretative repertoires or discourses, they do not do a detailed analysis of how the discourses are produced, reproduced and transformed through particular linguistic features. By contrast, Fairclough's example of the university job advertisements, summarised and discussed in Chapter 3, shows how discourses can be characterised on the basis of their linguistic make-up.

In finding and documenting an order of discourse, the concept of 'floating signifier' developed in Laclau and Mouffe's discourse theory is a useful tool: the floating signifiers that different actors fill with different content can be seen as indicators of orders of discourse. For instance, the floating signifier 'democracy' can point to an order of discourse of political discourses (here, politics is understood in a narrow sense), in which different discourses try to define 'democracy' in their own particular way. That a signifier is floating indicates that one discourse has not succeeded in fixing its meaning and that other discourses are struggling to appropriate it. The discourses in play and their relations with one another are what, in sum, constitute the order of discourse.

ANALYTICAL STRATEGIES

The three approaches which we have presented contain a mass of concepts which either directly, or on being operationalised, can be used in all stages of empirical research from the formulation of the research questions to the production and analysis of the material.[1] In relation to the analysis of the material, it can be difficult to know where to begin and which tools may be useful to apply. And the problem is not minimised, if – as we recommend – different approaches are combined in an attempt to make use of several of the approaches' strong points in analysis. In a specific analysis, it may be a problem where to begin and which tools to select. In this section we will present four strategies which can be used across all the approaches to provide an overall understanding of the material and identify analytical focus points for further investigation.

The nature of the analytical focus will hopefully have been preliminarily determined in the initial formulation of research questions, but the strategies may throughout the analysis help to operationalise and specify these questions. In the initial phase of analysis, the strategies can be used to get a first overall impression of an individual text or a corpus of texts, and to establish hypotheses worth a more detailed investigation. In later phases of the analysis, the strategies can help the researcher to ask more specific and precise questions of the material – questions which, in turn, may be explored by using more specific discourse analytical tools from any of the approaches. As an illustration of the strategies we use the texts which were reproduced in Example 2.1 in Chapter 2 (the letter to a magazine problems page and the agony aunt's reply).

Comparison

The simplest way of building an impression of the nature of a text is to compare it with other texts. The strategy of comparison is based theoretically on the structuralist point that a statement always gains its meaning through being different from something else which has been said or could have been said. In applying this strategy, the researcher asks the following questions: In what ways is the text under study different from other texts and what are the consequences? Which understanding of the world is taken for granted and which understandings are not recognised?

Such questions can be addressed through comparison with other texts on the same subject or texts on different subjects addressed to the same audience. Comparison is a strategy which is well-suited to facilitating the process by which analysts distance themselves from their material. The process of distancing is important as one of the aims of discourse analysis is to identify naturalised, taken-for-granted assumptions in the empirical material and this can be difficult if one shares those assumptions oneself. Comparison to radically different positions can help the researcher to recognise the contingent, culturally-relative nature of aspects of the texts under analysis.[2] Thus the comparison of the text under analysis with other existing possibilities is a first step towards arriving at a more precise description of the particular ways in which the text produces meaning.

Say, for example, the empirical focus is 'advice columns in magazines' and the topic of interest is the ways in which a women's magazine advice column creates identities and social relations for writers and readers. One way of beginning to pinpoint the nature of the identities constructed in advice columns is to compare the letter (Example 2.1) with letters in which one would expect other identities to be expressed and created, such as letters to the editor in which readers state their opinions rather than ask for advice. Or it can be compared with other types of text in which advice is sought – such as the transcripts of doctor/patient consultations – in order to come closer to a description of the particular ways in which the print medium of women's magazines shapes the identities which 'adviser' and 'client' can adopt.

Substitution

Substitution is a form of comparison in which the analyst herself creates the text for comparison. Substitution involves substituting a word with a different word, resulting in two versions of the text which can be compared with one another; in this way, the meaning of the original word can be pinned down (cf. van Leeuwen 1993). When 'Unhappy' in Example 2.1 says that she has 'dropped' her life in the religious community, how does the term 'dropped' affect the meaning of the statement? She could instead have said that she had 'left' her religious community. This would have implied a greater degree of voluntary decision making. Alternatively, she could have said that she 'had to leave' the religious community which would have implied a greater degree of force. Through such comparisons, a picture can gradually be formed of how the text establishes her identity in relation to the world around her including the decisions she constructs as within her control and the ones that she constructs as outwith her control.

In common with the strategy of comparison, substitution draws on the structuralist point that words acquire their meaning by being different from other words. The choice of one particular word entails the deselection of a range of other words and it is through this process that texts acquire their distinctive meanings. When one applies the strategy of substitution, one moves in the opposite direction: by inserting into the text some of the deselected words, one gains an impression of how they alter the meaning of the text, and thus – through the back-door, so to speak – one gains an impression of how the words that are actually selected create particular meanings in the text.

In the case of a long text, a single word can be substituted throughout the text in order to see how it changes the meaning of the text as a whole. But textual aspects other than single words can also be subject to substitution. For instance, the genre or the intended recipient of the text can be substituted in order to gain an understanding of the particular meanings produced by these features.

Exaggeration of Detail

The exaggeration of detail involves blowing up a particular textual detail out of proportion. The analyst may have identified a textual feature which appears odd or significant, but, as it is just one isolated feature, does not know what its significance is or how it relates to the text as a whole. To explore the significance of the feature, one can over-exaggerate it, and then ask what conditions would be necessary in order for the feature to make sense (cf. Knudsen 1989: 43) and into what overall interpretation of the text the feature would fit. Often interesting features occur at points in the text in which communication breaks down (see Chapter 4 on crisis points) but other features can also be subjected to exaggeration.

In the case of the problems page letters, both the reader and the adviser make use of terms relating to psychological problems (therapy, inferiority complexes). This detail can be enlarged to form a hypothesis that problems pages in women's magazines have a tendency to psychologise all problems. If one has a larger corpus of problems page material, then one can begin to read the other texts in order to establish what elements, if any, support this interpretation and what features are in conflict with it. And it may well be that it is found that some of the problems are not constructed as psychological but as financial or social or as something completely different. If this is so, the original interpretation of the material needs to be refined by addressing the following questions: Can the hypothesis be adjusted to take account of these additional elements? Do the elements that are not in line with the hypothesis have any common features? Perhaps certain parts of the text are governed by one logic and others by another. Such questions can be explored through use of the fourth and final strategy: multivocality.

Multivocality

The strategy of multivocality consists of the delineation of different voices or discursive logics in the text. The strategy is based on the discourse analytical premise concerning intertextuality – that is, the premise that all utterances inevitably draw on, incorporate or challenge earlier utterances (cf. Chapter 3). Intertextuality always involves the reproduction and transformation of different voices in new articulations, producing multivocal texts. Therefore, to merely note that a text is multivocal is not so interesting in itself, rather the aim of the strategy is to use the multivocality to generate new questions to pose to the text: What characterises the different voices of the text? When does each voice speak? What meanings do the different voices contribute to producing?

To return to our example of the texts from the problems page, the strategy of multivocality can be used to build on the results of the exaggeration of detail. The focus is on questions such as the following: When are the advice-seeker's questions incorporated into a discourse of psychological problems and when are other explanatory frameworks applied?

How is the boundary established between the problems the ordinary individual can cope with and the problems which demand psychological expertise, and how is the advice-seeker constructed as a person who, in certain contexts, is a free agent in charge of her own life and in others is a victim of circumstances?

From Strategies to Further Analysis

In the analysis of a single text or a corpus of texts, the researcher often has to test a wide range of hypotheses before arriving at a final interpretation of the material. At best, the testing of the first hypothesis gives inconclusive results: some aspects fit but there are still textual features which point in other directions and one is left with a feeling that the hypothesis cannot capture the central features of the material. So one has to try again.

The order in which we presented the four strategies was arbitrary. Analysis can begin with any one of the strategies, the analyst can switch back and forth from one to the other and it is not necessary to use them all. The purpose of the strategies is both to develop an overall understanding of the material and to give more specific ideas for how to apply the specific tools of the discourse analytical approach or approaches used. When, for example, the strategy of multivocality (see p. 151–152) leads to considerations about the reader's positioning as agent or victim within different explanatory frameworks, this line can be continued by using one or more of the approaches to discourse analysis, applying their specific tools in order to investigate this aspect of the text further. In Laclau and Mouffe's discourse theory, that we applied to the problems page in Chapter 2, the focus would be on the construction of different identities within different discourses, analysing the potentially antagonistic relations between the different identities as in the example from the problems page. In critical discourse analysis, positioning can be explored at the level of discursive practice in terms of the relations between different discourses that construct particular explanations of the world and identities. At the level of text, critical discourse analysis can cast light on the discursive nature of explanatory frameworks and identities through analysis of transitivity in the text; a focus on transitivity provides insight into how subjects are linked to (or detached from) objects or processes. In discursive psychology, insight can be gained into positioning by analysis of the ways in which people, through positioning themselves and being positioned by others, construct, negotiate and challenge different accounts which represent different understandings of the world, including different attributions of responsibility for actions and events. We illustrate the three different forms of textual analysis when presenting the application of a multiperspectival research framework based on all three approaches in the next section of this chapter.

Analysis can, then, be seen as a circular process, involving interplay between an overall understanding of the material and closer analysis of selected aspects of the material using specific discourse analytical tools. The strategies should help to establish the overall understanding and point to the relevant tools, and the specific tools are used for further investigation which might in turn lead to modifications of the overall understanding.

It is important that one goes about the process of interpretation in a way that enables the material to 'resist'. In using the term 'hypotheses' for the preliminary interpretations, we have sought to signal that the questions one asks of the empirical material have to be asked so precisely that it is possible to find out if the interpretation does not hold. Thus we distance ourselves *both* from an empiricism which claims that the empirical material itself supplies its own interpretation and does not recognise that interpretation is always a re-construction of the material *and* from a tendency to give such general, sweeping interpretations that one suspects that the answer was decided in advance.

We can see analysis as a circular movement between an overall understanding and closer textual analysis, and this begs the question of when to break out of the circle, and decide that the interpretation is final. We will return to this problem at the end of this chapter.

MULTIPERSPECTIVAL RESEARCH

Earlier in this chapter, we pointed out a range of strong points and weaknesses in the various discourse analytical approaches in general, and identified areas where it may be useful to combine components of the different approaches to discourse analysis. Such a combination represents a form of multiperspectival work in itself, since each approach represents a distinct perspective that produces a particular understanding of the phenomenon under study. Rather than drawing on different discourse analytical approaches, it is often more common for discourse analysts to use a single discourse analytical approach and to supplement it with non-discourse analytical theories about the specific social phenomenon under study – for example, theories about globalisation, nationalism, organisations or the media. By combining different approaches – whether that may be different discourse analytical approaches or different discourse analytical and non-discourse analytical approaches – to form a multiperspectival framework, research can cast light on a phenomenon from different angles and thus take more account of the complexity of the phenomenon. But a central problem is how to combine approaches based on different, and sometimes incompatible, ontological or episte-mological premises. We argue that it is necessary to relate the different approaches to one another, identifying the forms of (local) knowledge each approach produces and translating non-discourse analytical approaches into discourse analytical terms, in order to ensure that the philosophical premises, theories and methods of the different approaches are consistent.

First, we will discuss what we consider to be central issues related to the construction of the type of multiperspectival framework that is based both on different discourse analytical and on different non-discourse analytical approaches. The main issues covered are the questions of per-spectivism, compatibility and translation. Then we will present an empiri-cal illustration, concentrating on how to build a discourse analytical framework based on different discourse analytical approaches, how to import into that framework different non-discourse analytical approaches and how to apply the resulting multiperspectival framework in textual analysis of empirical material. In relation to the construction of a multiperspectival framework, the inclusion of each approach is jus-tified on the grounds of the knowledge each approach can produce about the social phenomenon under study. The combined application of the approaches in textual analysis is designed both to demonstrate the parti-cular form of knowledge each approach contributes and the explanatory power of the multiperspectival framework as a whole as a social research methodology.

Combining Different Approaches: Main Issues

In doing discourse analytical research, it is important to adhere to the social constructionist premise that the research object itself does not determine the theoretical and methodological choices made. Research does not reflect reality in this way. Rather, the philosophical and theore-tical framework contributes to constructing the field of study in a certain way, and the different approaches will therefore conceive the 'same' field of study differently, emphasising some aspects and ignoring others. The discourse analytical framework, then, ought to be based on dialogue with the field of study, whereby the analyst recognises and accounts for how the framework has created the object and vice versa and makes clear the contingent nature of the knowledge produced. In this process, it is important to ensure that philosophical premises, theory and method are integrated with one another – that is, that they together form a complete package, to use the expression introduced in Chapter 1.

Our starting point is that a combination of different theories and methods, forming a multiperspectival research framework, is well suited as a methodology for social constructionist discourse analysis partly because of constructionism's inherent *perspectivism*. If knowledge can only be obtained from particular perspectives, then different perspectives produce different forms of context-bound, contingent knowledge rather than universal knowledge based on a neutral, context-free foundation. When combined, the different forms of knowledge produce not a universal understanding but a broader, albeit contingent, understanding. And another ground for multiperspectival research is that it suits critical research as different perspectives demonstrate that the social world can be understood and constructed in various ways, thus pointing out that things could be different and opening up for the possibility for social change. Multiperspectival work, combining discourse analysis and other social theories, is correspondingly popular among discourse analysts, as noted above.

While the use of non-discourse analytical approaches together with discourse analysis is widespread, there is a strong tendency to ignore, or at least underplay, the epistemological, theoretical and methodological implications of incorporating non-discourse analytical theories into a discourse analytical framework. One exception to this is the work of Chouliaraki and Fairclough (1999) who explore theoretically ways in which non-discourse analytical social analysis and discourse analysis can cross-fertilise one another and argue for the use within a critical discourse analytical framework of many different types of theory, providing the overall perspective is critical. In relation to specific empirical studies, there are relatively few discourse analysts who tackle the question of compatibility when reporting on their use of approaches based on different philosophical premises.

We argue for a multiperspectival discourse analysis that takes account of the problems involved in combining different discourse analytical approaches and in importing non-discourse analytical approaches. Our position is that it is important that discourse analysts uphold a key principle of multiperspectival research, as mentioned in Chapter 1: that it is not based on a mish-mash of disparate approaches without serious assessment of their relations with each other (as in many types of eclecticism). Rather, multiperspectivalism requires that one weighs the approaches up against each other with respect to philosophical premises, theoretical claims, methodology and method, identifying what kind of contingent knowledge each approach can supply and modifying approaches in the light of these considerations. It is only by identifying their individual premises and comparing them that we can pinpoint the nature of that contingent knowledge, and what each approach can and cannot do. By identifying what an approach can do, we make clear to ourselves what we can use it for and also justify its inclusion; by identifying what it cannot do, we justify its use together with another approach. It may often enhance the research framework to *import* approaches which are based on different, and even apparently incompatible philosophical premises about the nature of language and social reality in order to form a research framework but – and this is quite a big 'but' – it is necessary to *translate* imported theories based on different premises into discourse analytical terms. The extent and nature of translation work depends, of course, on the premises of the researcher's discourse analytical framework – and, in particular, its view of the relationship between discourse and social practice. If, for example, the framework used is based on Laclau and Mouffe's discourse theory, then a great deal of translation work will often be necessary. According to discourse theory, all sociality is discursively constructed, and theories that recognise other forms of logic than discursive ones must be translated into discursive terms. For instance, theories which identify an economic logic functioning independently of the discursive logic have to be adjusted in order to fit into the universe of discourse theory.

If the research framework used is that of Fairclough's critical discourse analysis, sociological theory can be drawn upon in the analysis of the wider social practice of which the discursive practice is an integral part, *without* the analyst having to 'translate' the theories into discursive terms. This is because Fairclough sees discursive practice as just one dimension of the social in a dialectical relationship with other dimensions which function according to other logics. To understand these other dimensions, it is necessary to draw on relevant theories that can shed light on them.

We will now, by way of an empirical illustration, address the tasks of how to build and apply a discourse analytical framework based on different approaches to discourse analysis, how to import sociological theories into the discourse analytical research framework and how to apply the framework in textual analysis. We will highlight the nature of the contingent knowledge produced by each approach both to justify its inclusion in the framework and to pinpoint its contribution to the sociological understanding of the field of study. The aim in presenting this example is to provide ideas for how to carry out empirical research in which one combines different discourse analytical approaches and imports and translates non-discourse analytical theories.

The Environment and Political Action – an Example

The example is drawn from a study by Louise Phillips of the environment and political action in Denmark.[3] The study is based on 33 semi-structured interviews with individuals, couples and groups. The focus is on their discourse relating to the environment and political action in the light of societal developments in late modernity. These developments include the proliferation of risks, changed relations between the global and the local connected to the spread of mass mediated communication, and the rise of new forms of politics based on individualisation and consumer culture. A main motivation for the study is the view that there is a need for more empirical research that systematically draws on social theory in order to explore the links between the general societal developments and people's talk in everyday life. In this example, we concentrate on one of the central themes of the study: the ways in which environmentalist consumer practices are represented discursively. The main focus points are how people cope with living with the uncertainty associated with risks and how they negotiate responsibility for environmental problems. These questions are addressed by analysis of how different discourses ascribe different meanings to 'consumption' and different identities to actors as personally responsible for the problems or as politically unengaged.

Building the Discourse Analytical Framework

Drawing on all three approaches – Laclau and Mouffe's discourse theory, critical discourse analysis and discursive psychology – the research framework is based on the view of discourse as at least partly constitutive of social practices and subjects. Discourses are understood, broadly speaking, as limited ranges of possible statements promoting a limited range of meanings so that discourses shape what it is possible to say in particular situations. Discursive change – and thus social and cultural change – takes place as elements of existing discourses are articulated together to form new interdiscursive mixes. However, the framework diverges from Laclau and Mouffe's discourse theory, whilst still drawing on both critical discourse analysis and discursive psychology, in focusing empirically on situated language use in specific interactional contexts rather than focusing, in more abstract terms, on the discourses that circulate in society.

Norman Fairclough's critical discourse analysis is employed both as the main model of discourse as social practice and as the main methodology for detailed discourse analysis. Discourse is analysed in terms of three dimensions: discursive practice, text and social practice. For analysis of the discursive practice dimension, Laclau and Mouffe's approach to discourses and identity is also applied. Like Fairclough, Phillips distinguishes between the wider social practice and discourse, drawing on social theory in order to cast light on the wider societal developments of which discourse is a part. But in contrast to Fairclough, this move is not based on an *ontological* distinction between the discursive and the non-discursive. The establishment of an ontological distinction, according to Phillips, involves underplaying the role of discourse – the representation of social practice in meaning – as a *constitutive* dimension of every social practice. Instead, her framework is based on an *analytical* distinction between discursive practices – the object of empirical analysis – and broader societal developments – the background for analysis. In other words, the question of the ontological status of discourse is bracketed and discursive practice is treated as an analytically distinct dimension of social practice. Social theories about politics, mediatisation, risks and identity are imported into the discourse analytical framework in order to cast light on the social practice *and* as cues for analysis. They are imported only after undergoing a process of translation in order to fit the discourse analytical framework.

The approach to critical discourse analysis is supplemented by an approach to discursive psychology (Wetherell and Potter 1992) which places rather more weight on how discourses are used as flexible resources in creating and negotiating representations of the world and identities in talk-in-interaction. Wetherell and Potter's approach combines a poststructuralist, discourse-theoretical focus on the ways in which specific discourses constitute subjects and objects and an interactionist focus on the ways in which people use discursive resources actively to accomplish social actions in specific contexts of interaction.

Social Theory: Import and Translation

In incorporating sociological theories into a discourse analytical framework, the theories should be transformed through being translated into discourse analytical terms. The metaphor of translation, then, describes a process of *transformation* which takes place in the shift from one analytical discourse – sociological theory – into another – discourse analysis (see also Chouliaraki and Fairclough 1999: 112ff.). We will now sketch out some of the imported social theories and the translation work to which they were subjected.

The social theories drawn on in the study deal with the proliferation of risks and the mediatisation of culture and politics (e.g. Bauman 1991; Beck 1992, 1996; Thompson 1995) and new forms of politics (e.g. Beck 1996; Giddens 1991). Here, we will confine ourselves to a brief sketch of the contributions by Ulrich Beck, Anthony Giddens and Zygmunt Bauman. Beck describes contemporary society as a risk society in which industrial modernisation has created a range of risks which are unlimited in time and space and which have sources and consequences for which nobody can be held to account. As a result of these risks, people feel themselves to be dependent on scientific knowledge and rationality which the media play an important role in providing. But at the same time, we have lost our faith in science, and scientific rationality is increasingly challenged by social rationality that draws its arguments from outside the realms of elite politics and science. The media represent a key field of struggle between the knowledge-claims of the different forms of rationality over the sources and effects of risks and their possible solutions. We are constantly bombarded by a huge number of problems on which we have to take a stand. Many of the problems take the form of environmental risks such as 'There could be pesticides in my tea', or 'The over-felling of trees is causing global warming'. Through the rise in mediated experience, Beck claims people have become more aware of, and emotionally sensitive to, objects of which they only have mediated experience (such as global ecological risks).

Awareness of global problems – including ecological risks – that the individual gains through mass communication fosters a sense of personal moral responsibility for solving these problems, according to Beck. The increased focus on personal responsibility can be understood as part of a general tendency towards individualisation whereby traditional social constraints on individual agency, which previously were viewed as inevitable and fixed, are treated as objects of choice and responsibility. New forms of politics have arisen under conditions of individualisation which have been described by Beck as subpolitics and by Giddens as life politics. Subpolitics is an expression of one of the forms of reflexivity that characterise risk society. In subpolitics, agents outside the established political system participate in reflection and critique of existing forms of social organisation, in particular about moral issues concerning the environment, for example. The conflict in the media between competing knowledge claims represents a form of critical reflexive debate in its own right and also furthers subpolitical activity by supplying people with the necessary knowledge for informed critique of experts' arguments. Giddens' similar concept of life politics is based on people's recognition of the interplay between the local and the global in everyday life which dawns on the individual as globalising forces impinge on the self, and as self-actualisation shapes global forces. Political action based on life politics can involve consumption practices.

In contrast to the view that individualisation is leading to new forms of politics based on solidarity, Bauman stresses the corrosive effects of individualisation and commodification processes on forms of politics based on a sense of solidarity. Consumerism, spread through the media, fosters a self-centred individualism that disrupts the possibilities for solid and stable identities. Consumerism provides people with an easy way of meeting responsibilities. Consumer choice places weight on individual responsibility for public problems. This entails, in Bauman's terms, the 'privatization of human problems and of the responsibility for their resolution' (1991: 261). According to Bauman, consumer behaviour – private shopping concerns – does not represent an effective form of political action; in the postmodern consumer society, he argues, people act only as consumers, not as citizens, and the failure to solve social problems has not led to political protest but to guilt, shame and embarrassment (1991: 261).

When non-discourse analytical theories are imported into a discourse analytical framework, it is necessary to take account of the elements which are not in line with discourse analysis ontologically or epistemologically, and consider how much these elements pervade the rest of the theories. Our view is that it is possible to import the theories without incorporating all the elements, but the elements to be used have to be translated so that they can be applied in discourse analysis.

Giddens' theory of life politics is based on a cognitivist view of the subject which does not fit a discourse analytical framework. When the theory is imported into a discourse analytical project, it is necessary to distance oneself from his view of the subject and consider how heavily it has impregnated the rest of the theory. We believe that it is possible to import his theory of life politics without taking on board its model of the subject. But the theory has to be translated so that it can be applied in concrete analyses of discourse. The theory can be operationalised by investigating people's discursive constructions of 'politics' and 'consumption', rather than treating them as pre-given entities.

Beck's theory is overly rationalistic and insufficiently culturalist. Beck does not take sufficient account of the cultural dimension of processes involving the definition and contestation of risks (for example, Alexander 1996; Cottle 1998). According to Beck, it is the risks themselves which determine how they are defined socially and treated in practice.

This perspective stands in contrast to the cultural perspective to which discourse analysis belongs, which claims that the definition of risks depends on how risks are constructed in meaning. But while Beck sees risk definition as primarily a question of the real nature of the risks, he identifies the struggle between competing knowledge claims as a cultural activity that involves a struggle between different understandings of the environment and risk. The problem lies in his underemphasis on the role of cultural activity in defining the risks themselves. Nevertheless, our view is that Beck's approach can still be used as a starting point for empirical studies that focus on the cultural dimension. The struggle between different claims that Beck identifies can be seen as a struggle between competing discourses and can be analysed through discourse analysis. Responsibility can be treated empirically as something which is negotiated discursively in audience consumption of the media. The study focuses on the ways in which the people interviewed deal with, and participate in, discursive conflicts over knowledge and on the social and political implications of their discursive practices.

The potentially negative effects of consumerism, as put forward by Bauman, can be understood and explored in discourse analytical terms as a question of whether people construct consumption discursively as a viable form of political action and position themselves as active political consumers who meet their responsibility for public problems through consumption. Thus, in Bauman's case, the theory does not need translation in order to fit into a discourse analytical framework.

In addition to social theory, Phillips' study also draws on reception studies which show that viewers have difficulty in connecting the political agenda, which is presented on the news, with their own everyday life (for example, Hagen 1994; Jensen 1990). News viewing thus contributes to people's sense of distance from the sphere of institutionalised politics. But reception studies also have to be translated into discourse analytical terms. Many reception studies are based on a different epistemology from discourse analysis. Many reception analysts view interview statements as true or false reports about people's attitudes and activities – for example, statements about their actual interpretations of a particular programme. In contrast, the focus in discourse analysis is on the ways in which people construct and negotiate particular discursive representations of their practices, attitudes and identities in the interview situation.

Pulling together these resources from various non-discourse analytical approaches, Phillips can start building a research framework suited to deal with her particular area of interest. First of all, the sociological theories provide insight into the wider social practices of ecology and politics in late modern society, that form the background of her study. Secondly, the theories enable her to establish a preliminary idea of the relevant order of discourse, and, thirdly, provide cues about what particular discourses might be at work. Beck, Giddens and Bauman all point to the likelihood that one will find negotiations about environmental problems and what to do about them in media and everyday talk. Translating this into discourse analytical terms, Phillips outlines 'the environment and political action' as the order of discourse she is interested in studying. Concerning the content of this order of discourse, the different theorists have different suggestions, and these suggestions are translated into hypotheses to be investigated further in Phillips' empirical analysis. Translated into discourse analytical terms, Beck proposes a clash between scientific and science-sceptical discourses, and he suggests a specific kind of subject construction whereby responsibility is democratised and individual agents hold themselves morally responsible for environmental problems. Giddens suggests a subject construction whereby political action is linked to consumption in a world-view that interweaves the local and the global. Bauman points to a different construction of the subject where responsibility is privatised and awareness of public problems does not lead to political protest but to guilt and shame on the part of consumers. The reception studies offer yet another possibility as the subject here is distanced from the sphere of politics.

Taken together, the theorists thus provide a partly contradictory image of the field, indicating several discourses or elements of discourses that might be at play. And that is a very useful starting point for the empirical analysis, leading to questions such as the following: Can these elements be recognised in the empirical material? Are the elements articulated together in specific discourses? Is one discourse hegemonic or are there several competing discourses? During the course of analysis, Phillips, for instance, finds both an 'ecological discourse' in which subjects are constructed as morally responsible for environmental problems *and* a 'consumerist discourse' in which the individual is distanced from the environmental problems, and consumption is viewed as legitimate regardless of the environmental effects. And thus new questions can be asked: How are the two conflicting discourses distributed and negotiated? Do they clash or are the differences dissolved in new hybrid forms?

In this way, non-discourse analytical theories are imported into the project in order to gain a preliminary understanding of the order of discourse and cues as to what discourses to look for in the material. An important point to remember in this respect is that the imported theories may not fully cover the possibilities of the material: the discourses they point to may be absent and other discourses may prevail. Thus the empirical mapping of the different discourses and their interrelations may lead to a reformulation of the initial picture of the order of discourse, and to a critical dialogue with the theories that were imported to establish the research framework in the first place. Empirical discourse analytical research, then, may not just draw on sociological analysis but also enrich our sociological understanding of the phenomenon under study, by casting light on the discursive dimension of social practice.

To summarise, a multiperspectival framework has been constructed through the combination of different discourse analytical approaches and the import of theories of social practice into the discourse analytical framework, after their translation into discourse analytical terms. Within the multiperspectival framework, discourse analysis has been privileged in the sense that social theories and reception analysis have been translated into discourse analytical terms and not the other way round. But, at the same time, the form of knowledge which discourse analysis aims to produce is circumscribed. No attempt is made to give a general account of social practice in relation to individualisation, citizenship and democracy or to address the question of the efficacy of political consumption as a mode of political action; the scope of the study is restricted to the discursive dimension, a dimension that is treated as analytically (though not ontologically) distinct from other dimensions. Through the interviews, the study explores people's discursive construction of political action in relation to news coverage of ecological risks and the environment. We will now illustrate the application of the framework to analysis of a single interview extract in order to give an impression of how the tools of different discourse analytical approaches can be used in conjunction with the cues for analysis provided by social theory.

Textual Analysis Using the Three Approaches to Discourse Analysis: An Illustration

In the following interview extract, the four respondents (flatmates) in a group interview articulate different discourses that each construct different understandings of environmental questions and different identities for the speakers which point to and legitimate different courses of action:

1	**Interviewer**	:	*Oh no so your consumption. Oh, your choices.*
2	**Laurits**	:	*Mm there's no doubt about, I'm not in doubt that oh, the increased*
3			*focus on organic farm-goods, oh organic products has meant that*
4			*there's been an increase in the number of organic farmers.*
5	**Tim**	:	*Yes, that's (.) is completely (absolutely) definite (and)*
6	**Jonathan**	:	*Yes, I think so too, and you get, apart from that, you get, you get, I'd say*
7			*it's one of the things you have to say to yourself and that you have to*
8			*believe because, if, if, if <u>no-one</u> believed in it, so the world would look (1)*
9			*look terrible, if no-one believed that (.) anything could be changed (.)*
10			*with anything. Everyone has to take the starting point that changes <u>can</u>*
11			*take place (have to) take the starting point in themselves.*

12	**Tim**	:	Yes, so I think exactly
13	**Jonathan**	:	And so others also do the same hopefully
14	**Tim**	.:	That, that the example of ecology, it, it is simply the perfect example, in
15			my eyes. It has worked. You can see that. And that also persuades me
16			that (.) the next focus point that comes in the media that that if it's
17			something I of course, conditional on my seeing that it has any
18			relevance, ohm, so it will come to work, and so I will also be able much
19			more quickly to do the small things, in everyday life, for example, like
20			buying organic things instead of something else. I don't know, I don't
21			have any example but.
22	**Laurits**	:	Take another example, like (.) oh, sorting rubbish. Where there are
23			many places now where you sort out rubbish.
24	**Tim**	:	Yes
25	**Laurits**	:	And there you can say then that the problem is located where it does
26			not help because it is thrown together at some point anyway. Oh so the
27			only thing we (.) still really have (1) as separate rubbish is glass
28			treatment and paper. Oh and that's what you can (2) can get a little
29			irritated about, that more doesn't happen, oh, in that area, when (.)
30			consumers now (.) at least some places, are being put to work. Ooh.
31			That oh it's (1) in this case oh them who collect it together, who don't
32			(.) follow up on it.
33	**Jonathan**	:	Do they mix it together again when they collect it together, or what is
34			it you're saying?
35	**Laurits**	:	Yes, I mean that most of the rubbish which, I mean at home in (.) I
36			come from Skælskør, there they sort it into (1) green rubbish and (.) grey
37			rubbish and the kind of (.) thing which can be recycled. Things that, no
38			things that can (.)
39	**Christian**	:	Biodegradable waste
40	**Jonathan**	:	Organic?
41	**Laurits**	:	Biodegradable waste, and things that aren't biodegradable.
42	**Tim**	:	Yes.
43	**Laurits**	:	Oh and I have read at least that it's quite limited how much of what is
44			biodegradable that <u>is</u> broken down. You can say that
45	**Interviewer**	:	Could you (plural) think of going down there (.) to the yard down there
46			with your (.) biodegradable rubbish?
47	**Laurits**	:	(compost?)
48	**Jonathan**	:	Can you do that?
49	**Interviewer**	:	Yes, they have a compost container.
50	**Jonathan**	:	Compost machine? I didn't even know that, no.
51	**Tim**	:	No
52	**Interviewer**	:	There's also one in Gardner Street.
53	**Tim**	:	It has to be up here. It has to be when you stand and are just about to
54			throw something out, you mustn't have to do something extra for it.
55	**Laurits**	:	We can see we (still) have (1) problems enough going down with our
56			glass things [giggle] and oh, I don't think that (.) this household at least
57			would do anything (.) that is more than that.
58	**Interviewer**	:	Mm.
59	**Laurits**	:	That oh, yes the only thing I can, you do want to, but oh (.) you don't
60			get it done

61	Tim	:	So if (1) I would like to, oh, I could well think of (.) you could (.) sort
62			your rubbish, if we could do it up from here, just like (.) you have had
63			it down there, my grandmother
64	Laurits	:	If it wasn't any trouble, we could also do it, but the trouble is if you have
65			to go to three, go, three different places with your rubbish.
66	Tim	:	Yes, yes. Well, we completely agree with that. But well now (1) I know
67			that my (.) grandmother she lives in Vejle and they have had some trial
68			with it, that is, sorting of rubbish and it has actually worked. Oh, oh and
69			there is really a big difference (.) measurable tons oh of what ends up
70			in the rubbish tip and what ends up oh in the incinerator and different
71			places ohm. And it, it works by that, that there are two small bags, so
72			(1) and when you open the rubbish
73	Laurits	:	Mm
74	Tim	:	but anything other than that I don't believe in. It won't work.
75	Laurits	:	If it doesn't cost any extra work, I also think it can be done but oh (2) I
76			wouldn't oh (2) I would like to, but I (.) don't do it, if it causes (.) oh
77			more difficulties in daily life.

In order to highlight the particular form of knowledge produced by each of the different discourse analytical approaches, we will present separate analyses according to the three approaches rather than presenting a combined analysis as is the convention in accounts of discourse analytical research. In particular, it should be noted that in the study from which the following analyses derive, Laclau and Mouffe's discourse theory is incorporated into an analysis of the level of discursive practice in the terms of critical discourse analysis, whereas we present it as an independent analysis. While the three approaches have different emphases, there is a degree of overlap in relation to the types of analyses they tend to produce. The analyses we present are not in depth or comprehensive but aim to give an idea of how each of the three approaches can be employed in analysis. Also, it is important to note that this specific analysis is part of a larger analysis of a range of empirical material and the specific discourses referred to in the example have been established through the analysis of the larger material rather than just this specific extract. We will first apply Laclau and Mouffe's approach, followed by critical discourse analysis and then discursive psychology.

Laclau and Mouffe's Discourse Theory

Laclau and Mouffe, as noted in Chapter 2, do not supply concrete methods for analysis, but a range of analytical focus-points can be extrapolated from their model. What discourses are articulated in the text? What meanings are established and what meanings are excluded? What are the nodal points of the discourses (that is, the central signs, around which the other signs are organised and derive their meaning and which exclude other possible meanings)? Do different discourses define the nodal points in different ways, so that there is a struggle to fix meanings in terms of one discourse rather than another? And which meanings are taken for granted across different discourses? What identities and groups are discursively constructed?

In the first part of the interview, Laurits, Tim and Jonathan all talk within the terms of *an ecological discourse* (lines 2–21). The ecological discourse is a discourse which stresses the importance of protecting the environment on the basis of a holistic understanding of the world. Ecology is a nodal-point around which other signs such as rubbish-sorting, biodegradable waste and organic products are organised. The discourse ascribes to individuals a *green identity*, whereby they should be actively engaged in environmental problems and recognise their role as an integrated part of nature. The individual's identity then is constructed around the master-signifier 'ecological agent'. According to this discourse, engagement in protecting the environment is a *moral necessity* and lack of engagement is illegitimate:

Laurits: Mm there's no doubt about, I'm not in doubt that oh, the increased focus on organic farm-goods, oh organic products has meant that there's been an increase in the number of organic farmers.

Tim: Yes, that's (.) is completely (absolutely) definite (and) […] persuades me that (.) the next focus point that comes in the media that that if it's something I of course, conditional on my seeing that it has any relevance, ohm, so it will come to work, and so I will also be able much more quickly to do the small things, in everyday life, for example, like buying organic things instead of something else. I don't know, I don't have any example but.

Ecological discourse, then, is articulated together with a *consumer discourse*: personal engagement is defined as consumption behaviour – 'buying organic things' (line 20) and 'sorting rubbish' (line 22). All three speakers present media coverage of environmental issues as the catalyst for both their own and other people's adoption of environmentalist consumption practices.

When Laurits identifies a technical problem with rubbish sorting (lines 25–32), the discussion changes focus from expressions by all three speakers of their commitment to environmentalist consumer behaviour to an account by Laurits of a problem with rubbish sorting which threatens its effectiveness and reliability. Laurits claims that the sorted rubbish is mixed together again at a later stage. The claim which Laurits makes about the ineffectiveness of the sorting system is based on a *cynical, sceptical discourse* which characterises late modernity, whereby scientific and other authorities are questioned (this questioning of authority forms part of the basis for subpolitics). Here, he adopts the identity of *detached sceptic.*

Following Laurits' account of the technical problem with rubbish sorting and the other speakers' minimal responses to his account, Tim and Laurits justify their lack of environmentalist action – their failure to take their rubbish to be sorted – by drawing on a *discourse of everyday constraints.* For example, Laurits says: 'If it wasn't any trouble, we could also do it, but the trouble is if you have to go to three, go, three different places with your rubbish' (lines 64–5). Within the discourse of everyday constraints, the difficulties of everyday life represent a nodal point which functions as sufficient grounds for not acting more to protect the environment, and the individual is constructed as passively subject to everyday constraints rather than a moral agent: Laurits: 'If it doesn't cost any extra work, I also think it can be done but oh I wouldn't oh I would like to, but I don't do it, if it causes oh more difficulties in daily life' (lines 75–7). Tim and Laurits begin, then, by positioning themselves within an ecological discourse and end by positioning themselves within a discourse of everyday constraints. They construct a self-identity out of fragments of disparate discourses which are linked together in a jointly-constructed narrative and thus articulated together to form an interdiscursive mix or hybrid discourse. This is in line with a basic discourse analytical premise shared by all three approaches that people's identities are constructed across different, contradictory and often antagonistic, discourses. The hybrid discourse condenses fragments of an *ecological discourse* (acting to protect the environment on the basis of a recognition of the impact of micro actions on the whole) with elements of a *consumerist discourse* (acting through individual consumption – in this case, throwing out their rubbish instead of sorting it) and a *discourse of everyday constraints* (presenting the constraints of the everyday world as grounds for not acting more to protect the environment).

Critical Discourse Analysis

A similar account of the articulation of discourses will be produced by analysis at the level of *discursive practice* in critical discourse analysis. However, critical discourse analysis also casts light on the linguistic construction of the discourses through analysis of the *text* dimension, and, as noted earlier in this chapter, the focus on language also helps to identify and demarcate the discourses. Moreover, critical discourse analysis involves systematic analysis of *social practice* as an analytically distinct dimension of discursive practice. In the following, we present a brief analysis of the interview extract at the levels of *text* and *social practice*.

The ecological discourse is constructed linguistically partly through particular forms of transitivity. For example, the speakers ascribe themselves identities as personally responsible for solving environmental problems through positioning themselves as agents in active processes, such as in the following – 'I will also be able much more quickly to do the small things, in everyday life' (lines 18–19). In addition, Jonathan conceives moral responsibility as a general condition attributed to the individual as part of a collective (a holistic view of the individual as an integrated part of a whole). Thus he does not just attribute responsibility to himself but to a generalised 'you' that embraces both the speaker and people in general – 'It's one of the things you have to say to yourself' (line 7). While he begins with a subjective modality – 'I think so too' – signalling that his statement has roots in his own personal viewpoint, the rest of his turn is in an objective modality. Objective modality here works to reinforce the power of the statements, presenting them as facts independent of the speaker rather than as merely subjective opinions. In the accounts of the ineffectiveness of rubbish sorting in the terms of the sceptical discourse, objective modality is also used, again working to construct the statements as facts rather than views based on the speaker's own personal interests.

While everyday constraints work to justify lack of action, Tim and Laurits also signal that their lack of action is not fully legitimate – a position that belongs to the ecological discourse. Laurits does this, for example, through hedges – giggling and pauses – and the use of 'we' and 'this household' as the agents of the lack of action: 'We can see we (still) have problems enough going down with our glass things [giggle] and oh, I don't think that (.) this household at least would do anything (.) that is more than that' (lines 55–7). In this way, he assigns agency to the collective rather than to himself, so that inaction is accounted for by the consensus to which they are all bound as flatmates, rather than by the individual's own failure to meet his responsibility. Similarly, Tim signals ambivalence in relation to their inaction through a narrative about a successful case of rubbish sorting about which he has privileged knowledge (through his grandmother). By describing a situation where rubbish sorting works and by indicating that it is different from their situation – it is in another town and is a trial run – Tim suggests that the problem lies with the situation rather than with themselves.

But the hybrid discourse is not fully hegemonic in the terms of both Laclau and Mouffe and critical discourse analysis: it does not succeed in pinning down meaning in only one way so that its representation of the world is fully accepted as common-sense. Rather a conflict takes place between this discourse and another discourse that puts forward an antagonistic explanatory framework – an ecological discourse which is articulated by Jonathan. The discursive conflict is analysed below in terms of discursive psychology. The focus here is on the ways in which the conflict takes place through a negotiation of meaning in which each speaker participates through his discursive positioning of himself and others.

Before that, we will give an impression of how critical discourse analysis can be applied to analyse the dimension of *social practice* by summarising how it has been applied in Phillips' study. Drawing on theories of life politics and subpolitics and consumerism's negative effects on politics based on solidarity, the aim is to cast light on the social and political consequences of the discourses. In relation to the theory of life politics, it can be concluded on the basis of the analysis of discursive practice and of text, that there are different ways to relate to ecological problems: sometimes action in relation to greater environmental problems is understood as part of everyday practice while, at other times, it is held outside through arguments about everyday limitations. The articulation of the ecological discourse, consumer discourse, sceptical discourse and discourse of everyday constraints both jointly as a hybrid discourse and individually in conflict with one another can be seen as an expression of subpolitics whereby different discourses put forward different knowledge-claims including claims relating to the attribution of responsibility.

The hybrid discourse can be understood as a product of a process of negotiation between an ecological discourse which attributes responsibility for environmental problems to the individual, a consumer discourse whereby one acts through consumption and a discourse of everyday constraints that legitimates that one does not take responsibility for the problems. A sense of responsibility deriving from mediated experience was expressed but it was held in check by being articulated within the hybrid discourse which provided people with a way of justifying no engagement in life politics or subpolitics beyond a limited amount of political consumption. This seems to confirm Bauman's pessimistic view that the 'privatisation of human problems and of the responsibility for their resolution' mitigates against political action which challenges existing forms of social organisation.

Discursive Psychology

In common with Laclau and Mouffe's discourse theory and critical discourse analysis, Wetherell and Potter's form of discursive psychology can be used to identify the different discourses analysed above using Laclau and Mouffe's approach. In applying discursive psychology, researchers often identify linguistic features such as pronouns and modalities as one does in critical discourse analysis. However, discursive psychologists tend to place more weight on the ways in which speakers use discourses as flexible resources (interpretative repertoires) in particular contexts of interaction, and on the linguistic features that speakers apply as rhetorical strategies in order to establish their accounts of the world as solid and objective and competing accounts as false and subjective. As noted earlier, they also focus more on the speakers' flexible positioning within different discourses and on the ways in which speakers' positioning of themselves and others supports or challenges particular constructions of the world, producing either a meaning consensus or a negotiation of meaning. Here we illustrate how discursive psychology is used to explore the discursive production of consensus and the negotiation of meaning identified in the other analyses.

Laurits' account of the ineffectiveness of ecological action extends over four turns (from line 25–44), punctuated only by a question from Jonathan and minimal responses from Tim. Jonathan's question – 'Do they mix it together again when they collect it together, or what is it you're saying?' – divides Laurits' general account of the problem (lines 25–32) and his account of a specific case – the sorting process and its ineffectiveness in his home town (lines 35–8, 41, 43–44). Jonathan's question may have been interpreted by Laurits as a mild challenge, prompting him to provide backing for his general claims in the form of a narrative about a concrete case of which he had privileged knowledge based on his roots in the place in question. While Tim, Laurits and Jonathan all begin the discussion with propositions about the importance and value of ecology, only Jonathan presents a belief in change as a moral necessity: 'Everyone has to take the starting point that changes can take place (have to) take the starting point in themselves' (lines 10–11). This implies that the belief is a prerequisite for people's acceptance of responsibility for the problems. It also indicates a reflexive understanding of the uncertainty associated with people's actions. Tim expresses support for Jonathan's view over three turns (lines 12, 14–21). However, when Laurits then questions the efficacy of rubbish sorting, and the discussion changes tack to focus first on the ineffectiveness of action and then on the limits imposed by everyday constraints on their action, Jonathan disappears from the conversation apart from one early intervention in the form of the question mentioned above (lines 33–34) which can be interpreted as a mild challenge to Laurits, and apart from a few short interventions later (lines 40, 48, 50). During the whole of the final exchange – the exchange between Laurits and Tim about the limits to their action (lines 53–77) – Jonathan is silent. He does not belong to the consensus or community of meaning constructed by Tim and Laurits, since he presents support for the environmentalist system on the basis of a moral imperative which overrides the lack of trust in, or doubt about, science and authority which belongs to the sceptical discourse identified in the analysis drawing on Laclau and Mouffe's discourse theory.

In terms of discursive psychology, the analysis demonstrates, then, *how* expressions of personal responsibility are held in check and a failure to engage in political action is legitimated through people's flexible use of discourses as conversational resources: Laurits' and Tim's positioning within the hybrid discourse which legitimates a lack of engagement in political action leads to the exclusion of Jonathan's ecological discourse in which a lack of engagement is illegitimate. Thus discursive psychology's analysis of the rhetorical organisation of the interaction is in line with critical discourse analysis' view of the social consequences of the discursive practice – a view that, as noted above, supports Bauman's understanding of the privatisation of responsibility.

Our aim in presenting this example of the use of multiperspectival discourse analysis as a social research methodology has been to demonstrate the *mechanics* of the framework – how it combines different discourse analytical approaches, how it draws on sociological theory by importing and translating non-discourse analytical approaches and how the different approaches together can be applied in analysis to produce different forms of knowledge about the field of study. Discourse analysis is privileged in the sense that it is the discourse analytical framework used which determines the ways in which sociological theories are imported and translated. And the research field is defined strictly as the discursive dimension of the social changes relating to mediated experience of ecological risks and political action identified in sociological theory. At the same time, we have sought to demonstrate the explanatory power of multiperspectival discourse analysis, showing that it does not just draw on sociological analysis but may enrich that analysis, by casting light on the discursive dimension of social practice.

VALIDITY

From a number of different angles, this chapter has focused on the construction of specific research projects. The last issue to be discussed here is how to evaluate research, one's own as well as that of others. Validity is the question of what standards the research must meet in order to count as qualified academic research. By measuring research in relation to certain criteria, it can be evaluated as good or bad. These are common procedures in all scientifc work, but the criteria accepted differ. The discussion of criteria is part of a larger epistemological discussion of the character and status of scientific knowledge. In positivistic epistemologies it is assumed that knowledge can reflect reality without bias, and criteria are developed to ensure such a reflection. In discourse analysis, and in social constructionism in general, this assumption is rejected, but there is no agreement about which criteria to apply instead.

As our focal points in this brief discussion of validity we will use two of the criteria adopted by Potter and Wetherell (1987), and presented in Chapter 4: coherence and fruitfulness. Most social constructionists would agree to these criteria, although they are not uncontested. One objection to *coherence* as a validity measure is inherent in the argument that paradoxes and contradictions serve to demonstrate that two perspectives may be incompatible but both still valid (e.g. Ashmore 1989; Haraway 1991; Lyotard 1984). Here, the criterion of coherence would flatten out the message of the research, that opposing truths should be maintained as such. In some forms of dialogical research (see Chapter 6), for instance, *ironic validity* (Lather 1993) is introduced as a measure of the knowledge produced, whereby the aim is to represent the different, and perhaps contradictory, voices of researchers and informants alike, without privileging any single perspective.

Another problem with coherence as validity standard is the argument, along discourse psychological lines, that coherence is not an internal feature of a text: some readers might see an inconsistency where others see a stringent argument. A validity criterion, that takes this objection into account, is that the research should be *plausible to the community of scholars* (e.g. Howarth 2000: 130). Here the emphasis is on the collective aspect of knowledge production, and what is regarded as the better research product is seen as a consequence of the discursive processes to establish truth within a specific domain. However, taken alone, this criterion implies a potential conservatism, whereby knowledge is produced only along already recognised lines in order to gain acceptance and, hence, validity. Remembering Fairclough's point about social reproduction and change, it can be argued that representations that reproduce a given discursive practice also tend to reproduce the social order in which it is embedded, and the power relationships prevailing there.

The tendency to conservatism might be counterbalanced by the criterion of *fruitfulness*, emphasising the importance of the production of new knowledge. This criterion focuses on the effects of knowledge production; the way that research may foster new types of thinking and action. But there are different suggestions about the context in which the fruitfulness should apply. Potter and Wetherell's understanding is that fruitfulness refers to the ability of research to generate new scientific explanations of the phenomenon under study, whereas Karen Tracy (1995: 210) introduces the additional criterion of *helpful problem framing*, emphasising that research must be directly useful to the informants, helping them to reflect on their actions.[4]

Even from this brief extract of validity criteria, it is immediately apparent that the choice and combination of criteria hinge on one's perspective on scientific knowledge – what status one ascribes to scientific knowledge and what one thinks it should be used for. This is the discussion we turn to in the next chapter. Therefore, rather than anticipating this and taking an overarching stand at this point, we will limit our scope here to specific text analysis. Of course, the question of validity in text analysis cannot be isolated from the question of validity in the overall research project; but the pragmatic question of when to exit the circle arises if analysis, as we have suggested, is seen as a circular movement between an overall understanding of the empirical material and specific textual analysis. When is an analysis completed? When can the analyst break the interpretative circle and put a stop to the analysis? If the object of analysis is a large corpus or lengthy texts, or if one is carrying out a very detailed analysis of a single text, there is always more that can be analysed or new perspectives that can be explored. And how much of the analysis should be included in the research report? There are no definitive answers, but we suggest the following rules of thumb:

- The analysis should be *solid*. It is best if interpretation is based on a range of different textual features rather than just one feature.
- The analysis should be *comprehensive*. This does not mean that all aspects of the text have to be analysed in all the ways one could – which would be impossible in many cases – but that the questions posed to the text should be answered fully and any textual features that conflict with the analysis should be accounted for.
- As mentioned in Chapter 4, the analysis should be presented in a *transparent* way, allowing the reader, as far as possible, to 'test' the claims made. This can be achieved by documenting the interpretations made and by giving the reader access to the empirical material or at least by reproducing longer extracts in the presentation of the analysis.

In this section we have presented a number of validity criteria, some of them compatible, and some opposing each other. In this situation of no agreement, the single most important criterion is to *explicate and follow the criteria of validity* to which one adheres. By defining the standards that the research aims to meet, the research invites discussion and critique of the knowledge produced on its own premises. Explication of the guiding set of rules and the procedures one has followed enables the reader to conduct an *immanent critique* of the research – that is, an evaluation in terms of its inner consistency. Does the researcher do what she says she does? Do the philosophical premises, the theoretical claims and the methodology employed form a complete package? If not, the validity of the research is reduced, but perhaps new avenues for further research are opened.

But the discussion of a specific item of research may not end in immanent critique. Even on explication, the validity criteria of the research project may not be accepted by the reader. The limitation of the validity criterion of explicating and following one's own validity criteria is that it cannot judge what is the best validity criterion among different alternatives. It cannot answer the question of which one to go by if two research reports with different sets of criteria produce different results. If research could only be discussed in terms of inner consistency, each research report, or each school of research, would become an island, closed in on itself, unable to participate in a broader discussion about knowledge and society. If the researcher accepts the social constructionist premise that knowledge is always historically and culturally embedded, this also pertains to scientific knowledge, including the researcher's own results. This premise entails rejection of universal standards according to which all knowledge can be measured. But how can we then establish a meaningful discussion across different validity criteria, or more generally, across different worldviews? This is a central issue in the following chapter.

NOTES

1 This section is based on Jørgensen 2001.

2 See Chapter 6 for a more detailed discussion of how to unmask naturalised, common-sense assumptions.

3 For accounts of the study, see Phillips (2000a, 2000b).

4 For discussions of these and other validity criteria, see e.g. Denzin (1997: 7ff.), Potter and Wetherell (1987: 169ff.), Tracy (1995: 208ff.)

6 Critical Social Constructionist Research

What kind of knowledge does discourse analytical research produce? What is the status of its results, and what can they be used for? These questions, conventionally posed in all academic work, form part of a wider discussion about the nature of social scientific knowledge. In this chapter we will present aspects of this discussion in the form it has taken within social constructionism. In Chapter 1 on pages 21–3 we briefly outlined the issue of the status of research knowledge, introducing the anti-foundationalist premise adhered to in social constructionism that all knowledge is discursively produced and therefore contingent, and that there is no possibility of achieving absolute or universal knowledge since there is no context-free, neutral base for truth-claims. If all knowledge is historically and socially embedded, and if truth is a discursive effect rather than a transparent account of reality, how, we asked, do we treat our own knowledge? In Chapter 4, under the heading of reflexivity, we discussed how researchers try to acknowledge their own role in the research process and evaluate the results in relation to their consequences. These concerns represent attempts to take into account that the researcher can never just be 'a fly on the wall' who sees things as they really are, and that the researcher's knowledge production, as in the case of all other discourse, is productive – it creates reality at the same time as representing it.

But even if we were to follow such reflexive procedures conscientiously, we would never be able to produce fully 'transparent' knowledge, whereby our results would accurately depict reality one-to-one, and whereby we could somehow achieve full control over the effects of these results (cf. Rose 1997). It is precisely the possibility of absolute knowledge that is rejected in the social constructionist premises.

Some critics of social constructionism argue, therefore, that social constructionism is unusable, both scientifically and politically. It is scientifically unusable because it cannot determine what is true: every result is just one among many other possible stories about reality. And it is politically unusable because it cannot determine what is good and bad. When a social constructionist identifies social conditions that should be changed, this is just an expression of her own contingent view, critics argue (for example, Soper 1990).

Our position is that this reading of social constructionism is too pessimistic, and in this final part of the book, we will argue that discourse analysis is indeed well suited to critical social research. We will do this by presenting and discussing a range of different social constructionist positions in the debate and by locating the three discourse analytical approaches we have covered in the book within the wider social constructionist field. The focus will be on ways in which social constructionist researchers can tackle their own knowledge production. What status do the results have? How can research further social change? How can taken-for-granted, naturalised aspects of our world be revealed? How can researchers take their own role in knowledge production into account when conducting their research?

The overall aim of the chapter is to contribute to the overarching discussion of social research as critique. We will argue that social constructionist research, including discourse analysis, inevitably is, and *should* be, a critical enterprise. After an initial discussion about *what* discourse analysis claims to produce knowledge about, we will go on to present a classic understanding of critique: research as a critique of ideology. The conceptualisation of research as a critique of ideology has been strongly criticised within social constructionism, and the first point to address is whether critique should actually be the aim of research at all. Since our answer here is yes, we then go on to explore a minimal definition of critique as the unmasking of dominant, taken-for-granted understandings of reality. Our aim here is to theorise a position for the researcher from which he or she can discover what is otherwise taken for granted. We present three different strategies for the production of knowledge about the taken-for-granted, and we discuss the status of such knowledge. The discussion of relativism is inherent in the social constructionist premises, and we explore different positions in the negotiation of relativism at different phases of the research project. Here, an important point is that the question of critique and the status of scientific knowledge is not just about the declaration of epistemological principles in the introduction of research reports. Rather, it is necessary to think through the consequences of the epistemological principles for every stage of the research process, including the choice of theory and method and the presentation of the results in research reports; and conversely, it is important to consider how the choices one makes contribute to positioning the researcher in relation to epistemology. Finally, we gather the different threads of the argument in a presentation of our own position, arguing that following scientific criteria enables the researcher to produce a particular and valuable form of knowledge, and that the degree of authority ascribed to scientific knowledge in public debates should be the subject of ongoing negotiation.

'But What About Reality?'

When discourse analysts present their results, they are sometimes met with the question, 'Yes, but is it just a discourse, or...?' The question implies a distinction between discourses and something else which is not viewed as discursive, and, by the word 'but', it is also implied that this other entity is more fundamental than discourses. Let us deal with this question in two steps. First, what is outside discourses? And secondly, is the relationship between the two spheres hierarchical? There are a range of different dimensions which are supposedly not covered by discourse analysis. These dimensions include experiences, feelings and the body, the material world and people's actions. The three approaches, as we have discussed earlier, have different understandings of the relationship between the discursive and the non-discursive. Discursive psychology, for example, has made a point of treating as discursively constituted, psychological categories that traditionally have been viewed as non-discursive – such as attitudes, emotions and memory. Laclau and Mouffe's discourse theory generalises this position, seeing all reality as discursively constituted and, thus, making legitimate the use, in principle, of discourse analytical tools to analyse all aspects of the world including the body and the material world. But although categories such as the body can, in principle, be taken into account in a discourse theoretical analysis, this does not mean that discourse theory provides a satisfactory theorisation of the body. None of our approaches do that. So, if the focus of interest is the body, it is a good idea to read more sophisticated theory on the body and attempt to translate it into the discourse analytical perspective chosen.

Critical discourse analysis distinguishes more sharply between the discursive and the non-discursive. In relation to this approach, it therefore makes more sense to ask if something is 'just discourse' or if the relevant non-discursive practices have also been studied. But it does not make sense in any of the approaches to ask if something is 'just discourse' if one is implying that discourses are surface phenomena and that the core of the social has to be analysed at a more fundamental level. That is, if what one is really asking is 'Is it just a discourse, or is it also reality?' All the approaches view discourse as (at least partly) constitutive of the social, but that the social is constituted does not mean that it is not real. The constituted social world provides conditions of possibility for action and produces effects in just as firm a way as the physical world.

According to a caricature of social constructionism, reality is what we say it is. If we say it is different, then it is different. If I say in the morning, that I am a man, then that is what I am; if I then say in the afternoon that I am a woman, then I am. This caricature is both right and wrong. At the level of principle it is right; it is through ascribing meanings to ourselves and the surrounding world that we can understand and act in the world, and in that sense both ourselves and our world *are* the meanings we ascribe to them. Meanings are contingent and therefore changeable and, if they change, the subject and the surrounding world also change, making available other possibilities for thinking and acting. But, in a given situation, most meanings are relatively stable and individual subjects have only limited possibilities for manipulating them. Changes in meaning ascriptions are collective social processes. If a single individual declares that, during the afternoon, she has undergone a sex change, it is not likely that this identity change will be accepted by those around her or that our understanding of gender will suddenly change. The existing fixities of meaning are too stable for that.

Most discourse analysts (and probably most researchers in general) would like to contribute, through their research, to changing the world for the better. For discourse analysts, this ambition is often pursued through demonstration of the negative consequences of particular fixations of meaning designed to open up for other ways of understanding the world. They attempt, then, to destabilise prevailing systems of meaning. But an important reason why meaning systems are so stable is that many of our understandings of the world are naturalised; that is, we view them not as *understandings of* the world but *as* the world. Therefore, an important discourse analytical aim is to unmask and delineate taken-for-granted, common-sense understandings, transforming them into potential objects for discussion and criticism and, thus, open to change.

This application of discourse analytical knowledge suffers from an epistemological difficulty. How can researchers reveal common-sense understandings in their own society, if they, being part of society themselves, share many of those understandings? The question of the possibilities for identifying society's naturalised understandings is a central theme in the following, within the context of the overarching discussion about what critical research is and can be.

IDEOLOGY CRITIQUE

All the approaches to discourse analysis presented in this book understand themselves to be critical in some way or another. On the basis of research, they aim to criticise unjust social conditions and contribute to improvement of those conditions. Critical research has a long history in both the social sciences and the humanities, but the understanding of what critique is, and, in particular, what its foundations are, varies across the different traditions.

Ideology critique – widespread in the 1970s and with historical roots in Marx and the Frankfurt School – represents one important type of critique. In this view, power relations in society are accompanied by a hegemonic language that systematically masks reality. The aim of critique is to undermine power by revealing the reality behind ideology. For example, people may suggest that, in our society, there is sexual equality. At the same time, social research may reveal that men earn more than women and that women systematically spend more time on household tasks than men. There is, then, an inconsistency between how things really are and people's understanding of how things are, and this inconsistency provides the grounds for critique. People do not see reality properly because ideologies distort their world-view. For example, there may be an ideology that holds that the sexes, after many years of struggle, are now equal, and this ideology may reinforce a male-dominated hierarchy in the job market and, perhaps, a female-dominated home. Ideology, then, furthers unequal relations of power but people cannot see it because they suffer from false consciousness: what they see is ideology rather than reality. In the critique of the dominant ideology, the researcher's role is to reveal ideology as distortion, so that people gain the possibility of seeing behind ideology and changing reality.

Put briefly, the critique of the dominant ideology aims to unmask power with truth. This understanding of critique has been subjected to heavy criticism by social constructionist researchers. First of all, it has been criticised for its adherence to a classical Marxist conception of society, whereby the base determines the superstructure, or, in our terms, discourses are constituted by non-discursive conditions, primarily the economy. Second, it presumes that there is a truth about social conditions behind the discourses and that the researcher has privileged access to that truth. Thirdly, it assumes that this truth is free of power (cf. Foucault 1980: 118; see also Barrett 1991; Billig and Simons 1994).

These premises conflict with social constructionism, where truth is seen as intertwined with power and the truths which are produced (including those of the researcher) are seen as historically and socially contingent. But does this mean that critical social constructionist research is impossible? Does it mean that all truths are equally good (or equally bad)? According to Michael Billig and Herbert Simons' (1994) diagnosis, a great deal of critical research is being produced, but critique has gone overboard – anything and everything is criticised and every truth is subjected to criticism and deconstruction. Critique has become 'promiscuous', as they put it, as it is no longer connected to a political project, since we no longer have a firm belief in true, political principles as did critical ideology theorists (1994: 6).

This discussion of the relationship between science and politics, and hence of the possibilities for critical research, has been long and intense within social constructionism. And it seems as if the field of discussion suffers from a paradox, whereby research is seen *both* as more *and* as less political than before. On the one hand, it is implicit in the social constructionist perspective that research is always political. Research can never free itself from values as it is always situated in a specific cultural and historical context. And the research which is produced about the world is political by virtue of its performative character: that is, it acts on the world by constituting it in certain ways rather than others. For example, traditional anthropology with its division of the world into 'us' and 'them' has contributed to the legitimation of the dominance of the West through colonialism and neo-colonialism (Fabian 1983). From a social constructionist point of view, research cannot avoid being political.

On the other hand, the concern is voiced by theorists such as Billig and Simons that social constructionist premises render research less political. The argument is that if social constructionism no longer can deliver absolute truths or normative ideals, then research ends up in a relativism where people either criticise anything at all without having any political strategy, or accept everything without taking a political stand because they do not want to accord themselves a false authority by criticising the lives and opinions of others.

In the rest of the chapter, we discuss, on the basis of the question of critique, a range of different suggestions as to what social constructionist research can be used for. We cannot hope to exhaust the discussion and we do not try to give detailed accounts of the work of the authors we take up. Rather, we use the different authors to demarcate a range of key positions in the debate – and a range of possible answers to the question of critical research.

All the contributions to the discussion share a common concern with what research can and should be used for. They all agree that science cannot ascribe to its own knowledge the status of 'truth' in opposition to the 'false consciousness' of others. But the answers to what critique is and to how to view the relations between critique, science and society, are different. They have very different consequences, not just for what we do with the results when research is completed, but also for how we go about the research process itself – in particular, how we build an analytical framework, how we produce and analyse empirical material and how we write up and present our research. Thus, although there are no easy answers to the question of what status scientifically-produced knowledge has and how it can be applied in a responsible way, it is important to take a stand and tailor the research accordingly.

A Modified Ideology Critique

One response to the question of whether it is possible to do critical research can be labelled a 'modified ideology critique'. This approach retains the basic principles of ideology critique that people's worldviews are not always in line with reality, and that research should make better world-views available. At the same time, it modifies ideology critique by softening the hierarchy between the researcher's knowledge and other people's knowledge; access to truth is no longer viewed as a scientific privilege.

Fairclough's critical discourse analysis is an example of this modified version of ideology critique. According to critical discourse analysis, dis-courses can be more or less ideological. The more ideological discourses are those that give a distorted representation of reality (misrepresenta-tion) and thus contribute to the maintenance of relations of domination in society (Chouliaraki and Fairclough 1999: 32f.). In this, we hear the echo of ideology critique: discourse analysis should reveal ideologi-cal representations and attempt to replace them with more adequate representations of reality.

However, critical discourse analysis modifies traditional ideology critique in some respects, particularly in Chouliaraki and Fairclough (1999). The authors still maintain that certain representations are more true than others; however, they argue that what is true should not be determined by a scientific elite but by a public, democratic debate in which different representations are compared with one another in relation to both their content and their social consequences. It is the task of science to con-tribute to public debate kinds of knowledge which people normally do not produce or have at their disposal in everyday practices (1999: 33). Thus scientific knowledge here is treated as a contribution to the public debate rather than the final arbiter of truth.

But even with these modifications, critical discourse analysis articulates the question of critique in a way from which many other social constructionists distance themselves. For example, as we have already discussed in earlier chapters and will see on p. 186, there is disagreement as to the question of whether or not it is possible to distinguish between more or less ideological discourses. Before discussing further the modified critique of ideology formulated by critical discourse analysis, we map out a range of other positions in the debate. We begin by taking a step backwards. Until now we have presented the discussion as a question of *how* to produce critical knowledge. This question contains two presuppositions – that research can produce knowledge and that it should be critical. But not all social constructionists accept these two assumptions.

THE CRITIQUE OF CRITIQUE

Ideology critique used research to produce knowledge about the world that was in opposition to, and better than, people's understandings. Social constructionism distanced itself from this on the basis of the premise that knowledge is never a direct reflection of the world, a premise which applies to scientific knowledge just as much as to other forms of knowledge. There are two ways of taking the consequences of this premise. For most social constructionists, the purpose of research is still to know something about the world and to produce as good representations of the world as possible, and the premise that knowledge is historically and culturally specific can be tackled through various forms of reflexivity. But for a minority of social constructionists, knowledge, in the sense of representation, is impossible, and therefore it is not the task of research to produce knowledge in that sense. We will begin by discussing this latter position.

The anthropologist, Steven Tyler (1986) criticises the paradigm of representation followed by modern science – that is, the belief that reality can be reflected in scientific texts. By promising absolute truth, science has exerted power over ordinary people's lives and discounted their everyday knowledge. Representation or *mimesis* is impossible, according to Tyler, and therefore sciences such as anthropology should rid themselves of their scientific ideals and stop trying to tell us what the world is. Instead, they should more mystically and poetically 'evoke' what cannot be said, in order to make us think about who we are and what we ought to do.[1]

In this type of theory, the question of critique does not arise at all, since the purpose of science is not to produce a description of the world but to produce effects in the world. While also aiming to change the world, critique implies that one representation of the world is replaced by another, better representation – and it is this idea that Tyler considers naïve and even destructive.

Tyler's argument hinges on the possibility of writing non-representational texts. His own text is not written in a traditional, scientific form, rather it mixes arguments with more poetic narrative passages, and in thus it evokes its message rather than stating it explicitly. But even with this experimental form of presentation, we do not think that the text avoids representing the world. In the following passage, it is quite clear that a particular representation of the world is used as an argument for how to write ethnographies about it:

> A post-modern ethnography is fragmentary because it cannot be otherwise. Life in the field is itself fragmentary, not at all organized around familiar ethnological categories such as kinship, economy, and religion […] (Tyler 1986: 131)

Here, Tyler describes what life is like in the field – that is, fragmented – and how ethnography therefore should be – correspondingly fragmented. Thus, Tyler bases his argument on a description of reality, a representation. And in this particular passage, he even argues that ethnography should reflect the world (by being fragmented), in opposition to his claim that representation is impossible.

Our point is that even if it is impossible, according to social constructionist premises, to distinguish categorically between representation and reality, and even if representation is never a direct reflection of reality, in our texts we cannot avoid representing and thus giving some sort of picture of reality. Another problem in Tyler's theory is that he advocates the withdrawal of anthropology from science and instead its embrace of a kind of poetry or therapy. Although modern science might have followed naïve ideals and had negative consequences, we do not see any reason to reject all scientific rules and criteria. On the contrary, as we will argue, the humanities and social sciences must be maintained as a space for the production, discussion and evaluation of different representations of the world on the basis of a set of shared criteria.

If scientific texts, as we have argued, inevitably represent the world, this opens up the possibility of replacing one representation of the world with another through critique. But not everyone agrees with this ideal. The problem is that critique, in the main, involves an asymmetrical relationship between those who criticise and those who are criticised, as in ideology critique whereby the researcher is in possession of the truth while all others have false consciousness. If we are to research according to social constructionist premises, we cannot privilege scientific knowledge in this way. This raises the question of what scientific knowledge is and whether it can be said to be in any way better than other forms of knowledge, a question to which we will return later. Some researchers think that the asymmetrical relationship between researcher and researched that critique tends to entail is so problematic that we should be wary of making critique the goal we set for research.

Among those who problematise critique in this way is the anthropologist of science, Bruno Latour (1999), who argues that critique is not necessary as people already know what they should know; people do not need researchers running around revealing their illusions. The social psychologist, Kenneth Gergen, argues along similar lines. Although not dismissing the concept of critique altogether, he warns of the negative consequences of research as critique (Gergen 1994b, 1998). Gergen argues that critique implies what he calls a 'binary ontology' (1994b: 60). According to Gergen, critique is always dependent on that which it criticises. In criticising something, one reinforces it at the same time. The debate becomes polarised between 'for' and 'against' so that arguments which do not fit in one or other camp are excluded, and other debates are also kept off the agenda. Moreover, Gergen argues, discussion is often treated as a kind of war and critique as an attack on our inner essence. Therefore, critique does not lead to dialogue but to alienation. In another metaphor, when one criticises another person's opinions, one establishes a position as a wise parent who corrects a child, states Gergen (1994b: 63). In so doing, critique silences the opposing party, blocking democratic debate. This is particularly paradoxical in the case of critique by social constructionists since social constructionism strives to avoid all tendencies to totalisation (1994b: 67f.). The conclusion is, then, that critique freezes debate, restricting and polarising the voices which can participate in it.

Gergen's ideal is a debate consisting of different competing contributions. His starting point is that knowledge production is a social process in which decisions are taken collectively. This collectivity entails that, in discussing a specific topic, every single individual has knowledge of many different arguments. Gergen proposes, for example, that we do not polarise the debate about a specific topic in terms of 'for' and 'against' a single aspect of the topic but instead follow up the different arguments as a network of threads which gradually form a complex picture (1994b: 71ff.).

We fully agree with the social constructionist view put forward by Gergen that knowledge production should be understood as a collective process (cf. Calhoun 1995: Chapter 6), and his proposal that we take account of this in specific debates can be a good way of maintaining the complexity of the debated topic. However, while experiments of the kind Gergen suggests can be a fine supplement to critique as a scientific practice, we do not think that they are an adequate substitute for critique. Gergen's suggestions can contribute to viewing the topic under debate from many perspectives and to a better understanding of the arguments of the others. But, in our view, his suggestion also implies that all arguments are equally good and that, through understanding, we can resolve conflicts of meaning.

Gergen's scepticism about the concept of critique is based on the hierarchy it constructs between the researcher and the surrounding world. He formulates the relationship as one of patronising parent versus child and tries to replace it with more symmetrical relations. The implication of the parent/child metaphor is that the one party in the conversation is totally denied legitimacy. We agree that the concept of critique implies an asymmetry but we do not think that this necessarily entails the denial of legitimacy to the opposing party. Moreover, our view is that Gergen's equation of critique with binary ontology unfairly narrows down the concept of critique. In another metaphor, critique as scientific practice often involves 'unmasking' naturalised, taken-for-granted knowledge which may be shared by competing contributions to a given debate. To a large extent, we subscribe to this metaphor, and maintain critique as the aim of social research. But have these formulations brought us back to ideology critique's search for the truth behind all illusions? Not necessarily, and we will, in the following pages, explore some alternative possibilities.

CRITIQUE OF THE TAKEN-FOR-GRANTED

The unmasking of taken-for-granted, naturalised knowledge is often an explicitly formulated aim of social constructionist research (see, for example, Marcus and Fischer 1986: Chapter 6; cf. Brown 1994: 24). Here the critical project is a matter of denaturalisation of the taken-for-granted understandings of reality. The starting point is that our representations of the world are always contingent – they could have been different – and, in taking something for granted, we forget that it could have been different. As the taken-for-granted delimits the field of possibilities for thinking and acting, its unmasking can open up a political field to other possibilities and, therefore, can represent a critical research aim in its own right.

This is, for example, the case for Laclau and Mouffe's discourse theory.[2] In their theory of the hegemonic practices of discourse, Laclau and Mouffe conceptualise how reality comes to appear to be natural and non-contingent. They propose that discourses, by way of hegemonic closures, fix meanings in particular ways and, thus, exclude all other meaning potentials, and that, through myths about society and identity, the discursive constructions appear as natural and delimited aspects of reality. Laclau and Mouffe's aim is to challenge hegemonic closures by going in the opposite direction: through deconstruction, they strive to show that the entities which we see as objective and natural are, in reality, contingent combinations of elements which could always have been articulated differently.

As mentioned in Chapter 2, Laclau equates ideology and objectivity and, in some sense, the project of discourse theory is thereby a project of ideology critique, although very different from traditional ideology critique. While Laclau adheres to ideology critique's definition of ideology as a distortion of reality, he views this distortion as an unavoidable part of every representation of the world. In order to be able to engage in meaningful talk, we always have to reduce the meaning potentials of the words we use, and we must assume that there are objects such as society and subjects about which we can say something meaningful. And here lies the ideological distortion as these operations imply objectification that negates the contingency inherent in all ascription of meaning (Laclau 1990: Chapter 2; 1996a).

Laclau and Mouffe's discourse theory is therefore ideology critique in the sense that it aims to expose contingency and deconstruct objectivity but, in contrast to traditional ideology critique, it cannot offer any ideology-free truth – the researcher is also condemned to distort reality through the identification of objects and meaningful talk about them.

Discourse theory's formulation of the critical project provokes a number of questions. Craig Calhoun, for example, criticises the type of theory that sees power as all-pervasive and all utterances as ideological. By viewing all constructions as equally ideological, this type of theory, Calhoun contends, rules out the possibility of distinguishing between those contributions which improve the world and those which do not and, as a result, critique becomes unconstructively directed towards anything at all (Calhoun 1995: 64). From Calhoun's perspective, one can ask how discourse theory determines what to criticise, and what the researcher has to offer instead. Does Laclau and Mouffe's discourse theory deal only in 'negative criticism' (Brown 1994: 23f.), whereby existing conditions are criticised without the suggestion of a better alternative? Discourse theory does, in fact, present a positive utopia which research can help to realise – namely, the utopia of a 'radical democracy' (Laclau and Mouffe 1985, Chapter 4; Mouffe 1992). A democracy providing full freedom and equality for everyone is impossible and political communities can never include everyone as they always build on an opposition between 'us' and 'them'. But it *is* possible to have full freedom and equality as a horizon to strive towards and an attempt can be made to include more and more areas in the political debate about equality (Mouffe 1992: 378f.). Democracy provides us with a framework by which we can compare ourselves with one another and, in this way, identify injustices. If men have the vote, for example, why can women not have it also, feminists asked in the early 20th century. And the way towards a radical democracy lies in making it possible to ask more and more of that kind of question. If others have the freedom to be heterosexual, why can we not have the freedom to be homosexual? If others are accepted as white, why can we not be accepted as black? All these questions have been posed by new social movements and have contributed to opening up the domain for questions which can be discussed politically in terms of freedom and equality.

In a radical democracy, it is important that the political field never stiffens into firmly demarcated groups and standard positions on the political agenda. Every political question divides people into particular groups and gives them particular identities; it fixes the myth of society in particular ways. And since one way never exhausts all parts of our fragmented and overdetermined identities, and never realises all possible group formations, it is important that existing groups can be deconstructed all the time and new groups can be formed – and fresh questions can be placed on the agenda. Groups that engage in political activity over a particular question must therefore be understood not as groups of identical people who share the same essence but as temporary alliances in which particular aspects of the members' identity are constituted and activated in relation to the question at hand. Only if one keeps open the issues of which conflicts should be on the political agenda and which groups are in conflict, is it possible continuously to introduce new discussion topics in relation to equality and freedom. Laclau and Mouffe's critical project of unmasking the taken-for-granted can, then, be said to be a political project in which the deconstruction of objectivity keeps us aware of the ideological, contingent nature of the objectivity we ascribe to the world and, more specifically, exposes new areas for political discussion.

However, in response to Calhoun's question as to how one determines what should be criticised, discourse theory's vision of radical democracy provides only a modest answer. Discourse theory's critical project consists of the deconstruction of the taken-for-granted but the theory does not give any guidelines as to *which* taken-for-granted understandings are most in need of deconstruction and in terms of which political criterion. In our view, not setting *a priori* normative standards does not necessarily constitute an obstacle for critical research. However, if we operate along the lines of the social constructionist premise on which discourse theory itself is based, namely, that research does not just produce a representation of the world but also produces effects in the world, it is important to make the research aims clear to oneself and others.

This political dimension can be added to a discourse theoretical project by combining it with other approaches to research that enable the researcher to identify the aims and the political direction of the specific research project. *Action research*, currently gaining in popularity, is one such approach (see, for example Reason and Bradbury 2001; Tracy 1995; Willig 1999a). Action research relates much more intimately to the field of study than traditional scientific approaches, as it is argued that research should be carried out *with* people, rather than *about* them. This means that the aims of the research should be formulated in a specific context of social practice, together with the people in this context, whereby informants and researcher cooperate in identifying specific problems in the field that the research should help to solve. In many forms of contemporary action research, people in the field are seen as *participants* in the research process, contributing their knowledge of the field to a common development of new knowledge together with the researcher (for a related approach, see our discussion of dialogical research on p. 198–200).

Another, more traditional, way to integrate a specific political dimension into the research project is to incorporate a theoretical perspective that invests the concept of critique with a clearer political direction. In the following sections, we will present some feminist perspectives according to which the research, from begining to end, follows a political trajectory.

IDENTIFYING THE TAKEN-FOR-GRANTED

Let us first return to the question of the taken-for-granted and how it can be identified. The taken-for-granted, as noted earlier, is, per definition, that which is not problematised – that which one does not even think *can* be problematised. In order to identify the taken-for-granted, naturalised ascriptions of meaning, researchers need to distance themselves from them in some way or another. In this section we will present three different responses to the epistemological question of how to theorise a subject position for the researcher that enables her to identify the taken-for-granted.

The first response we call *analytical redescription*. Basil Bernstein suggests that we think of theories as 'languages of description' and the application of the theory as a translation of the empirical material into its language (Bernstein 1996: Chapter 6). Through this process of translation, some of the taken-for-granted aspects of the material are denaturalised (cf. Chouliaraki and Fairclough 1999). All the discourse analytical approaches presented in this book provide the possibility of redescribing the empirical material. Laclau and Mouffe's theory of discourse and articulation and its concepts of floating signifiers, myths and so on can, for instance, be seen as a form of language which can describe the empirical material in a different way from the way in which it describes itself. Likewise, the linguistic tools of critical discourse analysis and the rhetorical tools of discursive psychology can be seen as distinct languages which can create a distance between the researcher and the material.

As is the case with all translations, such a translation is neither neutral nor innocent, involving a kind of violence on the empirical material (Silverstone 1999: 14). And that is also the intention; the aim of discourse analysis is to extract other meanings from the material than those which are at the foreground. But the conceptualisation of discourse analysis as a form of translation also carries with it some limitations as to how, and how much, we can twist our material, since we have to confine ourselves to those interpretations which fit the discourse analytical language we have chosen as our analytical framework. Conceptualising the different approaches to discourse analysis (along with any other scientific theory) as languages of description, then, on the one hand, enables the researcher to establish a distance to the empirical material, transforming it through redescription, and on the other, guarantee a certain loyalty to the original empirical texts by limiting the interpretations that can be made of them.

Critique from the Periphery

In order to move on to discuss other means of identifying the taken-for-granted, we need to highlight an assumption common to most social constructionist research: the assumption that the taken-for-granted is organised around a centre of power. It can be more or less explicit or theorised. Laclau and Mouffe, for example, both discuss it explicitly and theorise it solidly, so let us use discourse theory as our illustration. According to discourse theory, discourses fix meaning by excluding all other meaning potentials. Two discourses can collide in an antagonistic relationship to one another when they try to define the same terrain in conflicting ways. Antagonisms are dissolved through hegemony, whereby the one discourse conquers the terrain and appears as the objective reality; the objective being that which has become taken-for-granted, that which we forget is contingent. The taken-for-granted emerges, then, when alternatives are pushed out of our vision.

The taken-for-granted is not, of course, omnipresent – it is a key point of social constructionism that there is nothing natural or given about the taken-for-granted world. But the point at which a particular taken-for-granted understanding begins and ends can be understood in two ways. Either the taken-for-granted can be understood as emanating from a centre and spanning a certain radius out to the periphery on which it is not quite so taken for granted. Or one can understand the taken-for-granted as an all-imposing structure containing gaps that provide potential footholds for dissension. These two metaphors do not exclude one another and we think, for example, that discourse theory can be understood in both ways. Nevertheless, we separate them in order to be able to distinguish between two different kinds of response to the question of how to disclose the taken-for-granted. Both metaphors *localise* the taken-for-granted. Thus they also localise points from which to identify otherwise oblique, taken-for-granted understandings. We now turn to feminist theory in order to illustrate some ways to establish such points.

The social constructionist premise of the cultural and historical specificity of knowledge entails that people who are positioned differently in time and space also view the world differently and have varying taken-for-granted understandings. It is this premise which feminists, among others, have used to theorise the knowledge they themselves produce. Feminist thinkers have been at the forefront in the development of theories about situated knowledge; the adoption of a specific site for knowledge production, among other possible ones, is the starting point for most feminist research.

The basic premise underpinning feminist research is that women represent a special group – a group that has been overlooked and oppressed both in society and in science. And, from the perspective of our analysis of critique, this premise has two major consequences. First, feminist research is normative, the aim being to make women and their lives and experiences visible and to fight against the oppressive structures. As to the question of what should be criticised, feminism provides an example of research with a much clearer political direction than, for instance, Laclau and Mouffe's discourse theory: that which should be criticised is that which oppresses women. Second, the feminist starting point has led to fruitful discussions about how one can make visible and criticise dominant, naturalised understandings by locating oneself in a particular position, and how the anchoring of the knowledge produced by the researcher can be theorised. One influential position in this discussion is *feminist standpoint theory*, as formulated by the sociologist Dorothy Smith.

Dorothy Smith (1987) contends that the ideals of modern Western science relating to objectivity and abstraction both reflect and reinforce the marginalisation of women in a patriarchal and capitalist society. Therefore, she suggests a sociology which is based on the standpoint of women. The argument is not that women can see reality differently because they are biologically different from men, but that women as a social group have separate experiences from men as a result of the gendered distribution of labour. It is often women, Smith argues, that do all the housework, make the food and look after the children (1987: 83). And this work is often invisible. Whereas women are continuously confronted with the immediate local world and the concrete experiences of bodies and basic needs, it is much easier for men to transcend their local surroundings and assume a distance from the immediate reality, just as scientists distance themselves from their object of study. Thus, although science presents itself as if it were gender-neutral, in reality it is based on, and furthers, the worldviews and interests of men.

Smith uses women's experiences to construct a platform from which she is able to observe the dominant, taken-for-granted understandings and criticise them. She does not think that women's experiences *necessarily* lead to a feminist and critical perspective on the dominant relations of power since both sexes have to understand themselves and the world around them through the dominant discourse. A feminist understanding of the world has to be actively constructed (1987: 107), but the conditions of possibility for a feminist understanding lie in the marginalisation of women's lives and work. Women's experiences fall outside patriarchal frameworks of understanding, and this 'outside' (62ff., 78ff.) provides the resource for the feminist critique of the dominant, unquestioned understandings.

Smith recounts how she herself as an academic and single mother experienced the splitting of her own consciousness into two: a scientific, abstract consciousness as an academic and an experiential, locally-oriented consciousness as a mother. Women are 'strangers' in the academic world, and here the possibility for a critical perspective emerges. Starting out from experience, women can potentially see *both* the dominant structure *and* what falls outside it, and by virtue of their bifurcated consciousness they can, then, criticise the ruling power apparatus.

Let us now return to the two metaphors for conceptualising the boundaries of the taken-for-granted: we argued that the taken-for-granted can either be understood as a structure spreading from a centre and identifiable at its periphery, or as a structure with gaps that can expose and problematise the taken-for-granted. Smith's theory is more in line with the first metaphor: women's experiences represent a site outside the dominant discourse which can be used as a starting point for the problematisation of naturalised understandings as oppressive to women.

A parallel theorisation can be used to denaturalise understandings with respect to other oppressed groups. The working class, ethnic minorities and homosexuals, for example, can also, on the basis of their experiences, deliver standpoints from which the dominant understandings can be identified and criticised (Smith 1987).

In sum, Smith provides a particular theorisation of the conditions of possibility for critique. However, there are some problems with her perspective. Although she points out that women are different from one another and have different experiences, she tends to present women as a homogeneous group, positioned in the same way vis-à-vis the ruling power-apparatus. Consequently, her standpoint theory risks making invisible the differences among women. For example, in a society in which ethnicity is a key category, there may be big differences among women of different ethnic groups in relation to their experiences and their positioning in society. Patricia Hill Collins' work is relevant in relation to this (for example, 1986). Collins formulates a version of feminist standpoint theory which adresses the issue of homogeneity. She introduces the concept of the *outsider within* in order to link gender and race. She suggests that black women historically can be seen as outsiders within societies such as the US, where they come into whites' homes as maids, for example, but are never accepted as equals. This shared experience of always being both outside and inside can form a basis, according to Collins, for black, feminist thinking, in which both a theory and a political strategy can be developed, directed to furthering equality betwen gender, classes and ethnic groups. Collins (1998) stresses that women are different and that black women do not represent a homogeneous group either. Nevertheless she insists that certain groups under certain circumstances can share so many of the same life conditions that these common conditions can form the basis for a specific view of the world, a specific standpoint.

However, a problem associated with both versions of standpoint theory is that they involve a privileging of the category of experience. Calhoun warns against tying the critical perspective too tightly to specific experiences, since, if experience fully determines what people can see, then we lose the possibility of discussion with people who have different experiences (Calhoun 1995: 180f.). The danger is that we implant a form of essentialism where, for instance, men are totally excluded from feminist thinking on the grounds that they would never be able to see the world from the standpoint of women. Calhoun may have a point here, although we believe that Smith is less categorical on this point: men *tend towards* more abstract and less context-specific experiences rather than being excluded from concrete, context-specific experiences altogether (cf. Smith 1987: 82).

Rather, the biggest problem we see with standpoint theory is that it risks the reproduction of what it criticises. In terms of our metaphor for the boundaries of the taken-for-granted, if one uses the dominant discourse's distinction between 'them' and 'us', centre and periphery, to reveal the naturalised knowledge of the centre (by positioning oneself on the side of 'them' – on the periphery), one quickly comes to reproduce the naturalised distinction between 'them' and 'us' as a taken-for-granted understanding which one shares with the centre. On the one hand, Smith's goal is to problematise and criticise the oppression of women in society but, on the other hand, she takes as her starting-point the lives and experiences of 'women'. In this way, and in spite of her assurances that neither men nor women represent homogeneous groups, she reproduces the very same patriarchal division of the world into 'men' and 'women' that she aims to criticise (cf. Prins 1997: 76).[3]

Standpoint theory provides a strategy for distancing oneself from the centre, in order to look at the centre from the periphery. Another strategy to establish such a distance is to 'move away' from the centre in time or space. Sexuality in a Western society can, for instance, be problematised through reading anthropological studies of sexuality in other societies where completely different views about sexuality, love, body and gender, may be found. Similarly, one can adopt an historical approach such as Foucault often did. By exploring the understandings of sexuality prevalent in the past and, through the distancing process inherent in this, Foucault was able to present contemporary understandings of sexuality as exotic constructions which could have been different (Foucault 1979, 1987, 1988). The historical perspective provides us with material that helps to cast light on how categories such as sexuality have taken a specific form.

By drawing upon historical and anthropological material 'foreign' to oneself and one's own empirical material, one can try to establish a site outside one's culture from which one can identify what is taken for granted within it. The 'outsideness' of this site must not, however, be taken to be absolute as one cannot completely escape one's own understandings. But while access to 'foreign' material is always mediated by one's existing understandings, our view is that consideration of completely different worldviews can, at least, make it possible to ask new questions of our own understandings and the understandings identified in the empirical material.

Critique from Gaps in the Structure

Still exploring the question of how to uncover the dominant naturalised understandings of reality, we will now present a final theorisation which attempts to establish an alternative understanding of the world, seeing the world through gaps in the structure rather than from its periphery. Such an attempt is made, for example, by the feminist theorist, Donna Haraway.[4] Haraway does not base her research on the perspective of 'women' or the 'working class' or 'black people', as these categories are already part of the structure she wants to criticise; instead she tries to position herself between the existing categories and view the world from there. Her universe is, therefore, populated by beings such as cyborgs, monsters and gene-manipulated mice, which do not fit into the usual divisions between human, animal, machine and so on. By taking the perspective of, and identifying herself with, such 'inappropriate/d others', as she states using Trinh Minh-Has' concept (Haraway 1992: 299), she is able to explore how the categories we normally employ are contingent articulations of elements strictly divided into, for example, 'nature' and 'culture'. And this disruption to the construction of categories makes it possible to imagine other (and better) worlds in which the elements are articulated differently (1992: 313f.).

In the classic essay 'A Cyborg Manifesto' (1991), Haraway uses the figure of the cyborg to explore, among other things, our ideas about identity. The cyborg is a mix of organism and machine, nature and culture, and it therefore collapses the categories we normally keep separated. The Western tradition operates with a long list of such dichotomies (self/other, man/woman, civilised/primitive and so on) that contributes to the maintenance of a system of domination in which men dominate women, the 'civilised' dominate the 'primitive' and so on (1991: 177). Haraway employs the metaphor of cyborg to identify and criticise the dichotomies. Her point is that we are all cyborgs – a hybrid of human and machine (1991: 150). Without all our technical aids, we would not be what we are and could not do what we can. And more generally, the idea is that our identities are always 'polluted' – they never quite fit the categories we construct.

Haraway criticises the structure from its gaps – a viewpoint based on that which falls between our categories. But this does not mean that she has found a place from which she can see reality as it 'really' is, completely free of all structure. That would, in her view, be impossible. By employing the cyborg, which also has a prehistory in the military industry, she tries to appropriate a figure which is already circulating in our material and linguistic practices in order to re-code it. She appropriates the cyborg, using it to tell a different story, a story that creates a 'political myth' (1991: 157) in order to give an account of how we create ourselves and the world by combining heterogeneous elements. By criticising Western dichotomies, she opens up the possibility that elements can be combined in new and hopefully better ways in the future. In her account, research, like our identities, can never be completely 'pure'; it is destined to navigate in a world that is already structured in many different ways. But what it potentially *can* do is disrupt our understandings and reassemble them in new ways.

THE STATUS OF KNOWLEDGE

We have now presented three different theoretical understandings of how researchers can identify the taken-for-granted, naturalised constructs they seek to uncover. First, we suggested that theories are languages of redescription entailing the translation of the empirical material, second, we discussed standpoints on the periphery from which to gain an outside perspective on the centre, and third, we pointed to gaps in the dominant structure from where naturalised categories can be problematised. The question of naturalised constructs and the possibility of unmasking them was relevant because critique in social constructionism is often – at least as a minimum – formulated as the denaturalisation of the taken-for-granted. And all of these strategies aim to theorise a distance between researcher and the taken-for-granted, wherein the taken-for-granted becomes visible as an object of study. In other words, these alternatives, used individually or in combination, provide an epistemological basis from which knowledge can be produced. But implicit in the social constructionist premises lies the question of which status to ascribe this new knowledge. Most social constructionist researchers would agree that research itself establishes new forms of taken-for-granted understandings, and that scientific knowledge is a contingent construction of reality, just as other representations are. How then can we guarantee that the understanding of reality we present is better than the one we criticise? How can we evaluate scientific knowledge? In sum, (how) can we invest our claims with academic authority and political force without reference to a fixed foundation for knowledge?

Relativism and Reflexivity

Does the relativism inherent in the social constructionist premises make it impossible to distinguish good descriptions of reality from the not so good, and progressive political principles from reactionary ones? And, if this is the case, is it something we should worry about? We will now present a number of positions in the debate, starting in discursive psychology. Here opinion is divided (cf. Chapter 4): one grouping views relativism as a political obstacle whereas another grouping does not. Members of the second grouping, Derek Edwards, Malcolm Ashmore and Jonathan Potter (1995) argue that relativism is unavoidable but nothing to worry about. Relativism, according to them, is not a scientific programme, but a fundamental scepticism vis-à-vis any claim to knowledge about reality, a scepticism which makes it possible to question everything. But this does not mean that we cannot make claims and judgements about this reality – indeed, we cannot avoid doing so. What it does mean is that all claims are open to discussion, and herein lies the possibility for ongoing democratic debate. In contrast, realistic arguments, trying as they do to pin down what the world really is, freeze the discussion.

Edwards et al.'s strategy is to *embrace relativism*, accepting it unconditionally as a condition for all knowledge production. Other discursive psychologists such as Parker (1992) and Willig (1999b) warn against this wholesale acceptance of relativism. They argue that critical research becomes impossible if all statements about the world in principle are equally good and, to avoid this danger, they choose a combination of social constructionism and the ontology of critical realism in order to take account of what they consider to be the non-discursive aspects of the world. Critical discourse analysis has also, to some extent, chosen this route. Chouliaraki and Fairclough (1999) distinguish between different forms of relativism, accepting a modest form of relativism endorsed by critical realism, and rejecting what they see as more radical forms. Drawing on the concepts of the critical realist, Roy Bhaskar, they accept *epistemic relativism*, according to which all discourses stem from a particular position in social life, and dismiss *judgemental relativism*, which holds that all discourses are equally good representations of reality. They dismiss judgemental relativism with the argument that the strengths and weaknesses of discourses are continuously being judged in every-day practices when, for instance, people test how good a discourse is to think with or to use as a framework for collective action (cf. Brown 1994: 27ff.).

It is a matter of interpretation whether Chouliaraki and Fairclough's position is actually different from the one espoused by Edwards, Ashmore and Potter. One interpretation is that Chouliaraki and Fairclough's rejection of judgemental relativism rests on the argument that, in every discursive situation, certain standards are implied as to what is right and wrong, useful or not. All discourses can never be equally good as one always argues within a discursive space in which there is already a set of criteria for what is accepted as a true statement. In this interpretation, the measurement criteria for which representations are the best are contingent; embedded in specific discursive spaces – a position close to Edwards et al.'s embrace of relativism. But if this were the case, why make the distinction between epistemic and judgemental relativism in the first place? In an alternative interpretation of Chouliaraki and Fairclough's position, this distinction makes more sense. According to this interpretation, Chouliaraki and Fairclough argue that some representations reflect reality more loyally than others according to some external measure. Such an interpretation is out of line with their definition of truth as a product of a democratic discussion but fits well with their distinction between more or less ideological dis-courses.[5] According to this interpretation, Chouliaraki and Fairclough *circumscribe relativism*, viewing all representations as socially con-structed (a relativist position), but seeing some as more loyal to reality than others (a non-relativist position). From a social constructionist perspective, the question arises here as to *who* should pass judgement as to which representations are better than others. If the choice of one representation over others is not the product of struggle in a discursive field, there must be someone – such as the researcher – who decides by virtue of their privileged insight.[6]

We have now discussed the difference between an embrace and a cir-cumscription of relativism at a metatheoretical, epistemological level and here, as we have seen, the difference is not always clear. But the discus-sion can also be conducted in relation to other stages of the research process and here the difference between Fairclough's critical discourse analysis and Edwards et al.'s approach to discursive psychology is more obvious. The discussion about relativism is not just about epistemological principles but also about how – and the extent to which – the researchers take account of the principles in constructing their research designs. Although Chouliaraki and Fairclough briefly mention the necessity of reflexive consideration of the role of the researcher in knowledge production (1999: 9, 29; cf. Chouliaraki 1995), the general tendency in critical discourse analysis is to apply conventional scientific methods in the production of empirical material and present research results in traditional academic texts without reflexive questioning of these practices. In contrast, the field of discursive psychology as a whole offers an extensive discussion of the possibilities for reflexive research.[7] As outlined in Chapter 4, reflexivity is an attempt to take into account the researcher's own role in knowledge production in the light of the relativist premise, inherent in social constructionism, that one's own knowledge is socially and culturally constructed. The aim is to redefine the classical relations of authority between the researcher and the people under study, and to avoid positioning oneself as a sovereign authority with privileged access to truth.

One strategy is to enlist the informants as co-researchers, and many discursive psychologists advocate *dialogical research* based on more dialogical methods for the production and analysis of empirical material (e.g. Condor 1997; Sampson 1991). Instead of viewing empirical material as something which exists 'out there' for a neutral researcher to observe and collect, this approach stresses that empirical material is a social construction, resulting from the interaction between researcher and researched. In other words, researchers create their objects of analysis and empirical material through ongoing dialogue with the field. Dialogical research is viewed as a more democratic alternative to traditional forms of research since more space is given to the informants' voices in the production of the material and in the writing-up of the results: for example, by presenting their empirical material as a product of a dialogue between researcher and researched, by reproducing longer interview extracts, by carrying out the analysis in cooperation with the informants, or by involving them as co-authors of the text. Although many discursive psychologists and other critical social psychologists play an active role in reflexivity debates and support the idea of dialogical research (see, for example, Ibáñez and Íñiguez 1997), their application of the principles in specific research projects tends to be limited, often restricted to a recognition that their empirical material is the product of a dialogue between the researcher and the researched. For example, they mostly discuss the material exclusively in relation to the informants, ignoring their own role as researchers in the construction of the material.

In particular, they often analyse interview responses without analysing the questions, thus overlooking the dialogical context to which the responses belong (Condor 1997).[8]

With respect to dialogical research's aim to challenge the authority of the researcher, the question is whether this is possible and desirable. Equality between researchers, informants and their respective forms of knowledge should supposedly make research more democratic. But, in our view, this equality can never be total: it is the researcher who decides that a project should be carried out and defines what it should be about and who should be involved as informants. And it is the researcher who coordinates the whole process and who gains any academic prestige which the project brings. As Susan Condor points out, there is a danger that dialogical researchers merely mask the asymmetrical relationship between researcher and informants, presenting themselves as neutral spokespeople for the informants (Condor 1997: 133; cf. Chouliaraki 1995).

Even if one could make the relationship between researcher and researched fully symmetrical, the question remains as to whether or not this is a good idea. We see a fruitful potential in the development of dia-logical research practices both in relation to the research design – whereby researchers try, to a greater extent, to take into account their own active role in knowledge production – and in relation to the con-struction of the researcher's role whereby researchers cast off part of their authority in order to take more account of the voices and interests of the informants. The discussion within dialogical research of what (and whose) knowledge is accepted as legitimate provides a central contribution to democratic debate, promoting awareness of who has the monopoly over knowledge of what, who is silenced and what knowledge is not recog-nised *as* knowledge. Furthermore, dialogical research may help to create common platforms on which to exchange knowledge between different discourses, such as scientific knowledge and everyday knowledge. But we find in dialogical research a tendency towards the total rejection of one's authority as researcher and the equation of scientific and other forms of knowledge. In contrast, we would emphasise the point that even if all knowledge can, in principle, be equated on the grounds that all knowl-edge is contingent, there are at a given point in a given society, different types of knowledge, constructed according to different logics and directed at different applications. We do not believe that these different forms of knowledge can or should be reduced to one another or, more specifically, that scientific knowledge and everyday knowledge can be measured according to the same standards or have the same authority in all cases. Despite its contingency, we believe that the legitimacy of science depends precisely on its being viewed as a distinctive form of knowledge with its own criteria for knowledge production and resulting authority.

Dialogical research is a reflexive answer to social constructionist relativism in the research phases of gathering, analysing and presenting empirical material, attempting to dismantle the hierarchical relation between researcher and informant. *Experimental writing*, to which we now turn, focuses on the presentation of research, thus problematising another hierarchical relationship, that between writer and reader. The traditional scientific research presentation is criticised for presenting scientific knowledge as neutral and objective and, therefore, for ascribing it undeserved authority. On the basis of this critique, some researchers strive to show the construction of the text *in* the text, so that the reader is constantly reminded that what she reads is not the truth, but a contingent representation of reality. For example, Edwards and Potter (1992) have interrupted the conventional flow of the text in their book on discursive psychology with 'reflexive' boxes in which they discuss the status of their knowledge and how they have arrived at it. One of the boxes, for instance, takes the form of a dialogue between the two authors in which they discuss what label they should give to the model they have developed (1992: 155). In this way, they show that knowledge does not just exist but rather is produced by choices made by specific people in specific situations.[9]

Even though the aim of such presentations is to challenge the hierarchical relations of authority between author and reader, the texts may have the paradoxical effect of appearing patronising, as they imply that if the reader is not alerted, she would believe anything she reads. If this is the effect, then the goal of a more equal relationship between author and reader has obviously not been achieved.

In more extreme experiments, it almost appears as if the aim of the text is to say as little as possible – or at least to undermine whatever one has said so that the reader is not enticed to believe in it (e.g. Woolgar and Ashmore 1988). Experimental texts of this type can consequently be difficult to discuss because it remains unclear what message the authors are willing to commit themselves to. Not taking a stand, then, in our view leads to a problem, because the texts thereby close themselves off to discussion and critique. Our ideal is that scientific texts function as a contribution to an ongoing discussion and that the author, therefore, should make clear what it is she wants to say and what criteria she accepts as the basis for critique and discussion.[10] This problem notwithstanding, experimental writing can be an effective and constructive reflexive strategy to redefine the relationship between knowledge production, author and reader and to express this textually. In the next section, we will briefly return to this question.

The aim of our discussion of dialogical research and experimental writing has been to illustrate how the question of relativism is not just about stating the epistemological position followed (an embrace or circumscription of relativism). At all stages of the research process, the issue of relativism is negotiated, and choices are made which have consequences for the degree of relativist positioning of the research. If one chooses traditional methods for the production and analysis of material whereby it is always the researcher who has the last word, and if one writes up the results in a traditional scientific text where the researcher - subject and the conditions for knowledge production are excluded, then the knowledge produced is presented as 'a view from nowhere' (Nagel 1986). If, in contrast, one makes use of one or more reflexive strategies, the research results are positioned instead as one form of knowledge among other possible forms. In the first case, the disadvantage is that one quickly appears as a truth-sayer who has privileged access to reality. In the second case, the risk is that the reflexive strategies mask an authority which the researcher is ascribed and ascribes to herself without acknowledgement.

Relativism and Objectivity

As we have seen, adherence to the premises of social constructionism involves a negotiation of relativism, both in the claims of principle made in research and in the way the different phases of the research process are conducted in practice. We will now return to the discussion of relativism at the level of principle, exploring the status of knowledge produced in relativist research. Often relativism is treated as the opposite of objectivity. Knowledge which is tied to a particular perspective – a view from somewhere – cannot be objective, and if all knowledge is historically and culturally sedimented, then objectivity is impossible. This opposition underpins the ways of tackling relativism which we presented in the previous section. When Edwards et al. embrace relativism, they imply the impossibility of objectivity. And when Chouliaraki and Fairclough attempt to circumscribe relativism, it is because they think that some descriptions of the world are better and, at least, less misrepresentational than others, and that a total relativism excludes the discussion of more or less ideological knowledge.

Within feminist research the very opposition between relativism and objectivity is problematised. Sandra Harding (1991, 1996), for example, argues that knowledge becomes more objective through being produced within a particular historical and cultural context. Or to be more precise: all knowledge is historically and culturally constituted but modern science presents itself *as if* its knowledge has no context; it has natural-ised itself as a pure reflection of the world. Harding introduces the con-cepts of 'strong' and 'weak' objectivity (1991: Chapter 6; 1996). Modern science represents 'weak objectivity' because it does not take into account its own cultural and historical conditions of possibility. Strong objectivity is achieved through *strong reflexivity* which involves an explo-ration of our own cultural and social locations as researchers (Harding 1991: 161ff.). By accounting in this way for where our own knowledge 'comes from', we can produce more objective and less distorted repre-sentations of the world (cf. Bourdieu and Wacquant 1996).

Donna Haraway (1996) introduces the related concept of *situated knowledge* as her answer to the question of how we, on the one hand, accept that all knowledge is historically contingent, but, on the other hand, want to produce convincing descriptions of the world (1996: 252). Knowledge, according to Haraway, is always partial and it is always produced by following a particular view of the world. And this view is always made possible by 'visualising technologies' to see with – whether these are spectacles, microscopes or theoretical constructions. By examining how one's view is situated and by describing the 'technology' which has made the view possible, one can show that one's own repre-sentation of the world comes from a particular location and that it itself is also a construction.

Harding and Haraway both propose, then, that giving an account of how and where one's own representation of the world comes into being makes the knowledge better. But they understand the concept of 'better' in slightly different ways. Harding is very optimistic with respect to the possibilities for a reflexive strategy whereby researchers explore all their assumptions critically and systematically (Harding 1991: 307). This understanding of reflexivity implies that it is possible for the researcher's role and his or her cultural and historical location to become transparent to the researcher, and this is, we think, too much to hope for, as it returns us to a researcher position from which one can produce a transparent, neutral description of reality (cf. Rose 1997).

Haraway is also sceptical on this point (Haraway 1997: 16, 37f.). Although she argues that researchers should make the best attempt they can to describe the conditions of possibility for their view of the world, she stresses at the same time that research is always performative in that it constitutes the world in particular ways and therefore privileges certain possible worlds over others (1997: 37). She tries to demonstrate this by using an experimental mode of presentation in which she switches between narrative accounts, detailed analyses and reflexive comments. As noted earlier, she defines her cyborg-construction as a 'political myth' and stresses that she does not just represent the world but articulates elements in particular ways (Haraway 1992: 313ff.). Thus, she maintains a basic relativism without circumscribing it, as she tries to make visible the status of her own knowledge as a contingent construction. But, in her case, the embrace of relativism does not result in the undermining of her own possibility to say something or in her rejection of all criteria for evaluation of her knowledge-claims. In our reading, she accepts both political and scientific criteria for knowledge production: certain representations of the world are better than others, and they can be evaluated in terms of the political aims that the researcher sets for her research and in terms of scientific criteria such as coherent argumentation and transparency in the presentation of the process of knowledge production.

CRITIQUE AS A POSITIONED OPENING FOR DISCUSSION

We will now try to collect all the threads we have followed through our discussion of the possibilities for critical research and weave some of them together to form a proposal for how social constructionist researchers can understand and tackle their own knowledge production. Our position is that research ought to contain a critical perspective. Also, in a very broad sense of the word, 'critique', we believe that it is impossible to avoid being critical. As we have argued earlier, in producing texts, we cannot avoid saying something about the world, representing the world in meaning. As Laclau and Mouffe's discourse theory claims, texts always contain assumptions about how the world is, and thus the production of objectivity (in discourse theoretical terms) is unavoidable. Therefore, we agree with both Steven Tyler and Donna Haraway when they emphasise the performativity of scientific texts; texts inevitably *do* something to the world, rather than just describing it. But, in opposition to Tyler, we do not agree that, in writing academic texts, one can, or should, try to avoid describing or representing the world. Representing the world, in one way or another, is unavoidable in any production of meaning. And such a representation of the world is always put forward at the expense of other representations that could have been made, and in competition with other representations that have already been made.

Thus, if critique is understood in a broad sense as the proposal of one understanding of the world at the expense of other possible understandings, we do not think that one can avoid being critical at all.

But we will also propose a narrower understanding of critique. In what sense can some views of reality be understood as better than others? Some of the contributions which we have presented have objected to the construction of asymmetry in scientific practice, whereby science traditionally has privileged its own knowledge over all other forms of knowledge. Tyler, for example, argues for a complete withdrawal from science and its truth-claims. Kenneth Gergen and Bruno Latour argue that critique always positions the researcher as in possession of superior knowledge. And some discursive psychologists and feminist theorists advocate the use of reflexive strategies which promote a higher degree of equality between researcher, researched, and reader. In all of these cases, the tendency is towards the undermining of scientific authority in favour of a more equal relationship between different kinds of knowledge and the knowledge of different kinds of people (cf. Jørgensen in press).

Our view is that such a levelling-out process both tends to mask authority relations, which are unavoidable in scientific practice, and overlooks the unique qualities and value of scientific knowledge. If it is a general condition for knowledge production that certain representations of the world are promoted at the expense of others, then we would rather that researchers acknowledge that they *are* saying something about something and take responsibility for these claims, instead of pretending that they are not putting forward any message of their own about the world (as is the tendency in the case of Tyler, Latour and some versions of reflexive research). Not to take responsibility in this way is to deny themselves an authority they already have ascribed themselves as producers of texts. Also, we distance ourselves from the related attempt to equate scientific knowledge with all other forms of knowledge (which is the tendency in the case of Gergen and parts of dialogical research); our position is that scientific knowledge represents, rightly, a specific form of knowledge that, by virtue of its 'scientificity', has qualities which distinguishes it from other forms of knowledge.

At the same time, we agree that science should not position itself as the truth in opposition to the 'false consciousness' of everybody else. We propose the division of the discussion into two levels. *At the level of principle*, it has to be accepted that the knowledge produced by ourselves as researchers is no better than all other forms of knowledge in the sense that the knowledge produced by science is subject to the same conditions as all other knowledge – that is, it is historically and culturally specific and therefore contingent (it could always be different). This implies that researchers should be open to listening to other people's representations of the world and to discussing with them; other representations cannot be rejected on the grounds that researchers have privileged access to truth. This symmetry at the level of principle is important to maintain as it becomes difficult to have a democratic political discussion if an *a priori* distinction is made between those people who have legitimate knowledge and those who do not. Contingency at the level of principle, then, provides an opening for continued discussion (cf. Butler 1992) and, at the same time, it is social constructionism's central motor: it is on the basis of the premise that all knowledge is historically and culturally contingent that social constructionist researchers attempt to distance themselves from the taken-for-granted and make it the object of critique and discussion. And the consequence at the level of principle is that researchers' own taken-for-granted understandings can also become subject to unmasking and scrutiny.

But neither life nor research takes place on this level of principle in which everything is contingent (cf. Hall 1993). Utterances are always articulated in specific contexts that set narrow boundaries for what is understood as meaningful and as meaningless, true and false. And at this *grounded, concrete level*, we have no choice but to put forward certain representations of reality at the expense of others. As Haraway claims, people always talk within an already regulated space, so that all talk – including that of the researcher – is subject to the prevailing discursive logics. The utterances one makes are always situated or positioned. Although it is the goal of social constructionism to identify these spaces and destabilise their regulative logics, social constructionist research is, like all other discourse, subject to these logics, for good or for bad.

Our proposal is to use the concept of critique to combine these two levels – the level of principle and the concrete, grounded level – and see critique as *a positioned opening for discussion* (Jørgensen 2001). In our view, critical research should take responsibility for providing a particular scientific description of reality on the basis of a particular epistemic interest; that is, critical research should explicitly position itself and distance itself from alternative representations of reality on the grounds that it strives to do something specific for specific reasons. At the same time, critical research should make clear that the particular representation of reality it provides is just one among other possible representations, thus inviting further discussion.

In relation to the discussion about relativism, our position means that we align ourselves closely to Haraway when she talks about her research as a 'political myth'. We do not try to circumscribe relativism, and we do not see how it can be circumscribed within the terms of the social constructionist premises. But neither do we want to embrace it to the extent of undermining all knowledge projects with an eternal 'it could all have been different'. That knowledge is political means that one can neither present the absolute truth nor completely avoid saying something. What one says through one's research can make a difference to the world, and one should take responsibility for this. And this can be done by considering the goals and possible consequences of one's research in a wider social context (for example, a form of 'explanatory critique', see Chapter 3).

We distinguish ourselves from Haraway, perhaps, by placing more weight on the value of *scientificity*. Just because knowledge production is political, does not mean that it cannot have scientific value. Haraway would probably agree on this point, but in defining her project as a 'political myth' she emphasises the contingency; the fact that the representation could have been different. This is also our emphasis on the level of principle, but the understanding of scientific knowledge we are advocating aims to keep the level of principle and the level of the concrete in perspective simultaneously, and thus a more adequate description of the status of scientific knowledge would be a *truth that can be discussed*. Here 'truth' refers to the concrete, grounded level according to which some stories are advocated as better than others, and 'discuss' refers to the level of principle according to which one should always be open to alternative truth-claims.

What, then, constitutes the value of scientific knowledge and how can we practise research as a truth that can be discussed? Science can be seen as one discourse among many others; a discourse which is characterised by the production of knowledge in particular ways on the basis of particular rules. The rules include the general principles that research steps should be made as transparent as possible, that the argumentation should be consistent, that the theory should form a coherent system, and that empirical support should be given for the interpretations presented. From a social constructionist perspective, these rules are viewed as contingent, entailing that they can be criticised and changed over time. Many of the theorists presented here, for instance, represent critiques of traditional scientific practice and its rules and procedures, and they also contribute to the discursive struggle over which rules to adhere to in social constructionist research. Scientific knowledge is, like all other knowledge, a contingent construction submitted to discursive regulation. What differentiates scientific knowledge from most other forms of knowledge is the attempt to adhere to one or another set of *explicit* rules. And within a given set of rules – that is, at the concrete, grounded level – all scientific descriptions of reality are *not* equally good. Specific research results can, and should, be evaluated as better or poorer scientific representations of reality by evaluating whether the procedure and the result live up to the rules it claims to follow (cf. Phillips 2001).

In specific research projects, then, we think that it is crucial to make explicit the foundations for the knowledge produced. Positioning oneself and one's research involves giving an account of what it is one aims to say something about, and what rules one is following in the research process. This applies both to the more general rules about transparency and coherence and the more specific rules set by individual theories. We suggested earlier in the chapter that the different discourse analytical approaches can be understood as different 'languages of redescription' into which one translates the empirical material. And it is important that one makes clear which analytic language one is applying and, thereby, which rules one is following in the process of 'translation'. Theoretical and methodological consistency is, in this way, a research constraint: the researcher understands the world in a particular way rather than in other possible ways. But this is a necessary constraint that is also productive. The use of a specific theory in the production and analysis of material enables researchers to distance themselves from their everyday under-standing of the material, a process which is crucial to social construc-tionist research.

Scientificity – understood as research that gives reasons for, and follows, a set of explicit rules – is precisely what distinguishes scientific knowledge from other forms of knowledge. This does not mean that the production of other forms of knowledge is not governed by rules – it is, in fact, such rules and regularities that discourse analysis aims to iden-tify. And neither does it mean that other forms of knowledge do not, from time to time, draw on and apply scientific procedures. For exam-ple, in everyday conversation, people can dismiss others' descriptions of reality on the grounds that they lack consistency: 'that's not in line with what you said before'. But the difference is that the researcher has an obligation, as a member of a scientific community, to follow a certain set of rules as systematically as possible, and this opens up the possibility of producing knowledge which is not normally produced within other forms of discursive practice. And this is what, in our opinion, gives scientific research legitimacy as a contribution to wider democratic dis-cussions about what society is and what it should be.

In the wider democratic discussions, different forms of knowledge come together and here, again, the principle of contingency as a condi-tion for all knowledge production becomes important. Different forms of knowledge operate according to different discursive logics and, when they come together in a wider democratic debate, it is not necessarily the scientific set of rules or discursive logic which functions – or ought to function – as the common platform for discussion. Such a privileging of science would authorise the scientific experts as the only group allowed to make knowledge-claims. To decide the rules for the common discussion is a crucial part of the struggle taking place in relation to public debate. What are considered to be 'scientific questions' in public debate must be seen as the product of an ongoing struggle between different forms of knowledge rather than something to be decided once and for all, and the research produced is itself part of this struggle.

We have presented our proposal for critical research as a balancing act between the level of principle and the concrete, grounded level; a balancing act between, on the one hand, treating all knowledge, one's own included, as contingent and open to discussion and, on the other hand, treating it as a contribution in specific contexts in which some accounts of reality are better than others. The balance between the two cannot be ultimately determined by these general considerations; rather, it must be determined in relation to the specific research project in question, in which one must decide how to position oneself as researcher and consider the consequences of the position taken for the research design and the presentation of the research. Thus how to present oneself and one's own knowledge in a specific situation is a specific and strategic choice. One has to consider where to position oneself on a scale, ranging from the position of researcher as equal participant in the debate, offering a contribution on a par with all other forms of knowledge, to the position of researcher as scientific expert, invested with the authority to provide a better representation of reality on the grounds that this representation is the product of scientific research on the topic under debate.

If one chooses to stress the contingency of research, different reflexive strategies can be used, as in dialogical research, to build bridges between different forms of knowledge. Such strategies can be very valuable from the perspective of particular epistemic interests, provided one does not imply that it is possible to neutralise one's own authority completely. In this book, we have chosen a more traditional, academic mode of presentation. We have wanted to produce and convey knowledge about discourse analysis and we have laid claims to a certain authority in this, signalling 'this is something we know something about'. We have, for instance, often positioned ourselves as knowledgeable about the field and the reader as less knowledgeable. In other places, we have tried to formulate ourselves so as to open up for important discussions and to keep them open. For example, in this conclusion to the discussion about critical research, we have applied a number of subjective modalities ('we believe', 'in our view' and so on) in order to indicate that here we recognise that there are other positions with good arguments. In line with our view of research as a truth that can be discussed, we have, in formulating the text, switched between a 'truth-position', some places plainly stating 'how things are', and a 'discussion position', indicating contingency, in places where we identify a need for further debate.[11] Whether or not we have placed the boundary between truth and discussion in the right place, is up to the reader to decide. The conception of critique as a positioned opening for discussion always contains an invitation to the reader to enter the discussion herself and carry it further.

In the above presentation of our position, we have written a lot about what we think the researcher should 'take into account' and 'take responsibility for' – as if researchers were faced with clear choices and were in possession of an overview of the conditions of production and the consequences of their research projects. We state, for example, that researchers should position themselves explicitly, making clear the nature of the research project's epistemic interest and theoretical and methodological framework. However, as we have also argued, it is important to acknowledge that these reflexive practices are subject to constraints set by the conditions of knowledge production. Researchers are always part of a wider social context and thus cannot just position themselves and their knowledge freely. As we have just noted, it is the reader who, in some sense, has the last word in relation to the text – without the readers and their varied use of texts, texts could just as well remain unwritten. The individual researcher, then, cannot claim sovereign control over her knowledge. And, as we have stressed throughout this chapter, the same applies at the other end of knowledge production: the researcher's knowledge is itself a product of social and cultural conditions of which she is not in control and cannot fully understand. Reflexive strategies can be used, as suggested by Sandra Harding, for example, to cast light on the social and historical circumstances under which one's knowledge has been produced, but they will not provide complete transparency. It is impossible to make all taken-for-granted understandings explicit, and one cannot avoid introducing new taken-for-granted understandings.

Being positioned, then, is something which the researcher, to a certain extent, just *is*, and the lack of transparency this entails has to be accepted. But positioning is also something that the researcher *does*. Standpoint theory understands knowledge as something that can be achieved by virtue of a particular position provided by particular experiences. We agree with this to a certain extent, but we believe that it is also important to treat positioning as an *active* effort in which the researcher strategically positions herself in a particular location in order to see the world from the perspective of particular aims and a particular theoretical framework (cf. Haraway). And we believe that it is important to give an account of the position in which one is standing and the technologies with which one is seeing the world, even if it is impossible to transcend the contingent conditions of production and give a complete account.

We will conclude by returning to the critique of ideology – the approach to critique which has become so criticised within social constructionism because it assumes that the researcher can reveal people's ideologies with the help of truth. In fact, in important respects, our proposal for a theoretical understanding of critical research follows in the footsteps of the critique of ideology. We do not distinguish, as does critique of ideology, between more or less ideological representations of reality as we do not consider some accounts of reality to be more objective accounts of the world than others. But we do retain the asymmetry which is integral to the critique of ideology. Although, in principle, there are always many other possibilities of representing the world, the writing of specific texts always implies a claim that reality is representable and that the representation offered in the text is better than other possible interpretations.

Social constructionist research is, as we have seen, often concerned with the unmasking of the taken-for-granted and, as such, it has the ambition of 'getting behind' people's everyday understandings. In this respect, too, it resembles the critique of ideology. The epistemological difference is that we do not see the goal as that of reaching the reality behind the masks; any unmasking contains itself a new 'masking' – a new contingent construction of reality. If scientific truth, as in the critique of ideology, is conceptualised as oppositional to the false consciousness of everyday life, a hierarchy is established that delegitimises other forms of knowledge in public debate. At the same time, the strength of science is to have the time and the theory to distance itself from some of our shared, taken-for-granted understandings; thus science at its best contributes to democratic debate by making visible areas which have hitherto been outside discussion because the state of things has been considered to be natural. The version of reality which one puts forward in research is not better than any other at the level of principle, and it can always be cast aside through discursive struggles both within the scientific field and in the public sphere as a whole. But by representing a qualified (that is, scientific) and *different* account of reality from those which are otherwise available, research knowledge can hopefully contribute to the addition of new perspectives to public debate.

What right do we have to contribute with such new and critical perspectives, one may ask. As social constructionists, we do not have the right endowed by possession of a final truth. But we do have the right that all people, in principle, have to intervene in democratic debate with a truth that can be discussed, in order to further our visions for a better society.

NOTES

1 See Deleuze and Guattari (1987: Chapter 1) for a conception of representation which is similar in many ways.

2 See also Butler (1993: Chapters 7 and 8) for a very similar understanding of common-sense, critique and radical democracy.

3 See Harding (1991) for a standpoint theory which tries to take account of these points of criticism.

4 See Butler (1993: Chapter 8) for a queer-perspective which is based on 'queer' as a category which falls between the dominant categories, and see Bhabha (1994: Introduction) for an attempt to think from the gaps in dominant understandings of culture.

5 See Potter (1996b: 224ff.) for a critical reading of critical discourse analysis along these lines.

6 But see Chouliaraki (2002) for a reformulation of the relation between discourse analysis and critical realism, which also affects the question of relativism.

7 Reflexivity is also, in slightly different versions, a topic of discussion within other disciplines, such as anthropology, feminism and science studies. We briefly present one feminist understanding of reflexivity in the next section, but in the present section we mainly focus on critical social psychology including discursive psychology.

8 More radical attempts to engage in dialogical research have been carried out in related fields of research, see, for example, poststructuralist feminist social scientists such as Lather and Smithies (1997).

9 See Ashmore (1989), Lather and Smithies (1997) and Woolgar (1989) for similar experiments with presentation forms. Lather and Smithies (1997), for example, is a poststructuralist text written by feminist theorists on several levels that privileges the knowledge of the informants over that of the researchers and which constantly tries to make clear to the reader that there

is never only one story and no story is fixed. Lather (2001) contains additional reflections based on the writing of Lather and Smithies (1997). See also Denzin (1997) for a discussion of different forms of experimental writing.

10 This criticism can also be directed at Steven Tyler's ideas that the texts should evoke rather than represent, as we already have mentioned.

11 See Harré and van Langenhove (1999) for a discussion of academic writing from the perspective of the theory of positioning.

References

Abrams, D. and Hogg, M. (eds) (1990) *Social Identity Theory*. Brighton: Harvester Wheatsheaf.

Alexander, J. (1996) 'Critical reflections on "reflexive modernization"', *Theory, Culture and Society*, 13(4): 133–8.

Althusser, L. (1971) 'Ideology and ideological state apparatuses', in L. Althusser *Lenin and Philosophy and Other Essays*. London: New Left Review.

Anderson, B. (1983) *Imagined Communities: Reflections on the Origin and Spread of Nationalism*. London: Verso.

Antaki, C. (1994) *Explaining and Arguing*. London: Sage.

Antaki, C. and Widdicombe, S. (eds) (1998) *Identities in Talk*. London: Sage Publications.

Aries, P. (1962) *Centuries of Childhood: A Social History of Family Life*. New York: Vintage.

Ashmore, M. (1989) *The Reflexive Thesis. Wrighting Sociology of Scientific Knowledge*. Chicago: The University of Chicago Press.

Atkinson, J. and Heritage, J. (eds) (1984) *Structures of Social Action: Studies in Conversation Analysis*. Cambridge: Cambridge University Press.

Austin, J. (1962) *How to do Things with Words*. London: Oxford University Press.

Azjen, I. (1988) *Attitudes, Personality and Behaviour*. Buckingham: Open University Press.

Bakhtin, M. (1981) *The Dialogical Imagination*. Austin: University of Texas Press.

Bakhtin, M. (1986) *Speech Genres and Other Late Essays*. C. Emerson and M. Holquist (eds). Austin: University of Texas Press.

Barrett, M. (1991) 'Ideology, politics, hegemony: from Gramsci to Laclau and Mouffe', in M. Barrett: *The Politics of Truth. From Marx to Foucault*. Cambridge: Polity Press.

Barthes, R. (1982) 'Inaugural lecture, Collège de France', in S. Sontag (ed.), *A Barthes Reader*. London: Jonathan Cape.

Bauman, Z. (1991) *Modernity and Ambivalence*. Cambridge: Polity Press.

Beck, U. (1992) *The Risk Society*. London: Sage.

Beck, U. (1996) *The Reinvention of Politics*. London: Routledge.

Berelson, B. (1971) *Content Analysis in Communication Research*. Glencoe, IL.: Free Press.

Berger, A.A. (1991) *Media Analysis Techniques*. London: Sage.

Bernstein, B. (1996) *Pedagogy, Symbolic Control and Identity. Theory, Research, Critique*. London: Taylor & Francis.

Bhabha, H. (1994) *The Location of Culture*. London: Routledge.

Bhaskar, R. (1986) *Scientific Realism and Human Emancipation*. London: Verso.

Billig, M. (1982) *Ideology and Social Psychology*. Oxford: Blackwell.

Billig, M. (1991) *Ideology and Opinions*. London: Sage.

Billig, M. (1992) *Talking of the Royal Family*. London: Routledge.

Billig, M. (1996) *Arguing and Thinking: A Rhetorical Approach to Social Psychology*, 2nd ed. Cambridge: Cambridge University Press.

Billig, M. (1997) 'The dialogic unconscious: discourse analysis, psychoanalysis and repression', *British Journal of Social Psychology*, 36(2): 139–59.

Billig, M. (1999a) 'Whose terms? Whose ordinariness? Rhetoric and ideology in conversation analysis', *Discourse and Society*, 10(4): 543–58.

Billig, M. (1999b) 'Conversation analysis and the claims of naivity', *Discourse and Society*, 10(4): 572–6.

Billig, M. and Simons, H.W. (1994) 'Introduction', in H.W. Simons and M. Billig (eds), *After Postmodernism. Reconstructing Ideology Critique*. London: Sage Publications.

Bourdieu, P. and Wacquant, L.J.D. (1996) *An Invitation to Reflexive Sociology*. Cambridge: Polity Press.

Bracher, M. (1993) *Lacan, Discourse, and Social Change*. Ithaca, NY: Cornell University Press.

Breakwell, G. and Canter, D. (1993) *Empirical Approaches to Social Representations*. Oxford: Clarendon Press.

Brown, G. and Yule, G. (1983) *Discourse Analysis*. Cambridge: Cambridge University Press.

Brown, R.H. (1994) 'Reconstructing social theory after the postmodern critique', in H.W. Simons and M. Billig (eds), *After Postmodernism. Reconstructing Ideology Critique*. London: Sage Publications.

Brundson, C. (1991) 'Pedagogies of the feminine: feminist teaching and women's genres', *Screen*, 32(4): 364–81.

Burr, V. (1995) *An Introduction to Social Constructionism*. London: Sage.

Butler, J. (1990) *Gender Trouble: Feminism and the Subversion of Identity*. New York: Routledge.

Butler, J. (1992) 'Contingent foundations: feminism and the question of "postmodernism"', in J. Butler and J. Scott (eds), *Feminists Theorize the Political*. New York: Routledge.

Butler, J. (1993) *Bodies that Matter. On the Discursive Limits of 'Sex'*. New York: Routledge.

Calhoun, C. (1995) *Critical Social Theory*. Oxford: Blackwell.

Cheesman, R. and Mortensen, A.T. (1991) *Om Målgrupper*. Papirer om Faglig Formidling, No. 15/87. Roskilde Universitetscenter: Kommunikation. [*Target Groups*. Communication Studies, Roskilde University: Papers on Specialist Communication.]

Chouliaraki, L. (1995) 'The constitution of ethnographic texts in social scientific discourse: "realist" and "polyphonic" representations', *Interface. Journal of Applied Linguistics* 10(1): 27–46.

Chouliaraki, L. (1998) 'Regulation in "progressivist" pedagogic discourse: individualized teacher–pupil talk', *Discourse and Society*, 9(1): 5–32.

Chouliaraki, L. (1999) 'Media discourse and national identity: death and myth in a news broadcast', in M. Reisigl and R. Wodak (eds), *The Semiotics of Racism*. Vienna: Passager Verlag.

Chouliaraki, L. (2002) 'Capturing the "contingency of universality": some reflections on discourse and critical realism', *Social Semiotics* 12(2): 84–114.

Chouliaraki, L. and Fairclough, N. (1999) *Discourse in Late Modernity: Rethinking Critical Discourse Analysis*. Edinburgh: Edinburgh University Press.

Collier, A. (1994) *Critical Realism*. London: Verso.

Collin, F. (1997) *Social Reality*. London: Routledge.

Collins, P.H. (1986) 'Learning from the outsider within: the sociological significance of Black feminist thought', *Social Problems* 33(6): 14–32.

Collins, P.H. (1998) *Fighting Words. Black Women and the Search for Justice*. Minneapolis, MN: University of Minnesota Press.

Condor, S. (1997) 'And so say all of us?: Some thoughts on "experiential democratization" as an aim for critical social psychologists', in T. Ibáñez and L. Íñiguez (eds), *Critical Social Psychology*. London: Sage.

Condor, S. and Antaki, C. (1997) 'Social cognition and discourse', in T. van Dijk (ed.), *Discourse as Structure and Process. Discourse Studies: A Multidisciplinary Introduction*. Vol. 2. London: Sage.

Cottle, S. (1998) 'Ulrich Beck, "risk society" and the media: a catastrophic view?', *European Journal of Communication*, 13(1): 5–32.

Davies, B. and Harré, R. (1990) 'Positioning: the discursive production of selves', *Journal for the Theory of Social Behavior*, 20(1): 43–63.

Deleuze, G. and Guattari, F. (1987) *A Thousand Plateaus. Capitalism and Schizophrenia*. Minneapolis, MN: University of Minnesota Press.

Denzin, N.K. (1997) *Interpretive Ethnography. Ethnographic Practices for the 21st Century*. Thousand Oaks: Sage.

de Rosa, A. (1994) 'From theory to metatheory in social representations – the lines of argument of a theoretical methodological debate', *Social Science Information*, 33(2): 273–304.

Derrida, J. (1998) *Of Grammatology*. Baltimore, MD: Johns Hopkins University Press.

Dyrberg, T. (1997) *The Circular Structure of Power. Politics, Identity, Community*. London: Verso.

Edwards, D. (1996) *Discourse and Cognition*. London: Sage.

Edwards, D. and Potter, J. (1992) *Discursive Psychology*. London: Sage.

Edwards, D., Ashmore, M. and Potter, J. (1995) 'Death and furniture: the rhetoric, politics and theology of bottom line arguments against relativism', *History of the Human Sciences*, 8(2): 25–49.

Fabian, J. (1983) *Time and the Other. How Anthropology Makes its Object*. New York: Columbia University Press.

Fairclough, N. (1989) *Language and Power*. London: Longman.

Fairclough, N. (ed.) (1992a) *Critical Language Awareness*. London: Longman.

Fairclough, N. (1992b) *Discourse and Social Change*. Cambridge: Polity Press.

Fairclough, N. (1992c) 'Text and context: linguistic and intertextual analysis within discourse analysis', *Discourse and Society*, 3(2): 193–217.

Fairclough, N. (1993) 'Critical discourse analysis and the marketization of public discourse: the universities', *Discourse and Society*, 4(2): 133–68.

Fairclough, N. (1995a) *Critical Discourse Analysis*. London: Longman.

Fairclough, N. (1995b) *Media Discourse*. London: Edward Arnold.

Fairclough, N. (1998) 'Political discourse in the media: an analytical framework', in A. Bell and P. Garrett (eds), *Approaches to Media Discourse*. Oxford: Blackwell.

Fairclough, N. (2000) *New Labour, New Language?* London: Routledge.

Fairclough, N. (2001) 'The discourse of New Labour: critical discourse analysis' in M. Wetherell, S. Taylor and S. Yates (eds). *Discourse as Data: A Guide for Analysis*. London: Sage Publications.

Fairclough, N. and Wodak, R. (1997) 'Critical discourse analysis', in T. van Dijk (ed.), *Discourse as Social Interaction: Discourse Studies: A Multidisciplinary Introduction*. Vol. 2. London: Sage.

Featherstone, M. (1991) *Consumer Culture and Postmodernism*. London: Sage.

Festinger, L. (1957) *A Theory of Cognitive Dissonance*. New York: Row, Peterson & Co.

Fielding, N. (1993) 'Interviews', in N. Gilbert (ed.), *Researching Social Life*. London: Sage.

Fishbein, M. and Azjen, I. (1975) *Belief, Attitude, Intention and Behavior: An Introduction to Theory and Research*. Reading, MA.: Addison Wesley.

Fiske, J. (1982) *Introduction to Communication Studies*. London: Methuen.

Fiske, J. (1987) *Television Culture*. London: Methuen.

Foucault, M. (1972) *The Archaeology of Knowledge*. London: Routledge.

Foucault, M. (1973) *The Order of Things. An Archaeology of the Human Sciences.* New York: Vintage Books.

Foucault, M. (1977) *Discipline and Punish: The Birth of the Prison.* Harmondsworth: Penguin.

Foucault, M. (1979) *The History of Sexuality.* Vol. 1. Harmondsworth: Penguin.

Foucault, M. (1980) 'Truth and power', in C. Gordon (ed.) *Power/Knowledge. Selected Interviews and other Writings 1972–1977.* Hemel Hempstead: Harvester Wheatsheaf.

Foucault, M. (1987) *The Use of Pleasure. The History of Sexuality.* Vol. 2. Harmondsworth: Penguin.

Foucault, M. (1988) *Care of the Self. The History of Sexuality.* Vol. 3. Harmondsworth: Penguin.

Fowler, R. (1991) *Language in the News: Discourse and Ideology in the Press.* London: Routledge.

Fowler, R., Hodge, B., Kress, G. and Trew, T. (1979) *Language and Control.* London: Routledge & Kegan Paul.

Gergen, K. (1985) 'The social constructionist movement in modern social psychology', *American Psychologist,* 40(3): 266–75.

Gergen, K. (1991) *The Saturated Self.* New York: Basic Books.

Gergen, K. (1994a) *Realities and Relationships: Soundings in Social Construction.* Cambridge, MA: Harvard University Press.

Gergen, K. (1994b) 'The limits of pure critique', in H.W. Simons and M. Billig (eds), *After Postmodernism. Reconstructing Ideology Critique.* London: Sage Publications.

Gergen, K. (1998) 'Constructionist dialogues and the vicissitudes of the political', in I. Velody and R. Williams (eds), *The Politics of Constructionism.* London: Sage Publications.

Giddens, A. (1991) *Modernity and Self-Identity.* Cambridge: Polity Press.

Gramsci, A. (1991) *Selections from Prison Notebooks.* London: Lawrence and Wishart.

Hagen, I. (1994) 'The ambivalences of TV news-viewing: between ideals and everyday practices', *European Journal of Communication,* 9(2): 193–220.

Hall, S. (1980) 'Encoding and decoding the television discourse', in S. Hall, D. Hobson, A. Lowe and P. Willis (eds), *Culture, Media, Language.* London: Hutchinson .

Hall, S. (1990) 'Cultural identity and diaspora', in J. Rutherford (ed.), *Identity. Community, Culture, Difference.* London: Lawrence and Wishart.

Hall, S. (1991) 'Old and new identities, old and new ethnicities', in A. King (ed.), *Culture, Globalization and the World System.* Houndmills: Macmillan.

Hall, S. (1993) 'Minimal Selves', in A. Gray and J. McGuigan (eds), *Studying Culture: An Introductory Reader.* London: Edward Arnold.

Hall, S. (1996) 'Who needs "identity"?', in S. Hall and P. du Gay (eds), *Questions of Cultural Identity.* London: Sage.

Hall, S., Hobson, D., Lowe, A. and Willis, P. (eds) (1980) *Culture, Media, Language.* London: Hutchinson.

Halliday, M. (1994) *Introduction to Functional Grammar.* London: Edward Arnold.

Haraway, D. (1991) 'A cyborg manifesto: science, technology, and socialist-feminism in the late twentieth century', in D. Haraway, *Simians, Cyborgs, and Women. The Reinvention of Nature.* London: Free Association Books.

Haraway, D. (1992) 'The promises of monsters: a regenerative politics for inappropriate/d others', in L. Grossberg, C. Nelson and P.A. Treichler (eds), *Cultural Studies.* New York: Routledge.

Haraway, D. (1996) 'Situated knowledges: the science question in feminism and the privilege of partial perspective', in E.F. Keller and H.E. Longino (eds), *Feminism and Science.* Oxford: Oxford University Press.

Haraway, D. (1997) *Modest_Witness@Second_Millennium. FemaleMan©_Meets_OncoMouse™.* New York: Routledge.

Harding, S. (1991) *Whose Science? Whose Knowledge? Thinking from Women's Lives*. Milton Keynes: Open University Press.

Harding, S. (1996) 'Rethinking standpoint epistemology: what is "strong objectivity"?', in E.F. Keller and H.E. Longino (eds), *Feminism and Science*. Oxford: Oxford University Press.

Harré, R. (1983) *Personal Being: A Theory for Individual Psychology*. Oxford: Blackwell.

Harré, R. and Gillett, G. (1994) *The Discursive Mind*. London: Sage Publications.

Harré, R. and van Langenhove, L. (eds) (1999) *Positioning Theory*. Oxford: Blackwell.

Harvey, D. (1996) *Justice, Nature and the Geography of Difference*. London: Blackwell.

Henriques, J., Hollway, W., Urwin, C., Venn, C. and Walkerdine, V. (eds) (1984) *Changing the Subject: Psychology, Social Regulation and Subjectivity*. London: Methuen.

Heritage, J. (1984) *Garfinkel and Ethnomethodology*. Cambridge: Polity Press.

Heritage, J. (1997) 'Conversation analysis and institutional talk: analysing data', in D. Silverman (ed.), *Qualitative Research: Theory, Method and Practice*. London: Sage.

Heritage, J. (2000) 'Goffman, Garfinkel and conversation analysis', in M. Wetherell, S. Taylor and S. Yates (eds), *Discourse Theory and Practice: A Reader*. London: Sage.

Hobsbawm, E. (1990) *Nations and Nationalism since 1780: Programme, Myth, Reality*. Cambridge, UK: Columbia University Press.

Hodge, B. and Kress, G. (1988) *Social Semiotics*. Cambridge: Polity Press.

Hollway, W. (1984) 'Gender difference and the production of subjectivity', in J. Henriques, W. Hollway, C. Urwin, C. Venn and V. Walkerdine (eds), *Changing the Subject: Psychology, Social Regulation and Subjectivity*. London: Methuen.

Hollway, W. (1989) *Subjectivity and Method in Psychology: Gender, Meaning and Science*. London: Sage.

Hollway, W. (1995) 'Feminist discourses and women's heterosexual desire', in S. Wilkinson and C. Kitzinger (eds), *Feminism and Discourse: Psychological Perspectives*. London: Sage.

Hollway, W. and Jefferson, T. (1997) 'The risk society in an age of anxiety: situating fear of crime', *British Journal of Sociology*, 48(2): 255–66.

Holsti, O. (1969) *Content Analysis for the Social Sciences and Humanities*. Reading, MA.: Addison Wesley.

Howarth, D. (2000) *Discourse*. Buckingham: Open University Press.

Howarth, D., Norval, A.J. and Stavrakakis, Y. (eds) (2000) *Discourse Theory and Political Analysis*. Manchester University Press.

Ibáñez, T. and Íñiguez, L. (eds) (1997) *Critical Social Psychology*. London: Sage.

Jensen, K.B. (1990) 'The politics of polysemy: television news, everyday consciousness and political action'. *Media, Culture and Society*, 12(1): 57–77.

Jensen, K.B. and Jankowski, N. (eds) (1991) *A Handbook of Qualitative Methodologies for Mass Communication Research*. London: Routledge.

Jodelet, D. (1991) *Madness and Social Representations*. Hemel Hempstead: Harvester Wheatsheaf.

Johannessen, H. (1994) 'The dance of ideas in the health service', in J. Liep and K.F. Olwig (eds), *Complex Lives. Cultural Plurality in Denmark*. Copenhagen: Akademisk Forlag.

Johannessen, H. (1994) 'Ideerness dans i sundhedssystemet', in J. Liep and K.F. Olwig (eds), *Komplekse liv. Kulturel mangfoldighed i Danmark*. ['The dance of ideas in the health service', in *Complex Lives. Cultural Diversity in Denmark*.] Copenhagen: Akademisk Forlag.

Jäger, S. (1993) *Kritische Diskursanalyse: eine Einführung*. [*Critical Discourse Analysis: An Introduction*.] Duisberg: Diss.

Jäger, S. and Jäger, M. (1992) *Aus der Mitte der Gesellschaft*. [*From the Middle of Society*.] Duisberg: Diss.

Jørgensen, M.W. (2001) 'Diskursanalytiske strategier', in H. Christrup, A.T. Mortensen and C.H. Pedersen (eds), *At begribe og bevæge kommunikationsprocessor. Om metoder i forskningspraksis.* Papirer om Faglig Formidling, No. 47/01. Roskilde Universitetscenter: Kommunikation. ['Discourse analytical strategies', in *To Understand and Influence Communication Processes. Methods in Research Practice.* Communication Studies, Roskilde University: Papers on Specialist Communication.]

Kellner, D. (1989) *Critical Theory, Marxism and Modernity.* Cambridge: Polity Press/Baltimore: Johns Hopkins University Press.

Kellner, D. (1995) *Media Culture: Cultural Studies, Identity and Politics between the Modern and the Postmodern.* London: Routledge.

Knudsen, A. (1989) *En Ø i Historien.* [*An Island in History.*] Basilisk.

Kress, G. and van Leeuwen, T. (1996) *Reading Images: The Grammar of Visual Design.* London: Routledge.

Kress, G. and van Leeuwen, T. (2001) *Multi-Modal Discourse: The Modes and Media of Contemporary Communication.* London: Arnold.

Kress, G., Leite-Garcia, R. and van Leeuwen, T. (1997) 'Discourse semiotics', in T. van Dijk (ed.), *Discourse as Structure and Process. Discourse Studies: A Multidisciplinary Introduction.* Vol. 2. London: Sage.

Krippendorff, K. (1980) *Content Analysis: An Introduction to its Methodology.* London: Sage.

Kristeva, J. (1986) 'Word, dialogue and novel', in T. Moi (ed.), *The Kristeva Reader.* Oxford: Blackwell.

Kvale, S. (1992) 'Postmodern psychology: a contradiction in terms?', in S. Kvale (ed.), *Psychology and Postmodernism.* London: Sage.

Kvale, S. (1996) *InterViews. An Introduction to Qualitative Research Interviewing.* London: Sage.

Lacan, J. (1977a) 'The agency of the letter in the unconscious or reason since Freud', in J. Lacan, *Écrits: A Selection.* New York: W.W. Norton & Co.

Lacan, J. (1977b) 'The mirror stage as formative of the function of the I as revealed in psycho-analytic experience', in J. Lacan, *Écrits: A Selection.* New York: W.W. Norton & Co.

Laclau, E. (1990) *New Reflections on the Revolution of Our Time.* London: Verso.

Laclau, E. (1993a) 'Discourse', in R. Goodin and P. Pettit (eds), *The Blackwell Companion to Contemporary Political Philosophy.* Oxford: Blackwell.

Laclau, E. (1993b) 'Power and representation', in M. Poster (ed.), *Politics, Theory and Contemporary Culture.* New York: Columbia University Press.

Laclau, E. (1996a) 'The death and resurrection of the theory of ideology', *Journal of Political Ideologies*, 1(3): 201–20.

Laclau, E. (1996b) 'Universalism, particularism and the question of identity', in E. Laclau, *Emancipation(s).* London: Verso.

Laclau, E. and Mouffe, C. (1985) *Hegemony and Socialist Strategy. Towards a Radical Democratic Politics.* London: Verso.

Laclau, E. and Mouffe, C. (1990) 'Post-Marxism without apologies', in E. Laclau, *New Reflections on the Revolution of Our Time.* London: Verso.

Laclau, E. and Zac, L. (1994) 'Minding the gap: the subject of politics', in E. Laclau (ed.), *The Making of Political Identities.* London: Verso.

Larrain, J. (1994) *Ideology and Cultural Identity. Modernity and the Third World Presence.* Cambridge: Polity Press.

Larsen, H. (1999) 'Danish and British policies towards Europe in the 1990s: A Discourse approach'. *European Journal of International Relations* 5(4): 464–91.

Larsen, H. (forthcoming) *Still A Danish Foreign Policy? Danish Foreign Policy in an EU Context.* Houndmills: Palgrave/Macmillan.

Lather, P. (1993) 'Fertile obsession: validity after poststructuralism', *Sociological Quarterly*, 34(4): 673–94.

Lather, P. (2001) 'Postbook: working the ruins of feminist ethnography', *Signs: Journal of Women in Culture and Society* 27(1): 199–227.

Lather, P. and Smithies, C. (1997) *Troubling the Angels: Women Living with HIV/AIDS*. Boulder, CO: Westview/Harper Collins.

Latour, B. (1999) *Pandora's Hope. Essays on the Reality of Science Studies*. Cambridge, MA: Harvard University Press.

Leech, G. (1983) *The Principles of Pragmatics*. London: Longman.

Lunt, P. and Livingstone, S. (1996) 'Rethinking the focus group in media and communications research', *Journal of Communication*, 46(2): 79–98.

Lyotard, J.-F. (1984) *The Postmodern Condition*. Minneapolis, MN: University of Minnesota Press.

Maas, U. (1989) *Sprachpolitik und politische Sprachwissenschaft*. [*Language Politics and the Political Science of Language*.] Frankfurt am Main: Suhrkamp.

Marcus, G.E. and Fischer, M.M.J. (1986) *Anthropology as Cultural Critique. An Experimental Moment in the Human Sciences*. Chicago: The University of Chicago Press.

Mey, J. (1993) *Pragmatics: An Introduction*. Oxford: Blackwell.

Middleton, D. and Edwards, D. (eds) (1990) *Collective Remembering*. London: Sage.

Mills, S. (1997) *Discourse*. London: Routledge.

Mishler, E. (1986) *Research Interviewing: Context and Narrative*. Cambridge, MA.: Harvard University Press.

Morgan, D. (1997) *Focus Groups as Qualitative Research*. London: Sage.

Morley, D. (1992) *Television, Audiences and Cultural Studies*. London: Routledge.

Moscovici, S. (1984) 'The phenomenon of social representations', in R. Farr and S. Moscovici (eds), *Social Representations*. Cambridge: Cambridge University Press.

Moscovici, S. (1988) 'Notes towards a description of social representations', *European Journal of Social Psychology*, 18(3): 211–50.

Moscovici, S. (1994) 'Social representations and pragmatic communication', *Social Science Information*, 33(2): 163–77.

Mouffe, C. (1992) 'Feminism, citizenship and radical democratic politics', in J. Butler and J. Scott (eds), *Feminists Theorize the Political*. London: Routledge.

Mumby, D. and Clair, R. (1997) 'Organisational discourse', in T. van Dijk (ed.), *Discourse as Social Interaction. Discourse Studies. A Multidisciplinary Introduction*. Vol. 2 London: Sage.

Nagel, T. (1986) *The View from Nowhere*. New York: Oxford University Press.

Norval, A.J. (1996) *Deconstructing Apartheid Discourse*. London: Verso.

Ochs, E. (1979) 'Transcription as theory', in E. Ochs and B. Schieffelin (eds), *Developmental Pragmatics*. New York: Academic Press.

O'Shea, A. (1984) 'Trusting the people: how does Thatcherism work?', in *Formations of Nation and People*. London: Routledge.

Parker, I. (1992) *Discourse Dynamics: Critical Analysis for Social and Individual Psychology*. London: Routledge.

Parker, I. and Burman, E. (1993) 'Against discursive imperialism, empiricism and construction: thirty two problems with discourse analysis', in E. Burman and I. Parker (eds), *Discourse Analytic Research: Repertoires and Readings of Texts in Action*. London: Routledge.

Pecheux, M. (1982) *Language, Semantics and Ideology*. London: Macmillan.

Phillips, L. (1993) *Reproduction and Transformation of the Discourse of Thatcherism across Socio-political Domains*. Ph.D. thesis. London School of Economics and Political Science.

Phillips, L. (1996) 'Rhetoric and the spread of the discourse of Thatcherism', *Discourse and Society*, 7(2): 209–41.

Phillips, L. (1998) 'Hegemony and political discourse: the lasting impact of Thatcherism', *Sociology*, 32(4): 847–67.

Phillips, L. (2000a) 'Mediated communication and the privatization of public problems: discourse on ecological risks and political action', *European Journal of Communication*. 15(2): 171–207.

Phillips, L. (2000b) 'Risk, reflexivity and democracy: mediating expert knowledge in the news', *Nordicom Review*, 21(2): 115–35.

Phillips, L. (2001) 'Forskning i tvivl – en refleksiv evaluering af det diskursanalytiske interview som metode til kritiske studier', in H. Christrup, A.T. Mortensen and C.H. Pedersen (eds), *At begribe og bevæge kommunikationsprocesser. Om metoder i forskningspraksis*. Papirer om Faglig Formidling, No. 47/01. Roskilde Universitetscenter: Kommunikation. ['Research in doubt – a reflexive evaluation of the discourse analytical interview as a method for critical research', in *To Understand and Influence Communication Processess. Methods in Research Practice*. Communication Studies, Roskilde Universtiy: Papers on Specialist Communication.]

Pomerantz, A. (1986) 'Extreme case formulations: a way of legitimizing claims', *Human Studies*, 9(2/3): 219–29.

Potter, J. (1996a) 'Attitudes, social representations and discursive psychology', in M. Wetherell (ed.), *Identities, Groups and Social Issues*. London: Sage.

Potter, J. (1996b) *Representing Reality: Discourse, Rhetoric and Social Construction*. London: Sage.

Potter, J. (1997) 'Discourse analysis as a way of analysing naturally occurring talk', in D. Silverman (ed.), *Qualitative Research: Theory, Methods and Practice*. London: Sage.

Potter, J. (2001) 'Wittgenstein and Austin: developments in linguistic philosophy', in M. Wetherell et al. (eds), *Discourse Theory and Practice. A Reader*. London: Sage.

Potter, J. and Reicher, S. (1987) 'Discourses of community and conflict: the organisation of social categories in accounts of a "riot"', *British Journal of Social Psychology*, 26(1): 25–40.

Potter, J., Stringer, P. and Wetherell, M. (1984) *Social Texts and Context: Literature and Social Psychology*. London: Routledge and Kegan Paul.

Potter, J. and Wetherell, M. (1987) *Discourse and Social Psychology*. London: Sage.

Prins, B. (1997) *The Standpoint in Question. Situated Knowledges and the Dutch Minorities Discourse*. Utrecht.

Reason, P. and Bradbury, H. (eds) (2001) *Handbook of Action Research. Participatory Inquiry and Practice*. London: Sage Publications.

Richardson, K. (1998) 'Signs and wonders: interpreting the economy through television', in A. Bell and P. Garrett (eds), *Approaches to Media Discourse*. Oxford: Blackwell.

Rose, G. (1997) 'Situating knowledges: positionallity, reflexivities and other tactics', *Progress in Human Geography*, 21(3): 305–20.

Rosengren, K. (ed.) (1981) *Advances in Content Analysis*. Beverly Hills/London: Sage.

Sacks, H. (1992) *Lectures on Conversation*. 2 Volumes. Edited by G. Jefferson. Oxford: Basil Blackwell.

Sampson, E.E. (1991) 'The democratization of psychology', *Theory and Psychology*, 1(3): 275–98.

Saussure, F. de. (1960) *Course in General Linguistics*. London: Peter Owen.

Schegloff, E. (1997) 'Whose text? Whose context?', *Discourse and Society*, 8(2): 165–83.

Schegloff, E. (1999a) '"Schegloff's texts" as "Billig's data": a critical reply', *Discourse and Society*, 10(4): 558–72.

Schegloff, E. (1999b) 'Naivete vs sophistication or discipline vs self-indulgence: A rejoinder to Billig', *Discourse and Society*, 10(4): 577–82.

Schrøder, K. (1998) 'Discourse analysis and the media-society nexus: towards a notion of discourse ethnography?' Paper presented to the international conference 'Discourse and Social Research', Sørup Herregård Denmark.

Shotter, J. (1993) *The Cultural Politics of Everyday Life*. Buckingham: Open University Press.

Shotter, J. and Gergen, K. (eds) (1989) *Texts of Identity*. London: Sage.

Silverman, D. (1985) 'The articulation of elements: the parts and the whole', in D. Silverman: *Qualitative Methodology and Sociology*. Brookfield: Gower.

Silverstone, R. (1999) *Why Study the Media?* London: Sage Publications.

Smith, D.E. (1987) *The Everyday World As Problematic. A Feminist Sociology*. Boston: Northeastern University Press.

Smith, J. (1995) 'Semi-structured interviewing and qualitative analysis', in J. Smith, R. Harré and L. van Langenhove (eds), *Rethinking Methods in Psychology*. London: Sage.

Soper, K. (1990) 'Feminism, humanism and postmodernism', *Radical Philosophy*, 55(1): 11–17.

Tajfel, H. (1981) *Human Groups and Social Categories*. Cambridge: Cambridge University Press.

Taylor, S.J. and Bogdan, R. (1984) *Introduction to Qualitative Research*. New York: John Wiley.

Ten Have, P. (1999) *Doing Conversation Analysis: a Practical Guide*. London: Sage.

Thompson, J. (1984) *Studies in the Theory of Ideology*. Cambridge: Polity Press.

Thompson, J. (1990) *Ideology and Modern Culture*. Cambridge: Polity Press.

Thompson, J. (1995) *The Media and Modernity: A Social Theory of the Media*. Cambridge: Polity Press.

Torfing, J. (1999) *New Theories of Discourse: Laclau, Mouffe and Zizek*. Oxford: Blackwell.

Tracy, K. (1995) 'Action-implicative discourse analysis', *Journal of Language and Social Psychology*, 14(1–2): 195–215.

Tyler, S.A. (1986) 'Post-modern ethnography: from document of the occult to occult document', in J. Clifford and G.E. Marcus (eds), *Writing Culture. The Poetics and Politics of Ethnography*. Berkeley: University of California Press.

van Dijk, T. (1991) *Racism and the Press*. London: Routledge.

van Dijk, T. (1993) *Discourse and Elite Racism*. London: Sage.

van Dijk, T. (ed.) (1997a) *Discourse as Social Interaction: A Multidisciplinary Introduction*. Vol. 2. London: Sage.

van Dijk, T. (ed.) (1997b) 'Introduction', in *Discourse as Structure and Process: A Multidisciplinary Introduction*. Vol. 1. London: Sage.

van Dijk, T. and Kintch, W. (1983) *Strategies of Discourse Comprehension*. London: Academic Press.

van Leeuwen, T. (1993) 'Genre and field in critical discourse analysis: a synopsis', *Discourse & Society* 4(2): 193–223.

Walkerdine, V. (1990) *Schoolgirl Fictions*. London: Verso.

Walkerdine, V. (1993) '"Daddy's gonna buy you a dream to cling to (and mummy's gonna love you just as much as she can)": young girls and popular television', in D. Buckingham (ed.), *Reading Audiences: Young People and the Media*. Manchester: Manchester University Press.

Watson, R. (1997) 'Ethnomethodology and textual analysis', in D. Silverman (ed.), *Qualitative Research: Theory, Method and Practice*. London: Sage.

Wernick, A. (1991) *Promotional Culture*. London: Sage.

Wetherell, M. (1982) 'Cross-cultural studies of minimal groups: implications for the social identity theory of intergroup relations', in H. Tajfel (ed.), *Social Identity and Intergroup Relations*. Cambridge: Cambridge University Press.

Wetherell, M. (1995) 'Romantic discourse and feminist analysis: interrogating investment, power and desire', in S. Wilkinson and C. Kitzinger (eds), *Feminism and Discourse: Psychological Perspectives*. London: Sage.

Wetherell, M. (1996) 'Group conflict and the social psychology of racism', in M. Wetherell (ed.), *Identities, Groups and Social Issues*. London: Sage.

Wetherell, M. (1998) 'Positioning and interpretative repertoires: conversation analysis and post-structuralism in dialogue', *Discourse and Society*, 9(3): 387–412.

Wetherell, M. and Maybin, J. (1996) 'The distributed self: a social constructionist perspective', in R. Stevens (ed.), *Understanding the Self*. London: Sage.

Wetherell, M. and Potter, J. (1988) 'Discourse analysis and the identification of interpretive repertoires', in A. Antaki (ed.), *Analysing Everyday Explanation*. London: Sage.

Wetherell, M. and Potter, J. (1992) *Mapping the Language of Racism: Discourse and the Legitimation of Exploitation*. Hemel Hempstead: Harvester Wheatsheaf.

Wetherell, M., Stiven, H. and Potter, J. (1987) 'Unequal egalitarianism: a preliminary study of discourses concerning gender and employment opportunities', *British Journal of Social Psychology*, 26(1): 59–71.

Widdicombe, S. and Wooffitt, R. (1995) *The Language of Youth Subcultures: Social Identity in Action*. Hemel Hempstead: Harvester Wheatsheaf.

Willig, C. (ed.) (1999a) *Applied Discourse Analysis: Social and Psychological Interventions*. London: Sage.

Willig, C. (1999b) 'Beyond appearances: a critical realist approach to social constructionist work', in D. Nightingale and J. Cromby (eds), *Social Constructionist Psychology: A Critical Analysis of Theory and Practice*. Buckingham: Open University Press.

Wittgenstein, L. (1953) *Philosophical Investigations*. Oxford: Blackwell.

Wodak, R. (1991) 'Turning the tables: antisemitic discourse in post-war Austria', *Discourse and Society*, 2(1): 47–64.

Wodak, R. and Menz, F. (eds) (1990) *Sprache in der Politik – Politik in der Sprache: Analysen zum Öffentlichen Sprachgebrauch. [Language in Politics – Politics in Language: An Analysis of Public Language Use.]* Klagenfurt: Drava.

Wodak, R., de Cillia, R., Reisigl, M. and Liebhart, K. (1999) *The Discursive Construction of National Identity*. Edinburgh: Edinburgh University Press.

Woodward, K. (ed.) (1997) *Identity and Difference*. London: Sage.

Wooffitt, R. (2001) 'Researching psychic practitioners: conversation analysis'; in M. Wetherell, S. Taylor and S. Yates (eds) Discourse as Data: A Guide for analysis, London: Sage Publications.

Woolgar, S. (1980) 'Discovery: logic and sequence in a scientific text', in R. Krohn, K. Knorr and R. Whitley (eds), *The Social Process of Scientific Investigation*. Dordrecht: Reidal.

Woolgar, S. (1989) 'The ideology of representation and the role of the agent', in H. Lawson and L. Appignanesi (eds), *Dismantling Truth. Reality in the Post-Modern World*. New York: St. Martin's Press.

Woolgar, S. and Ashmore, M. (1988) 'The next step: an introduction to the reflexive project', in S. Woolgar (ed.), *Knowledge and Reflexivity. New Frontiers in the Sociology of Knowledge*. London: Sage Publications.

Index